Scotticisms
in Grammar and Vocabulary

Their sense, that aince was braw an' plain,
Tint a'thegether,
Like runes upon a standin' stane
Amang the heather.

R. L. Stevenson

Scotticisms
in Grammar and Vocabulary

'Like runes upon a standin' stane'?

MARINA DOSSENA

JOHN DONALD PUBLISHERS

To My Mother

First published in Great Britain in 2005 by
by John Donald Publishers
an imprint of Birlinn Ltd
West Newington House
10 Newington Road
Edinburgh
EH9 1QS

ISBN 10: 0 85976 605 5
ISBN 13: 978 0 85976 605 0

British Library Cataloguing in Publication Data
A catalogue record for this book is available
on request from the British Library

The publishers thank the Scotland Inheritance Fund
for their generous support in the publication of this volume

Typeset in Sabon by Koinonia, Manchester
Printed and bound by Antony Rowe Ltd, Chippenham, Wiltshire

Contents

Preface

*The general cast of the Scotish Dialect cannot be deemed, without injury
to the national character, the result of ignorance and vulgarity.*

James Adams, 1799

In 1855 James Paterson expressed his view, according to which Scots was not
'a mere dialect' of English, but 'a distinct branch of the great Teutonic family',
thus assigning it the status of a language distinct from English. At the same
time he also expressed his concern because it seemed doubtful 'that the
vernacular of Scotland can long maintain its ground in the face of so many
opposing circumstances' (1855: 164), the most powerful of which was possibly
school education. A few years later, Robert Louis Stevenson had also perceived
Scots as a 'dying language', and after more than a century many scholars still
claim the same. Despite all this, there is an incessant tide of debate on linguistic
questions in Scotland – definitely a token of the continuing topicality of Scots,
which adapts to different social contexts while maintaining its traditional
features and connotations.

The 'opposing circumstances' to which Paterson referred had long been
present. The aim of this study is to investigate the ways in which grammar
books and dictionaries, travelogues and such popular texts as proverb collections, allow us to gain insights into the history of progressive anglicisation on
the part of Scots and, at the same time, provide evidence of its continuing
identity. It is well-known that, especially in the eighteenth and nineteenth
centuries, grammatical forms and vocabulary items were stigmatised if their
usage was restricted either from the geographical or the social point of view,
while their acceptability was admitted in literary contexts. This study,
however, will attempt to go beyond this time span and will consider a broader
range of sources from different points of view.

The terminology used in this type of study has often proved controversial,
especially when the terms 'anglicisation' and 'standardisation' are used interchangeably; indeed, Aitken (1979 and 1991) and Bailey (1991) have shown the
extent to which this is misleading. First of all, the assumption that northern
varieties in general and Scots in particular need(ed) to be 'standardised' (i.e.,
brought close to the southern standard) has evaluative connotations which

may no longer be acceptable.[1] Secondly, the process through which English and Scots have become closer and closer has not always followed a consistent path of convergence. Divergence has occurred whenever features of one variety or the other have been emphasised for specific communicative purposes (i.e., whenever there have been 'vernacular revivals') or when the process of internal change (i.e., the historical development of the language) has resulted in the development of local features. Finally, it is incorrect to assume that convergence has always been in terms of northern forms becoming more like southern ones. In fact, modern standard English has derived many forms from northern English ones shared with Scots. Evidence of this is provided by the use of northern pronouns like *they* and the use of *-s* ending in the third person singular present tense, in addition to various lexical acquisitions that will be discussed in this book.

My purpose is not to provide a survey of all bibliographical sources concerning the connection and mutual influence of Scots and English in Scotland, but to try to outline how the debate on linguistic issues concerning Scots has developed over the centuries. Starting from an analysis of the linguistic situation in present-day Scotland, where English, Scots and Gaelic interact, I shall focus on the features of contemporary Scottish Standard English (SSE), and particularly I shall analyse the actual incidence of so-called 'Scotticisms', as defined by A. J. Aitken. The description of today's situation will be followed by an analysis of the concept of 'Scotticism' from the historical point of view. This will start from a description of the overall process of anglicization that developed in Scotland after the Union of Crowns; the main part of the historical study will then be centred around the eighteenth century. The role of prescriptive grammarians will be discussed, together with an outline of the ambiguous sociolinguistic attitudes that Scotticisms provoked at the turn of the century, when new literary figures sought to return status to 'the vernacular'. Finally, I shall consider the nineteenth century, in order to investigate what kind of features were still stigmatised. This will take me back to the present-day variety, allowing me to verify what items have changed their status, from 'proscribed Scotticisms' to 'covert' or 'overt Scotticisms'. To this end, an investigation of the Miller-Brown Corpus of Scottish English will allow me to assess the extent to which markedly Scottish forms occur in spontaneous speech. This investigation includes issues which I have also discussed elsewhere. However, in this volume they are resumed so as to present my results in a context which encompasses socio-historical views on linguistic change. In particular, this study will concentrate on syntax and vocabulary.

---

1 Crawford (1998: 7) points out that whenever conscious decisions were made, in order to bring one language closer to another, 'issues of cultural politics were involved. If, today, English writers were made to use American spelling and diction for the sake of global clarity, then many in England might feel a heightened sense of cultural imperialism'.

While this book was still in its early stages, I learned of the sad news of Professor Adam J. (Jack) Aitken's death; it was certainly a great loss for the community of Scottish scholarship and, more generally, for the academic world of historical dialectology. It had been a very special pleasure and an honour for me to meet Professor Aitken at the 1997 Aberdeen Conference on Languages of Scotland and Ulster. All his comments were appreciative and helpful, as he truly believed in encouraging researchers through guidance and a positive attitude. It is therefore suitable, in my opinion, that even a small contribution towards the continuation of research in the field of Scottish studies (such as the present one) should gratefully acknowledge the extent to which it is indebted to his example.

As the greatest part of my research was carried out in Scotland, it would be easy for me to borrow Thomas Pennant's words to express how much I have always appreciated the observations of all my Scottish colleagues, friends and acquaintances. As in the case of the traveller of more than two centuries ago, 'Gratitude forbids my silence respecting the kind of reception I universally met with; or the active zeal of everyone to facilitate my pursuits; or their liberal communication of every species of information, useful or entertaining'. First of all, I am extremely grateful to Prof. Jim Miller (University of Edinburgh) for allowing me to access the Miller-Brown Corpus of Scottish English. I also wish to thank Prof. Alexander Fenton (University of Edinburgh) for drawing my attention to a very rare collection of proverbs by Andrew Melville; to both of them I also owe the acknowledgement of invaluable advice. Then, the pleasant conversation of Tony and Miriam Dilworth, Dr. Margaret Laing, Dr. David Stevenson, Mrs. Thelma Jones and Mr. Ken Gourlay often provided a precious opportunity to gather instances of authentic Scotticisms and to discuss them in a friendly environment. So warm and enjoyable has always been their hospitality that I have grown to think of Edinburgh as my 'spiritual home', as I do not doubt they will have realised during my frequent visits.

Finally, I wish to express my sincerest thanks to those who (at various stages) patiently read earlier drafts of this book: Professors Maurizio Gotti and Richard Dury (University of Bergamo), John Phillips (University of Yamaguchi), Jim Miller, Alexander Fenton and Dr Keith Williamson (University of Edinburgh). Their encouraging comments certainly helped me clarify my ideas throughout the writing process. Participants at various conferences also provided stimulating challenges on various parts of this study: Mr. Derrick McClure and Dr. Caroline Macafee (Aberdeen University) and Dr. Anneli Meurman-Solin (University of Helsinki) provided specially valuable observations. In spite of all this, however, I remain solely responsible for any omissions and misinterpretation of data.

CHAPTER ONE

The Languages of Present-Day Scotland

Varieties of English in Britain are a fascinating subject, whether we consider them from the geographical or the social point of view; research carried out in Norwich by Trudgill (1974) and in Belfast by J. Milroy (1992), for instance, has marked turning points in the field of British dialectology and socio-linguistics. The case of Scotland, however, seems to have been underestimated in its potential for investigation: as Görlach (1988a: 221) points out,

> We are faced with a unique situation of a national language which was gradually eroded by its southern neighbour (...). What appears to be an ideal ground for socio-historical linguistics, with six centuries of change of functions, domains, registers and evaluations of Scots vis-à-vis English, has been neglected to an astonishing degree.

To some extent this is confirmed by the fact that such an important collection of studies as Cheshire (1991) does not include any discussion of varieties of English in Scotland, while their importance is implicitly acknowledged in the description of other varieties where Scots has influenced phonological or lexical features (for instance, very obviously, in Irish English, but also in American English, Canadian English, Australian English and New Zealand English).[1]

Yet Scotland has often been in the spotlight of linguistic inquiry for non-linguistic reasons, since the (apparently endless) debate on the status of Scots, whether it is a language or a dialect,[2] and its range of uses, whether literary or

---

1 On the influence of Scots on other varieties of English see, among others, Gunn (1970), Milroy (1982), Crozier (1984), Trudgill (1986: 141), Montgomery (1989 and 1997), Kingsmore (1995), Montgomery and Gregg (1997), Bauer (1997), Tulloch (1997a) and Robinson (1997: 56).

2 This issue is deeply felt even outside specialist circles, as is shown by the frequent 'Letters to the Editor' concerning this topic that appear in newspapers like *The Scotsman* or magazines like *The Scots Magazine*. However, there have been cases in which academic debate has totally disregarded this issue: for instance, no mention is made of the Scottish situation in the Proceedings of the Colloquium on Dialect and Standard Language held in Amsterdam in October 1990 (cf. van Leuvensteijn and Berns 1991), though the high degree of regional variation within Scots (cf. Johnston 1997b) certainly contributes to its definition as a language. Pollner (2000) also highlights the fact that scholarly interest in Scottish and Irish English has increased in relatively recent times.

non-literary, has often been biased by socio-political stances that, in some cases, have even overshadowed the linguistic focus (Macafee 1985). Scholars have often found it necessary to provide a political background for the socio-historical perspective of their analyses: as stressed by McClure (1995: 4), the inherent political importance of language is related to language being an aspect of the communal identity.

It is certainly true that Scotland represents one of the most distinct cases of linguistic co-existence: though a publication of the European Bureau for Lesser Used Languages focusing on Scots and Gaelic (Macleod and MacNacail 1995) describes Scotland as 'a linguistic double helix', the picture is much more complex. First of all, we should bear in mind that Scottish culture actually encompasses two broad categories defined by the geographical terms 'Highland' and 'Lowland', whose division was deepened with the advent of Anglo-Norman feudalism (McClure 1994: 30) and has represented a funda-mental dichotomy since then. While these two areas have always had close connections with each other, there have also been tragic clashes in many periods of Scottish history, Highlanders being stereotypically portrayed as 'barbarous' by Lowlanders from their political and religious perspective.

It is therefore impossible to discuss Scotland as a unit; it should always be pictured in its complexity. Consequently, any description of English in Scotland must also account for difference between Lowlands and Highlands, as the latter remained Gaelic-speaking till quite recently[3] and the kind of English that is spoken in that area – usually called 'Highland and Island English' (Shuken 1984 and 1985) – is closer to Southern English both from the phonological and the grammatical point of view.[4]

My description will be centred around Lowland Scotland, since this is the area where Scots and English interacted most and where the issue of their convergence, which is at the basis of my investigation, was felt most acutely; and yet, for the purposes of this study, the presence of Gaelic ought not to be excluded, in consideration of the influence it has had on the vocabulary and syntax of Scots and, consequently, on the Scottish varieties of English both in the Lowlands and in the Highlands.

Smith (1996: 166–167) identifies three groups of 'speakers of Anglo-Saxon-derived languages[5] in Scotland':

---

3 Language policies for this area will be discussed in the next section.
4 However, Trudgill (1974/1995: 47) points out that 'One can detect lexical and grammatical differences even in the speech of Highlanders who have never spoken Gaelic in their lives'. The issue of Highland English is also discussed by Speitel (1981). As regards the idea that the Highland variety is 'better' than the Lowland one, or indeed than English ones, this was stressed as late as 1927 in a tract of the Society for Pure English (Bradley and Bridges 1927: 11).
5 Note that this excludes Gaelic.

1. speakers of Scots, who – we are told – are those thus 'signalling their identity with Scottish working-class culture';[6]
2. speakers of 'so-called *Scottish Standard English* [henceforth SSE] (...) frequently defined as "Standard English with a Scottish Accent"';
3. speakers of 'a variety which might best be termed *standardised Southern English*, consisting of the grammar and vocabulary of Standard English transmitted in an accent focused on Received Pronunciation (...)'. Smith identifies these speakers as 'some English immigrants, and members of the Scottish aristocracy', but of course this is also the variety generally encountered 'through audio-visual media such as radio and television'.[7]

These varieties being very closely connected from the point of view of grammar and vocabulary, it is more convenient to follow a taxonomy of three groups of speakers of non-immigrant languages: Scottish Gaelic, Scots, and SSE, although for most speakers there have been overlappings involving all of these three languages. As a result, it is important to be aware of their main features, in order to understand in what ways they may have influenced each other and, in particular, in order to understand what characterises SSE today as a result of the interactions of these languages. While a detailed study of the phonology, vocabulary, morphology and syntax of all three in a present-day and historical perspective would be far beyond the scope of this book, I will try to clarify some aspects that appear to be particularly meaningful, in order to explain contemporary phenomena in their socio-historical framework.

In the description of Anglo-Saxon languages in Scotland the issue of terminology is also crucial, since a superficial identification of Scots with SSE might lead to the assumption that phonological, syntactic or morphological features of one are also shared by the other,[8] when in fact we are faced with a case of dialectal co-existence, and mutual influences have allowed both varieties to develop in a unique way.

Scottish Gaelic

While the linguistic structure of Gaelic has been the object of numerous studies in recent years (for instance, Clement 1984, Macaulay 1992, Ball and Fife 1993 and Williamson 1995/96), its survival through the centuries has attracted less attention beyond the circle of highly specific research (Durkacz 1983). Besides, the old distance between Lowlands and Highlands seems to have prevented Gaelic from ever being accounted for as a national language, while

6 Evidently the assumption is that Scots is more widely used by working-class speakers.
7 However, there are frequent exceptions in Scottish channels.
8 For instance, this is the case of Brown (1991), where a description of double modals in Hawick Scots could be taken to refer to SSE.

Lowland Scots (or *Lallans*, in its poetic denomination)[9] has recursively been held up as a badge of national(istic) identity.[10]

Scottish Gaelic is a Celtic language that was brought to Scotland from Ireland in the third-fifth centuries AD (Thomson 1984). Apparently the distinction between Scottish and Irish Gaelic began around the tenth century.[11] In Lowland Scotland, however, the use and prestige of Gaelic had begun to decline already in the twelfth century (cf. McClure 1984/1995: 6), when the influence of Northern English (i.e., Older Scots)[12] increased, and continued steadily until the twentieth century.

The language policy of the Stuart monarchs first, and of Hanoverian and subsequent governments later, seriously jeopardised Gaelic's chances of

---

9 *Lallans* was adopted as a distinct label by the writers of the Scottish Renaissance movement in the 1920s (most notably, Hugh MacDiarmid) borrowing it from Burns' postscript to his epistle 'To William Simpson of Ochiltree':

> In days when mankind were but callans
>   At *grammar*, *logic*, an' sic talents,
> They took nae pains their speech to balance,
>   Or rules to gie,
> But spak their thoughts in plain, braid Lallans,
>   Like you or me. (ll. 115–120)

The aim was to return proper poetic status to the language by revitalising it and even making up what was called *synthetic Scots* on the model of Nynorsk, the language that was created by the language scholar Ivar Aasen, primarily from the dialects of the western rural districts, after Norway's independence from Denmark in 1814. Nowadays Dano-Norwegian (Bokmål, or Riksmål), which stems from the written Danish introduced during the union of Denmark and Norway (1380–1814), and New Norwegian (Nynorsk) coexist, but the use of Dano-Norwegian is more widespread, since it is used in all national newspapers and in most of the literature. Both of these mutually intelligible languages are used in government and education. On lexical innovation in synthetic Scots, cf. McClure (1981b/1995).

10 However, 'nationalism does draw upon [Gaelic culture] as a source of symbols' (Macafee 1985: 8).

11 The extent to which labels may be difficult to attribute is shown by a famous quotation from the *Anglo-Saxon Chronicle*, in which the following languages are listed: 'englisc. 7 brittisc. 7 wilsc. 7 scyttisc.7 pyhtisc. 7 bocleden' (i.e., English, British, Welsh, Scottish, Pictish, Latin – cf. Culpeper 1997: 83). Skene (1867: 341) quotes a passage from the Metrical History by William Bosche, Archbishop of York, 1450–1460, which states: 'In cunctis planis : Anglorum lingua choruscat / Ast in montanis : barbara Scota sonat.' (In the Lowlands the language of the Angles is spoken : In the mountains that of the Scots). Cf. also Chapter 3.

12 Aitken (1985/1996: xiii), in his introduction to the *Concise Scots Dictionary* (CSD), provides the following dates for a chronology of Scots and English:

Old English	to 1100	Old English	to 1100
Older Scots	to 1700	Middle English	1100 to 1475
Pre-literary Scots	to 1375	Early Middle English	1100 to 1250
Early Scots	to 1450	Late Middle English	1400 to 1475
Middle Scots	1450 to 1700	Early Modern English	1475 to 1650
Early Middle Scots	1450 to 1550	Modern English	1650 onwards
Late Middle Scots	1550 to 1700		
Modern Scots	1700 onwards.		

survival. Already in 1609 James VI of Scotland, by then also James I of England, passed the Statutes of Iona,[13] which – among other impositions – forced the clan chiefs to withdraw their patronage from the bards (McClure 1994: 44). The Statutes were then ratified by an Act of 1616, which prescribed the teaching of English in local parish schools in the Highlands, with the explicit aim of extirpating the Gaelic tongue, seen as a source of 'barbarity':

> The Kingis Majestie haveing a speciall care and regard that (...) the vulgar Inglishe toung be universallie plantit, and the Irishe language, whilk is one of the chief and principall causis of the continewance of barbaritie and incivilitie amongis the inhabitantis of the Ilis and Heylandis, may be abolisheit and removit (text in Görlach 1991c: 384).[14]

In later times, the worst blows for Scottish Gaelic were possibly the aftermath of the Jacobite rebellion in 1746, when the Disarming Acts also had dramatic effects on lifestyle and culture, and the Highland Clearances in the nineteenth century, when thousands of people were forced to leave the Highlands and migrate overseas.[15] As a matter of fact, the main causes for decline identified by McArthur (1992b: 202) for all Celtic languages are the following:

1. disunity among the Celts in the face of colonisation, cultural domination and assimilation, and the pressure of governments often regarded as alien and regarding Celts as alien;
2. loss of linguistic status as English and French gained in strength and prestige;
3. shortage of reading material;
4. lack of adequate instruction and back-up;
5. loss of the language in religious life;
6. immigration into Celtic areas by speakers of English and French, often to hold important posts;
7. emigration, often under pressure;
8. the impact of the media;
9. a sense of increasing irrelevance (...) and assumptions of social and linguistic inferiority in the dominant culture that many Celts have slowly come to accept.

13 The name is due to the fact that the chiefs had to meet Andrew Knox, Bishop of the Isles, at Iona. One of the main aims was to persuade Highlanders to abandon their Catholicism and, to this purpose, the eldest child of each chief was to be educated in the south (Steel 1984: 110).

14 Grillo (1989: 85) presents the Statutes of Iona and the 1616 Acts as different, but the text he quotes for the latter (based on Nicolson 1866: 171) is the same. According to Romaine (1989: 217), they 'might well be the first instance of legislation designed to promote linguistic and cultural assimilation.'

15 The impact of the Clearances on language loss is described by Dorian (1981). This study, according to Grillo (1989: 51), not only gives an account of how linguistic change has occurred in Sutherland, but also how survival has been possible after tenant farmers began to develop new activities in socially separate fishing communities.

In this list we recognise a variety of reasons (which actually refer to different historical periods) that play simultaneous roles on different levels; for instance, loss of linguistic status is connected with the sense of irrelevance caused by the lack of reading and teaching materials, while, at the same time, the media provide much wider coverage in the dominant language. The role of language in religious life is also very important: the Statutes of Iona clearly associated linguistic policy with political and religious assimilation. Subsequent policies also followed similar criteria, and it was only in 1801 that the first complete Bible in Gaelic was published, although Meek (1988: 12; 15) states that 'by 1673 a complete translation of the Old Testament evidently existed' and the New Testament first appeared in Gaelic in 1766.[16] Although the literary tradition of Gaelic, especially in the eighteenth century, was remarkable (Watson 1984), the lack of such an important text in the local language for many centuries certainly proved crucial in the process of decline.[17]

Nowadays Gaelic is used as a community language in the north-west only; however, even data on this issue ought to be assessed carefully, because, as Romaine (1994: 40) points out, 'speakers who have a very limited productive control of the language still participate in the speech community of Gaelic speakers by virtue of their communicative competence', so official figures might not correspond to the real number of people whose abilities to understand and speak the language are homogeneous. Also Grillo (1989: 48) stresses the fact that 'there are always problems with statistical data collected in censuses and surveys which seek to record ('yes/no') who speaks a particular language'; the same author emphasises the fact that 'over the last hundred years or so monolingual speakers of Welsh and Scots Gaelic have virtually disappeared. In Scotland there has also been a major decline in the number of bilinguals'. Besides, Romaine (1989: 40–41) points out that

> None of the Celtic languages has secured a major urban area which is predominantly monolingual. The Isle of Lewis is the major stronghold

16 This was also linked to a strategic change on the part of the Society in Scotland for Propagating Christian Knowledge (SSPCK). Founded in 1709, the Society had always prevented the use of Gaelic as a medium for religious instruction, but it gradually became obvious that only rote learning could take place if the children did not understand what they read, so in 1766 the Society decided to allow learners to translate the English text into Gaelic ('Irish', as it was still called) though it was still forbidden to use it in conversation (Withers 1982; Leneman 1982). At the beginning of the twentieth century its activities were praised as forerunners of the Education Act of 1872, which brought greater occupational opportunities through a know-ledge of English. With this, commentators also associated 'wider social and political interests, a brighter intelligence and brighter outlook, freedom from mental vacuity and traditional superstitions' (Holmes 1909: 185). Besides, one observer specified that the young did not wish to be taught 'the language of their forefathers' (Holmes 1909: 196).

17 As we shall see in the next chapters, in the case of Scots the lack of Bible translations also played a major role in the process of anglicisation and, consequently, in the Scottish speakers' perception of their language as inferior.

for Scottish Gaelic, with over 85 percent of the population speaking the language. However, Stornoway, its capital, is in no sense a Gaelic town. In effect, this means that Gaelic does not claim a town of even 12,000, and thus, the language is largely rural rather than urban in its spread.

If we refer to census data, Douglas (1995) stated that Gaelic was spoken as a first language by 2% of the population. However, the exact figures resulting from the 1991 census are reported in the 'Gaelic Factsheet' included in the Scottish Executive website.[18] According to these, 69,510 people could speak, read and write Gaelic in Scotland, corresponding to 1.4% of the population; these figures may seem low, but Macleod and MacNacail (1995: 28) claimed that, if these data were compared with earlier ones, 'the number of Gaelic speakers in some areas of Scotland aged between five and fifteen actually increased': a phenomenon which may be due to a renewed literary interest, especially in Glasgow and Edinburgh. According to current data in the Scottish Executive website, 'The 2001 Census recorded 65,674 people aged three or over as being able to speak, read, or write Gaelic – 1.3 per cent of the Scottish population. The number of people aged two or over who could speak, read, write or understand Gaelic was recorded for the first time and found to be 92,396, or 1.9 per cent of the population'.

Current policies are directed to preservation of Gaelic (cf. MacKinnon 1984 and Macleod and MacNacail 1995); for instance, through broadcasts on radio and on TV (Henderson 1993: 74–79). However, it is undeniable that the constant spread of English has caused numerous cases of accommodation between the two languages and many degrees of variation even within the same language; in this respect Gaelic neologisms prove particularly interesting, in that they adapt typical English sounds and pronunciation to Gaelic grammar and spelling (e.g. *càr* = car, *telebhisean* = television); Ball and Fife (1993: 216) even report 'English *so* infiltrating the Gaelic of younger speakers'.

In education, a field that should prove crucial for language survival, some steps are being taken in order to cater for native and non-native speakers of Gaelic: a document of the Scottish Executive available in its website mentions the following among several others:

Under the Education (Scotland) Act 1980, education authorities have a duty to secure adequate and efficient provision of school education and further education and both of these include the teaching of Gaelic in Gaelic-speaking areas.

Under the Grants for Gaelic Language Education (Scotland) Regulations 1986, made under Section 73 of the Education (Scotland) Act 1980, The Scottish Office and local authorities have operated a scheme of specific grants for Gaelic education since 1986. (...)

18 The site is located at the following Internet address: <http://www.scotland.gov.uk>.

Gaelic features at all levels of education: pre-school, primary, secondary, further and higher education, and as part of teacher training. Education through the medium of Gaelic is well established at pre-school, primary, and further education levels and there is growing provision at secondary level. The provision of Gaelic medium education, like all education provision in Scotland, is determined by demand for the service balanced by the educational and economic viability of each educational unit. Gaelic language and Gaelic medium education are not confined to the traditional Gaelic-speaking areas of Scotland but are also established in the main urban areas. The culture, history, religion and belief of national minorities can all be taught in the general curriculum which is determined locally by education authorities and the managers of educational units.

A scheme of specific grants for Gaelic education was introduced in 1986.

The extent to which these policies will be successful will be seen in the future. At the time of going to press a new Gaelic Bill is being discussed in the Scottish Parliament. Cf. <http://www.scotland.gov.uk/pages/news/2003/10.SEED316.aspx>.

Scots

The status of Scots as a language or a dialect of English is still controversial: McArthur (1998: 138-159) provides a thorough overview of the statements that have been made to support one or the other stance at different times. Leith (1997: 150) points out that the choice has often been made difficult for both linguistic and political reasons, and he concludes that the 'stance on this issue will depend on the relative weight we attach to different kinds of criteria'. He also finds that 'the terms *dialect* and *language* are not fine enough to apply unequivocally to Scots' (1997: 157), since 'differences between Scots and English are often (...) not absolute, but may be expressed in terms of general tendencies and frequencies of items' (1997: 158).

Görlach (1991c: 22) reminds us that there have been criteria for accepting either option (language or dialect) since the sixteenth century: while several statements indicate that some users considered Scots an independent language,[19] 'the reciprocal intelligibility of Scots and English was [never] seriously endangered' and educated speakers were constantly aware of the historical relationship of Scots and northern English. Besides, 'structural differences were most marked in phonology/orthography and – in some texts – in lexis, but much less so in inflexion and syntax'. Görlach's conclusion is that

---

19 These will be discussed later and in the chapters pertaining to the various stages of the process of anglicisation.

It can therefore be argued that Scots is and has always been a subsystem of English, whose incipient separation from EModE [Early Modern English] was slowed down as a consequence of political, economic and cultural factors in the sixteenth century and finally blocked by the adoption of English as the written (and, later, the spoken) language of higher prestige (1991c: 23).

The label of 'subsystem' might also be challenged, in that it seems to imply a degree of inferiority which is in fact denied by the very argument of parallel, though asynchronous, development. Present-day Scots is certainly distinct enough to be dealt with separately, and recent scholarship seems to have devoted increasing attention to its features and traits; a very thorough summary of research carried out in the fields of linguistic surveys, sociolinguistics, grammar and vocabulary is presented by Aitken (1994),[20] where we also find indications of the renewed interest in the languages of Scotland through the organisation of conferences and papers presented in scholarly journals.

As McClure (1994: 24) points out, 'the distinction between Scots and Scottish English (...) is soundly based on historical facts', since Scots is derived from Northumbrian Old English, so 'in the course of the linguistic history of Scotland (...) first one and then two speech forms, both descended from Old English, have been used within the national boundaries.[21] (...) This situation has no exact parallel in the English-speaking world' (McClure 1994: 23). In addition, according to Görlach (1996a: 14), Scots is 'the most conspicuous case of what Kloss[22] called a *Halbsprache* in the sphere of English'. In his view, 'the degree of independence from English' may be determined on the basis of what he calls 'the four A's':

abstand – the greater the distance of the underlying system from Standard English (StE), the greater is the justification for classifying the speech form as a language (rather than a dialect);

ausbau – the greater the homogeneity of the speech form and the degree to which it has achieved linguistic norms on the one hand, and the range of functions in written and spoken forms on the other, the greater the claim to language-ness;

20 A similar study on Older Scots phonology appeared in Aitken (1991). An overview of the most comprehensive primary research in regional grammar in Britain and Ireland is provided by Kirk (1985).

21 As we mentioned before, we should remember that this actually describes the Lowlands, because the overall picture was multilingual: apart from Gaelic, more widespread in the centre and to the west, and varieties of OE, Norse was spoken in the north (Orkney and Shetland) and Latin was the language of the church and the law.

22 Görlach refers here to Heinz Kloss's work of 1978, *Die Entwicklung neuer germanischer Kultursprachen seit 1800* (Düsseldorf: Schwann) and, as a matter of fact, he draws a parallel with the development of Low German (cf. Görlach 1985b) and Jamaican (cf. also Gorlach 1991b and Smith 1996: 166).

attitude – if [speakers] wish to regard widely divergent speech forms as
varieties of one language, or minimally different ones as distinct
languages, the linguist cannot tell them they are wrong;

acquisition – incomplete language learning by entire groups of speakers can
cause the vernacular to drift away from the initially intended aim so that
new norms emerge (Görlach 1996a: 2).

Görlach (1996a: 15) finds that Scots 'has the potential for an independent
language as far as *abstand* (degree of divergence) and *ausbau* (functional
range) are concerned, only that the most important factor, attitude, is
underdeveloped'. This view seems to emerge from many of McClure's studies
(for instance, McClure 1995) and, as we have seen, the issue has often been
addressed in political terms. As Milroy (1996) points out, the connection
between ideology and language history is hardly negligible: the traditional unilinear view of historical linguistics 'was influenced very strongly by positions
that can be seen in retrospect to be ideologically influenced, valuing uniformity
above diversity, monolingualism above bilingualism and purity above mixing'
(1996: 184). However, 'the principles of variation studies can be held to
contradict the notion that languages develop in a unilinear continuum through
time (...). Even if a language were not influenced by external varieties, its true
history would be the history of its varieties as they intersect and overlap
through time, and phenomena like dialect-shift would play a central part in
historical description' (1996: 172). What Milroy calls 'the ideology of the
standard language' is related to 'the tendency to purism', the effects of which
may sometimes run counter to the belief that conservative rural dialects are purer
than the standard language (1996: 170–171). This view describes a division that
has often been identified in the description of Scotland's linguistic situation.

The debate on the status of Scots concerns both its historical development
and its present-day situation.[23] The first sources date from the seventh century
and they are based on the Old English of the Kingdom of Bernicia and the
Scandinavian-influenced English of immigrants from Northern England. As we
shall see in greater detail in Chapter 3, one of the earliest labels for the Scots
language was actually *Inglis*, thus making no distinction between the two
varieties of Old English that had been developing, as opposed to *Irishe*, which
designated the Gaelic language. It was only in 1494 that the use of *Scottis* was
recorded for the first time in Adam Loutfut's writings (McClure 1981a/1995:
44; Romaine 1982: 57), and 'the first major writer to make a point of insisting
on the independent status of 'Scottis' as compared to 'Inglis' was Gavin
Douglas in 1513' (McClure 1994: 32). Indeed, the political overtones of either
label actually emerge in the General Prologue to *Eneados*, in which Douglas
stresses the distinction between *Scottis*, 'our awin language', and the language
of England, which he calls *Inglis* or *Sudron* (McClure 1981a/1995: 44), the

23 Miscellaneous studies often discuss both aspects; for instance, this is the case with Aitken (1973).

latter 'having stronger negative connotations', as is shown by the fact that 'in Hary's *Wallace* the preferred name for the hero's opponents is *Southeron men* or *Southerons*' (McClure 1981a/1995: 50).

We could argue that the awareness of this distinction was the actual beginning of the progressive trend towards anglicisation that will be the object of the next chapters[24] and which Barber (1993) summarises in a few paragraphs emphasising the prestige value of English from the sixteenth century onwards; he also adds a sociolinguistic comment when, referring to today's situation, he says that 'having a dialect literature (...) is not the same as having a standard literary language' (1993: 174). At the same time, he acknowledges the existence of SSE without actually mentioning it explicitly when he states that 'since the eighteenth century (...) there have been works of literature in Scots, but the history-books and the contracts and the chemistry text-books have been written in what is essentially the southern literary language, though with a few specifically Scottish variations'. However, Barber does not go on to say what these variations are, whether they are lexical, morphological or syntactic, thus implicitly reflecting Milroy's view of the typical historical description as the account of unilinear developments in what is assumed to be the norm.

Gachelin (1995: 51) defines the words *Inglis* and *Scots* as 'historical chameleons'. He then denies the existence of SSE, but he does not base this statement on any linguistic consideration; instead, he equates SSE with 'equally non-existent "Norwegian Swedish" or "French Italian"' which are supposed to exist only 'as mispronounced by foreigners or in mixed couples' (1995: 52). What Gachelin does not seem to realise is that he is mixing linguistic elements like the historical development of two varieties of Old English into Scots and English respectively, and issues like language-contact and register-variation (the reference to foreign phonological realisations and interlanguages used by bilingual spouses are quite revealing in this respect). These issues, which are both important elements in the internal and the external history of Scots, seem to be overlooked because of the fuzziness of Gachelin's argument. A slightly better case is made by Shearer (1995), who presents the specificity of Scots vocabulary in its various registers and dialects (Central Scots, Northeast Scots, and Southern Scots),[25] highlighting the influence of other European languages, particularly French, Dutch, Gaelic and the Scandinavian languages.

24 This is the reason why Douglas's text is not discussed here in any detail, but in Chapter 3.
25 Cf. Romaine (1982: 66); information on dialect distribution is available through the work carried out since the 1950s through the Linguistic Survey of Scotland at the University of Edinburgh and available in the *Linguistic Atlas of Scotland* (Mather and Speitel 1975-86). The territory of Central Scots includes the cities of Edinburgh and Glasgow, thus having the highest number of speakers. The *Concise Scots Dictionary* (Robinson 1985-96) bases its distribution of dialect districts on work carried out for the *Scottish National Dictionary* (*SND*) (Grant and Murison 1931-76), and has the following, more detailed, distribution: Insular Scots (Shetland and Orkney), Northern Scots (Caithness, Sutherland, Ross and Inverness), North-East Scots (Nairn, Moray, Banff, Aberdeen and Buchan), East Mid Scots (Angus, Perthshire, Stirling, Fife

The high number of French loanwords in Scots has often been emphasised, again possibly for historical and political reasons, since most of these date from the times of the Auld Alliance, i.e., the Franco-Scottish alliance that lasted from 1296 to 1560; among these vocabulary items we find *cummer, houlet, tassie,* and *ashet*; according to the previously mentioned publication in the Scottish Office website, even 'the celebrated Scottish dish of haggis, (...) derives from the French 'hachis' (meaning minced beef)'. The same source provides another continental connection for the origin of golf: in the fifteenth century '(reputedly) Scots soldiers returning from the Hundred Years War brought back a game played with a stick and ball which was very popular among the Dutch and known as 'het kolf''; in fact, the contribution of Dutch to Scots vocabulary was quite extensive, as Murison (1971) has shown, though mainly restricted to the semantic field of trade.

The results of close contact between Scots and the Scandinavian languages has been shown through lists of vocabulary items – cf. Douglas (1995) and Stevenson (1963/1990). The former is very short and only presents Scots and Danish lexemes without providing an English translation; the latter is much more detailed, including lexical phrases, idioms, notes on pronunciation and the English equivalent of each item. For instance, Douglas has

SCOTS	DANISH
bairn	barn
brent	braende
kirk	kirke
lang	lang
ligg	ligge
mair	mer
smaa	smaa
stane	sten
starn, stern	stjerne

whereas in Stevenson's list we find

---

and Kinross, Edinburgh, the Lothians, Berwick and Peebles), West Mid Scots (Dumbarton, Argyll, Bute, Renfrew, Glasgow, Lanark and north Ayr), South Mid Scots (south Ayr, Kirkcudbright, Galloway and west Dumfries), Southern Scots (Roxburgh, Selkirk, east and mid Dumfries) and Ulster Scots. The *Concise Scots Dictionary* is an abridgement of the *Scottish National Dictionary*, which contains entries for Scots words and Scots usage of English words attested since 1700, and of the *Dictionary of the Older Scots Tongue* (*DOST*) (Craigie, Aitken *et al.* 1931 – 2002), which includes entries from the twelfth century to the end of the seventeenth century.

SCOTS	NORWEGIAN	ENGLISH
bigg	bygge	build
birk	bjørk	birch
blae	blå	blue
braw	bra	good
flit	flytte	move house
fremmed	fremmed	foreign
gate	gate	street
hals	hals	neck
hoast	hoste	cough

In neither case do we find an attempt to account for these similarities in actual philological terms, but in Stevenson's case the purpose of the list is simply to point out the analogy between the two languages, because 'The folk an lands o' Scotland an Norway are sib i mony gates ither than their leids, an aiblins we can lear muckle fra each ither gin we ken each ither better' (1963/1990: 1). Douglas, instead, wishes to underline the European dimension of Scots vocabulary and she provides even shorter lists of lexical items in common with French, Dutch and Gaelic, but her very slender pamphlet (9 pages altogether) simply summarises points that have been discussed in greater detail elsewhere – for instance by McClure (1994).

The Scandinavian influence is also obvious in the pronunciation of non-Scandinavian words like *kirk, kist, meikle* and *brig*, while McClure (1986/1995) has shown that Gaelic elements in Scots vocabulary are far more numerous than is generally assumed.[26] As a matter of fact, language contact, together with the issue of the relationship between internal and external elements in the process of anglicisation, which is further discussed by Görlach (1997a), is one of the factors that will be analysed in the historical chapters of this study. For the time being, it is important to stress the fact that a terminological distinction between Scots and SSE has to be drawn very clearly and explicitly in order to avoid confusion.

Scottish English

While it is true that phonological, morphological, lexical and syntactic features of a language all contribute to the specificity of that language, the case of SSE seems unique in the closeness of its texture. Miller (1993: 99) remarks: 'Scottish English may share one construction with Tyneside English, a second with Hiberno-English and a third with the West Midlands, but it may be alone in possessing all three constructions'. A similar case of variation between the standard

---

26 The relationship between Scots and Gaelic vocabulary is also discussed by Ó Baoill (1991 and 1997) and Macdonald (1994); on the Norse elements in Scots, cf. Smith (1994).

language and the local dialect also appears in English regions like Yorkshire. However, Aitken (1984b: 527) asserts that 'the Scots use more (...) non-standardisms more often and over virtually the whole social range, than are similar non-standardisms used elsewhere in the English-speaking world, including creole-speaking areas'. In fact, Aitken (1979: 85–86) identifies a range of speech options available to speakers, varying from 'broad dialect' to 'English'. Within this range options may be chosen according to a number of criteria: for instance, they may be related to register selection in different social circumstances, and in this case speakers may be called *dialect-switchers*; on the other hand, variation may be less predictable, in which case speakers may be defined as *style-drifters*. For this reason Macafee (1985: 7) finds that 'the coexistence of the Scots dialects with StE can be described as improper bilingualism, since speakers of both varieties cannot be said to operate with two linguistic systems, but rather with a variable bi-polar linguistic system, or dialect-standard continuum'.

As a matter of fact, SSE presents many features of Scots, though most of its grammar and vocabulary belong to general English. These features are specially prominent in pronunciation, since this is where it is easier to notice traits of SSE that are especially close to Scots. First, SSE is rhotic (i.e., the /r/ sound is heard after the vowel in such words as *car* or *there* and all the vowels and diphthongs appear unchanged before /r/); secondly, it retains the voiceless velar fricative /x/ represented by <ch> in borrowings like *loch, dreich, MacLachlan*, etc. Various studies have been carried out on the pronunciation of SSE: most notably, Abercrombie (1979), Aitken and McArthur (1979), Aitken (1984a) and Romaine (1975, 1978 and 1985) have focused on individual sounds, whereas McClure (1980) has examined intonation. As far as individual sounds are concerned, Scots and SSE share an important feature described as the 'Scottish Vowel-Length Rule', or 'Aitken's Law' from the name of the scholar who first identified it (cf. Aitken 1981 and Anderson 1993).[27] Of course this trait has been investigated in a number of subsequent studies (for instance, Agutter 1988a and McMahon 1992, where the former actually challenges the Scottishness of the rule), but we are not aware of any studies that investigate the relationship between realisations of the rule in cases of code-mixing between Scots and SSE.

The syntax and morphology of SSE and Scots are also worth examining in greater detail, as they may show interesting shared patterns, for instance in the use of modal verbs and negatives;[28] however, vocabulary is possibly the area in

---

27 According to this rule, 'originally long vowels are generally shortened except in stressed open syllables and when preceding a voiced fricative or /r/; and originally short vowels show a tendency to lengthening in the same environments' (McClure 1994: 50). This means that, for example, /i/ is long in *here, leave, see* and *agreed*, but short in *beat, feel* and *cease*; the same applies to /u/, which is short in *brood* but long in *brewed* (examples in McArthur 1992a: 910).

28 Typically, the lack of *may, shall* and *ought* and the presence of negative forms such as *disnae, dinnae* or *cannae* are taken to be exemplary cases of 'Scottishness': cf. Brown (1991) and Miller (1984 and 1993).

which Scots items are most likely to appear even in the language of people who have English as their principal adult language. All SSE utterances seem to place themselves at different stages along the cline between Southern Standard English and Scots, the type and quantity of Scots insertions depending on the speakers' attitude, their relationship with the interlocutor, the topic, etc. Romaine (1982: 65) considers five major dimensions of variation in her examination of 'the spoken English of Scotland today': 'region, social class, style, sex, and age', thus identifying SSE as a system of sociolects, or socially-defined varieties.

While the distribution of lexical items in the area of the Scottish-English border has been thoroughly examined by Glauser (1974), the variation within a geographical (but also a social) variety presents features of novelty that are just beginning to be investigated. The concept of continuum is also taken up by McClure (1994 and 1998) and Miller (1993). Both Aitken (1984b) and McClure (1994) claim that this situation of linguistic wavering between two codes is unique to Scotland, and this feature, which will be discussed in greater detail in the next chapter, is also identifiable in Iseabail Macleod's answer in a recent interview:

> Scots covers everything from dialects which the English – or even other Scots – wouldn't understand, to the way we're speaking just now, which is English with a Scottish accent. (*The Scots Magazine*, Dec. 1997, electronic edition).[29]

Apart from political considerations, the high degree of interchangeability that Scots has always shown with English (which makes it specially difficult to measure the location of an utterance or a sentence along the continuum that we have been describing) may possibly be one of the reasons why, unlike Celtic languages, it has never appeared in census returns (Leith 1997: 151).[30]

Scholars thus seem to agree on the difficulty of drawing a line between Scots and SSE, because of the constant switching (or drifting) in speakers' habits. Especially on the lexical level, SSE includes many items that are specifically Scottish because they are related to specific features of Scottish culture. Since the educational system, the law, and the church are organised differently from those in England and Wales,[31] there are a few lexical items pertaining to these areas that are not used elsewhere (unless it is with reference to a specifically Scottish context). For instance, in Scotland people talk about the *provost* and the *minister*, whereas in England the words *mayor* and *vicar* are used; to these we may add *laird*, *advocate*, *deacon*, *manse*, *stipend* and *glebe*.[32]

---

29 For *The Scots Magazine* the Internet address is <http://www.scotsmagazine.com/>.

30 This point will be resumed in Chapter 7.

31 As Macafee (1985: 8) points out, this is because, unlike Wales and Ireland, Scotland 'entered voluntarily into union with England (in 1707)'; cf. Chapter 4.

32 Of course the denotations of the various items are different in Scots and English in view of the different cultural phenomena which they express.

Borrowings from Gaelic are quite prominent in other cultural areas, for example in traditional folk music, where we have *clarsach*, *bodhran*, and *pibroch*; words like *clan, slogan, bard, sporran* and *ceilidh* are quite well-known even outside Scotland. The most obvious acquisitions, however, concern place-names: apart from world-famous instances like *Loch* (= lake, as in *Loch Ness*), we have *Ben* (= mountain, as in *Ben Nevis*), *Strath* (= valley, as in *Strathmore*), *Inver* (= mouth of a river, as in *Inveraray*), *Mull* (= promontory, as in *Mull of Kintyre*), *Kyle* (= strait, as in *Kyle of Lochalsh*) and many others.

Other elements appear in syntax; for instance, in cleft sentences. Shuken (1984: 155) identifies this device in Highland and Island English[33] constructions:

> Gaelic influence would seem to be reflected in the following constructions: those in which items are focused by using clefting, e.g. *It was always Gaelic I spoke in the home, Is it this here you want me to read?*; sentences beginning *There is/was*, where the focused item is brought forward in the sentence, e.g. *There's not many in Invernesshire are Gaelic-speaking, There's that many English people here now, it's English you talk mostly.*

Her suggestion that the general discourse strategy of thematic highlighting (of which clefts are an example) may be due to Gaelic influence is also discussed by Sornicola (1991), Dossena (1998a) and in various articles by Filppula (1991 and 1999).[34] The structure of Gaelic, in which the typical sequence is Verb-Subject-Object, is obviously the first element that seems to provide a historical background to the kind of constructions we have been identifying. However, a slightly closer investigation may provide even more clues. Ball and Fife (1993: 219) throw some light on relative clauses in Scots when they say that

> [Genitive relation] is expressed by means of subject/object or dative constructions, there being no direct Scottish Gaelic equivalent to English 'whose'. Thus *am fear a thàinig 'athair* 'the man whose father came' (lit. 'the man who his father came').

This feature might account for the limited use of *whase* in Scots, and indeed, its general substitution with *that + possessive adj.*[35] beyond literary contexts.

33 'Hebridean English' is possibly a more precise label for 'Island English' (Sabban 1982, 1984 and 1985), since by 'islands' Orkney and Shetland may also be meant, but in those areas Scandinavian influence was much more pervasive.

34 While most of Filppula's research has focused on Irish, the common root of Irish and Gaelic allows his findings to be reliably extended to phenomena in Scots and SSE: for instance, cf. Filppula (1997 and 1999) on the connections between Hiberno-English and Highland and Island English. The existence of a general family of 'Celtic Englishes', however, has been ruled out by Görlach (1998c).

35 Cf. Aitken (1992a: 896–897): '*The man that's hoose got burnt; the wumman that her dochter got mairrit*'.

The influence of Gaelic is perhaps easier to trace in the subordinate clauses beginning with *and*. Aitken (1992a: 896) provides the following examples of 'Verbless subordinate clauses that express surprise or indignation':

She had tae walk the hale lenth o the road and her seven month pregnant;
He tellt me tae run and me wi ma sair leg.

The analogy with Gaelic is perceived in three sentences analysed by Macaulay (1992: 169):

   a. Chunnaic Iain Anna agus i aig an dorus
      saw   Iain Anna *and she at the door*
   (= Iain saw Anna at the door)
   b. Chunnaic Iain Anna aig an dorus (= Iain saw Anna *at the door*)
   c. Chunnaic Iain Anna agus e aig an dorus
      saw   Iain Anna and *he* at the door
   (= Iain saw Anna as he was at the door).

The same strategy is discussed in its historical roots by Klemola and Filppula (1992), Dossena (1998a) and by Filppula (1999: 196-208); although it does not seem to be very frequent in SSE, it is certainly worth including it among those features that characterise this variety thanks to its connection with Scots, where it seems to be more widespread.

Of course this brief overview does not claim to represent all the phenomena due to language contact and interference between Gaelic, Scots and English, but simply to provide a context for some of the essential terminology that will be used in the next chapters. Some of the phenomena that were simply mentioned very briefly in this chapter will therefore be discussed in greater depth at later stages in this study.

Chapter Two

Scotticisms Today

Historical reasons have caused Scots and SSE to be closely connected, with Gaelic contributing to the vocabulary and syntax of both language varieties and acquiring vocabulary from the other two. Tulloch (1997b: 378–379) discusses the issue of identifying specific Scots vocabulary in the light of this very close connection with English: especially in speech, it is hardly likely that there will be 'pure' forms of either language, since speakers of SSE may use Scottish pronunciation, idioms or lexical items, while speakers of Scots are aware of the English language of education, the media and bureaucracy. His study, therefore, chooses to focus on 'the elements in Scots and English in Scotland which are not shared with English Standard English'. This definition of Scots vocabulary encompasses items whose cultural specificity makes them available to speakers of English, but only when referring to definite Scottish contexts; on the other hand, the choice to exclude items which 'seem to be confined to Scottish Standard English' limits the opportunity to compare the two codes on a communicative level, since the use of one item instead of another may be dictated by sociolinguistic and psycholinguistic reasons and may influence its pragmatic force.[1]

The distinction between one code (Scots) and the other (SSE) may be based on the density of items belonging to either: the lower the number of specifically Scottish elements in a text or in discourse, the closer this is to English Standard English. The connection between Scots and SSE is certainly easier to perceive on the phonological level and, as a matter of fact, also the range of options available to users on the syntactic and lexical levels seems to be wider in spoken language, since anglicisation appears to have been more effective in the codification of written language.[2]

What is a Scotticism?

The features of Scots generally present in SSE grammar and vocabulary are labelled as 'Scotticisms'. Algeo discusses the function of this and similar labels in the definition of geographical varieties, i.e. their use 'to denote a feature

---

1 The pragmatic value of Scots features in contemporary SSE will also be discussed in Chapter 7.
2 Macafee (1985) deals with this issue from the point of view of the influence that it has had on literacy in Scots as a consequence of literacy in English.

belonging to a national standard of an international language' (1989: 140) (for instance, *Americanism, Canadianism, Britticism* or *Australianism*), or 'the imitation in one language of the manner of expression typical of another' (1989: 141) (for instance, *Anglicism, Gallicism,* or *Latinism*).

Though both meanings may apply to the word 'Scotticism', the latter sense seems more appropriate for the object of our study, and indeed this becomes apparent when we consider that it was on the basis of this meaning that the word *Americanism* was coined by Witherspoon in 1781. As a matter of fact, this early value was seriously pejorative: Aitken seems to be the first scholar to use the word *Scotticism* in a contemporary academic context without over-loading it with the negative connotation it has had since its first appearance.[3] In fact, Aitken (1979) identifies a close connection with a psycholinguistic perspective that is mirrored in the speakers' sociolinguistic perceptions. While the latter will be resumed in Chapter 7, in these paragraphs we shall focus on the distinction that is drawn on the basis of the speakers' awareness of the specificity of the items that they use.

Speakers of SSE are generally taken to be unaware of their own code-mixing or style-drifting, but lexical choices are made more self-consciously and speakers may choose one item of vocabulary instead of another for stylistic or pragmatic purposes. This is what is argued by Aitken (1979: 104–110 and 1984a: 105–108) in his distinction between *covert Scotticisms* and *overt Scotticisms*. The former are used unselfconsciously; the latter, instead, are specially chosen to convey specific meaning: they are selected 'for special stylistic effect', for special emphasis or on specific occasions. This analysis certainly seems to be a very appropriate description of the phenomena occurring in SSE grammar and vocabulary, since it identifies the specificity of these phenomena, which are precisely those that mark a text as more or less broad. However, the distinction between one category and the other is not always very clear, and different studies have put forward different views.

McClure (1994: 85–86) points out that the distinction between overt and covert Scotticisms 'was recognised long before the introduction of the terms. John Sinclair[4] (...) observed that whereas many 'broad Scotch' words in wide use are easily recognised, numerous expressions are liable to be innocently 'mistaken for English' – by which he meant that they were used in the belief that everybody spoke so'.

As we saw in the previous chapter, lexical items pertaining to the legal system, to education and to religion are unique in their cultural specificity, but also the language of folklore, as may be expected, provides instances of words that have no direct equivalent in English: as an example, we may quote *fey* (=

---

3 The *Oxford English Dictionary* (*OED*) dates the first occurrence of this word to 1717; Aitken (1979: 94-95), however, has traced an earlier source in *Ravillac Redivivus*, of 1678 (cf. Chapters 3 and 4).

4 An eighteenth-century prescriptivist (cf. Chapter 4).

eerie, uncanny). All these, though overt Scotticisms, are not normally used to convey any special stylistic effect *per se*. Others, instead, are more markedly 'unusual', and are normally found in contexts that emphasise the fact that they are non-standard, though they may also appear in Northern English. For instance, this is the case of *bonnie* (or *bonny*), often found in collocations that have become almost idiomatic (e.g. *Bonnie Prince Charlie*, Charles Edward Stuart).

On a general level, we find that Scotticisms concern both grammar and vocabulary. The first summary of items (which is obviously not exhaustive, but simply underlines a few traits) is provided by Aitken (1979: 104–108, also discussed by Aitken 1984a: 105–108).[5] Since the article presents them in what appears to be random order, it may be useful to subdivide them into grammatical categories:

COVERT Scotticisms

Nouns / noun phrases	ashet = large serving plate
	bramble = blackberry
	burn = brook
	haar = thick sea mist
	pinkie = little finger
	rone-pipe = drainpipe
	to give someone a row = a scolding
	rowan = mountain ash
	he has a good conceit (= concept) of himself
	the whole jingbang or bangshoot = caboodle
Verbs / Verb phrases	I can see Christmas far enough (= I've had enough of it)
	I doubt (= I think) he's got lost
	don't let on (= reveal by your actions) you've seen him
	I put her gas at a peep[5] = I quashed her
	if it comes up my back = comes to hand, occurs to me
	to undertake something
	to jag = prick
	to miss oneself = to miss sth., e.g. a treat
	to shed (= part) one's hair
	to sort = mend
	to stay (= to live) in a (housing-) scheme = local authority housing estate
	to swither = hesitate

5 Aitken (1982: 31) points out that this and other Scotticisms, such as *fantoosh, high-heid-yin, housing-scheme*, or *to be up to high doh about something* are relatively recent, their first appearance being recorded in the twentieth or late nineteenth century. This is then a clear indication of the vitality of the language, which – in spite of past prescriptive attitudes – continues to adapt itself to a changing world in its own specific way.

Aspect	the walls were living (= alive) with bugs
	how's he keeping? (= how is he?)
Articles	to take the flu
Possessive adj.s	what would you like for your Christmas?
Preposition + adj.	I'm away to my bed
Prepositions /	
Prep. phrases	a week on Sunday
	the back of (= not long after) nine
	I'll see you the length of (= as far as) the bus stop
	to be up through (= during) the night
Adverbs	are you never out of your bed yet?
Conjunctions[6]	and him an elder of the kirk too
Exclamations	ach! och! mphm ['m:mm?]

OVERT Scotticisms

Nouns / noun phrases	a dram = a drink of whisky
	bairns = children
	chuckiestanes = pebbles
	clamjamfry = a confused mixture
	darg = a job of work
	hame, hoose = home, house
Adjectives	couthy = homely
	dreich = dry, tedious
	orra = odd
	peelie-wallie = somewhat ill, sickly
	shoogly = shaky, unsteady
	thrang = busy, engrossed
	wabbit = exhausted
	wersh = bitter or insipid
Verbs	birl = to spin
	coup = to capsise
	ken = to know
	stot = to bounce
	stravaig = to wander aimlessly
Affirmation	aye = yes
Negation	dinna = don't
Adverbs	gey = very
Prepositions	ben the hoose = in the house

---

6 This refers to the subordinating use of *and* described in Chapter 1.

Stereotypes[7] is he still to the fore = alive?

he's a right old sweetiewife = gossip, chatterbox

a bit of a feardie = a coward

a drop o the auld kirk / o the craitur = a small amount
of whisky .

that'll not set the heather on fire = cause any stir

let that flee stick to the wa = say no more about that
matter

it's back to the auld claes and parritch (= to
humdrum everyday life) tomorrow

come into the body of the kirk = come and join the
main company

to keep a calm sough = to keep quiet or not to get
excited

slàinte-mhath[8] = good health!

To these, McClure (1994: 86–87) adds the following items of vocabulary:

COVERT Scotticisms	OVERT Scotticisms
byre = cowshed	bonny = handsome
cleg = horsefly	blether / haver = talk nonsense
close = passageway between buildings	dwaam = daydream
forenoon = late morning	deave = deafen or exhaust
granny = chimney cowl	fantouche = affectedly flamboyant
mavis = thrush	jalouse = deduce
skelf / spelk = splinter in the skin	Sasunnach = native of England
stirk = bullock or heifer	kenspeckle = conspicuous
whin = gorse	shilp = insignificant person
	trauchled = overworked
	yokin-time / lowsin-time = beginning and end of a working day

As we see in this addition, covert Scotticisms are mainly nouns, whereas overt
Scotticisms also include adjectives and verbs. McClure also mentions the lore
of children, together with the other items that are specifically Scottish because
they belong to the vocabulary of church, law, education and Highland life and
culture. We find that this area is certainly worth investigating in greater detail,
because the preservation of traditional usage is quite likely in rhymes, games
and riddles. Among these lexical items McClure (1994: 87) includes the following:

---

7 What Aitken calls stereotypes might in fact be described as idioms.

8 The inclusion of a Gaelic phrase in Aitken's list of 'stereotypes' is remarkable because it shows
that, in this case, Gaelic has been adopted as a mark of Scottishness outside the context of its
typical usage, i.e. the Highlands and their culture.

- guising = children's practice of visiting homes in disguise on Halloween
- coalie-bag = ride on the back
- coxie-cusie / cockerty-hooie = ride on the shoulders
- leavie-o = a chasing game
- hi-spy = hide-and-seek, 'in which the seeker is *het* and 'home' is the *den* or *dell*.'

Among idioms, or 'unobtrusive habits in phrasing', McClure includes *the likes of you, mind and not lose it, go the messages, up to high doh* (= approaching panic), *come and give us your crack* (= chat with us), *does he always get Bandy?* (= Is he always known as Bandy?), *Jock Tamson's bairns* (= common humanity), *to gang agley, auld lang syne, aa the airts* (= all localities or directions).[9]

Görlach (1990: 130–133) presents a different classification of Scots lexical items in contemporary Scottish usage. In his study he investigates the issue of lexical survival in Scots and SSE through the analysis of 100 items (which 'had an obvious OE etymon and were apparently not current in ModE') recorded from post-medieval Scots and classified according to a usage test carried out by Derrick McClure as 'a competent speaker of Scots'. Görlach's categories for the usage test are as follows:

o	unknown	I would use it
1	known as (probably) obsolete	A not unless forced to by the context (e.g. for a rhyme)
2	known exclusively from literature	B only in writing
3	not common in speech, but regular in literature	C in speech as a conscious Scotticism
4	common in Scots	D regularly in speech
5	also part of ScE	

The usage test allows Görlach to draw up a correlation table that provides insights into the diffusion of these lexical items:

		A	B	C	D	
o	15	–	–	–	–	15
1	–	13	1	–	––	14
2	–	2	18	2	–	22
3	–	–	8	4	–	12
4	–	2	3	13	–	18
5	–	3	1	4	11	19
	15	20	31	23	11	100

As we can see, most items belong to categories C and D, which refer to spoken usage, but the highest number in one category appears in B2, thus showing the

---

9 Some of these phrases also occur in Aitken (1979), where they are presented along with sociolinguistic judgements about the degree of their acceptability.

persistence of items in literary usage. Category A1 shows items disappearing and C4 those which are more marked: in fact, these categories implicitly assume that the user is a speaker of SSE.

As a matter of fact, Görlach's comments on these results emphasise the specificity of the test and the fact that some lexical items may not be widespread because they are strictly local and speakers from other areas may not be aware of them, as in the case of *spelk* (= splinter), which becomes *skelf* in other areas, or because they may be restricted to certain domains and registers, as in the case of *dempster* (= law officer). For the purposes of our study, categories 4 and 5 are obviously those in which we may seek confirmation of the perceived specificity of a certain item from the geographical point of view. The lexical items that are included in these categories are the following:

4A = common in Scots, not used unless forced to by the context: *bairn, spelk*;

5A = also part of ScE, not used unless forced to by the context: *hamesucken* (= assault), *smeddum* (= pith, spirit), *dempster*;

4B = common in Scots, used only in writing: *barm* (= yeast), *lear* (= teach), *reird* (= uproar);

5B = also part of ScE, used only in writing: *Yule*;

4C = common in Scots, used in speech as a conscious Scotticism: *ben* (= inwards), *dree* (= endure), *dwine* (= pine, fade), *leed* (= language), *lew* (= lukewarm), *ream* (= cream), *sicker* (= safe, reliable), *snell* (= quick), *souch* (= sound), *stey* (= steep), *sye* (= filter), *threap* (= rebuke, argue), *wyte* (= blame);

5C = also part of ScE, used in speech as a conscious Scotticism: *handsel* (= gift), *neb* (= beak, nose), *quean* (= girl), *speir* (= ask);

5D = also part of ScE, used regularly in speech: *bannock, daft, darg* (= day's work), *dicht* (= arrange, wipe), *ken, neep* (= turnip), *redd* (= save, tidy),[10] *souter* (= cobbler), *sweir* (= lazy, loath), *thole, wersh*.

Categories C and D are those which correspond to Aitken's definition of overt and covert Scotticisms respectively and, as a matter of fact, in these categories we also find:

2C = words known exclusively from literature, used in speech as a conscious Scotticism: *flyte* (= chide), *nesh* (= soft);

3C = words not common in speech, but regular in literature, used in speech as a conscious Scotticism: *fey* (= doomed), *fouth* (= abundance), *haffet* (= temple), *weird* (= fate).

Despite apparent conflicts existing with previous classifications (for instance, *bairn* belonging to A, rather than C) we find that this categorisation may be

---

10 Although Görlach presents this as a noun, this is obviously a misprint, because the translation provided, based on the *CSD*, shows it to be a verb.

more accurate than others from various points of view. First of all, it relates items to usage in speech or in writing, on a more or less conscious level, so it is more specific as far as tenor and mode are concerned; then it accounts for the influence of literary sources on vocabulary, which, in the case of Scots, is certainly not negligible; finally, it identifies a sample of the Old English core in Scots vocabulary. Unfortunately, such a taxonomy is not extended to grammatical features, whereas we saw that previous classifications of covert and overt Scotticisms also included these elements.

In a subsequent study, Aitken (1992c: 904–905) presents a classification of vocabulary that is closer to Görlach's and goes beyond the distinction between covert and overt Scotticisms:

1 = words of original Scottish provenance used in the language at large for so long that few people think of them as ScoE;
2 = words widely used or known and generally perceived to be Scottish;
3 = words that have some external currency but are used more in Scotland than elsewhere, many as covert Scotticisms;
4 = general words that have uses special to ScoE and Scots;
5 = Scottish technical usages;
6 = colloquial words used and understood by all manner of Scots and by the middle class as overt Scotticisms;
7 = traditional Scots words occasionally introduced into StE contexts in the media and known to minorities.

This subdivision allows the author to classify various lexical items according to their degree of proximity to StE and, consequently, to their degree of opacity from the point of view of users both within and beyond Scottish contexts. The following items are included:

1 caddie, collie, cosy, croon, eerie, forebear, glamour, golf, gumption, lilt, golf links, pony, raid, rampage, scone, uncanny, weird, wizened, wraith;
2 bannock, cairn, ceilidh, clan, clarsach, corrie, first-foot, glengarry, gloaming, haggis, kilt, pibroch, sporran, Tam o'Shanter, wee, whisky;
3 bairn, bonnie, brae, burn, canny, douce, Hogmanay, kirk, peewit (= lapwing), pinkie, skirl;
4 astragal (= glazing bar on a window), close (n.), stair, stay, tablet (= sweet), uplift (= collect);
5 advocate (= barrister), convener (= chairman of a committee), induction (of an ordained minister to a ministerial charge), janitor, jus relicti (= the relict's share of a deceased's movable property), leet (= list of selected candidates for a post), procurator-fiscal (= official combining the offices of the coroner and public prosecutor), provost, timeous;
6 ach (= dismissive interjection), braw, chuckiestane, footer (= to mess about), gillie (= hunting attendant), girn (= to whine), glaikit (= stupid),

haar, howf (= public house), och, pernickety (= fussy), scunnered (= sickened), wabbit, wannert (= mad);

7 bogle, dominie, eident (= diligent), forfochen (= exhausted), furth of/ outwith, gardyloo, hochmagandie (= fornication), leid, makar, owerset (= translate), Sassenach (= Englishman / Lowlander), southron, yestreen.

Among these categories, no. 1 seems particularly interesting because it acknowledges the full standardisation of items that have kept their meaning while losing their geographical specificity.[11] In the other categories we find Gaelic items in no.2 and Scots cultural elements in no. 5, while categories 3 and 6 echo the previous distinction between overt and covert Scotticisms.[12]

In general, we see that present-day descriptions of (spoken) English in Scotland focus on those features that seem specific because of their closeness to Scots. In addition to other items clearly based on Aitken's list, Trudgill and Hannah (1985: 87) provide the following lexical items, for the totality of which they provide English equivalents and notes on usage: *carry-out* (= takeaway), *folk, infirmary, to mind* (= to remember), *to shoogle,* and *through* (= across). As far as phrases and idioms are concerned, they list *That's me away, He gave me a fright, I'm finished it, I'll get you home, Cheerio just now!, To go the messages.* However, the morpho-syntactic features of these idioms are not described.

Scotticisms in morphology and syntax

Some elements in these classifications of Scotticisms actually refer to different grammatical patterns, for instance in the use of the article in *I've got the cold.* Trudgill and Hannah (1985: 85–86) point out a number of features that are shared by SSE and other varieties, such as American English (AmE), but their study does not go into any depth. Lass (1987: 261–262) also presents 'a number of lexical and grammatical features characteristic of most varieties of Scots, including SSE', and he subdivides them into four broad categories:

1. lexical items unique to Scotland: *gean* (= wild cherry), *jag, whin* (= gorse), *rones, roup* (= public auction), *haar, aye* (=always),[13] *gey, swither, blether, weans,*[14] *thole, peelie-wallie;*

11 This category seems to have been neglected in previous studies on the interaction of Scots and English, though it is discussed briefly by Beal (1997) and Tulloch (1997b). The same might apply to category no. 4, which emphasises the role of cultural connotation in lexical choices; to these items we might add *water* (= river), as in *Water of Leith.*

12 Aitken (1992b: 901) integrates previous lists with *work for sweeties* (= for a pittance) [overt] and *cast out* (= quarrel), *cast up* (= reproach), and *handless* (= clumsy) [covert].

13 Lass identifies *aye* (= yes) as general northern; we should also remember that this usage is preserved in British parliamentary language.

14 Lass distinguishes this item from its synonym *bairn*, which he classifies as 'General Northern'; however, these two items are often used to distinguish varieties of Scots, *wean* being more widespread in the West.

2. Scots senses for General English items: *bramble, sort, while* (= until), *messages, cry* (= call by a name), *clap* (= pet an animal), *stay*;
3. idiomatic features: 'a kind of 'third person' self-portraiture (for want of a better term), in narration and comment: e.g. *there's me sitting on the floor after the chair broke, that's me away home; what like; the cat needs/ wants out; the now; back of* (= just after), e.g. *I'll be there the back of ten*';
4. grammatical features: these refer to negation and modals, but both are described very briefly, without specifying that phenomena like double modals actually belong to Scots, rather then SSE.

Although Lass also provides the translation of each lexical item and intersperses the text with occasional comments on usage and similarities with AmE or Northern varieties of English, no comments are made on the textual or pragmatic function, if any, of the use of these items.

Most of the studies that we have been describing so far include syntax and morphology in their description of the specificity of SSE. However, the most comprehensive account in this respect is offered by Miller (1993).[15] Although phonology and vocabulary are not described in any detail, Miller's analysis of morphology, syntax, and, most interestingly, of discourse strategies proves particularly fruitful for an account of the connections between Scots and SSE today.

Miller's own terminology is admittedly flexible from this point of view, in consideration of the high degree of variability within the SSE / Scots linguistic continuum. In Miller's words,

> Scottish speakers draw on Broad Scots and standard written English to varying degrees, depending on degree of formality (topic, location of con-versation, participants in the conversation) but also on the inclinations of the individual speaker. (...) As it is not our purpose here to define and delimit different varieties, we will use the terms 'Scots', 'Broad Scots' and 'Scottish English' fairly freely in reference to our data. (1993: 100)

Miller does not discuss the issue of awareness on the part of the speakers in any considerable detail, so he does not mention the contrast between overt and covert Scotticisms, but he always points out the analogies with other varieties of English,[16] thus shedding light on the possible perception of the features that he describes as more or less specifically non-standard. In the following para-graphs we shall provide a brief account of the phenomena that are described as markedly Scottish.

15 Cf. also Miller and Brown (1982), Miller (1984) and Kirk (1987). Häcker (1998), instead, limits her study to adverbial clauses.
16 For instance, as regards the use of *what* as a relative pronoun, as in *like the other birds what takes Dexedrine* (Miller 1993: 111), Miller refers to Macafee's studies on Glasgow usage. Another instance of non-standard usage shared by Scots and other varieties of English is the use of *them* as a demonstrative adjective, as in *them cakes was awfy dear* (Miller 1993: 108).

As far as morphology is concerned, we find:

a. the regularisation of irregular verbs: e.g. *gaed* instead of *went*, *sellt* instead of *sold*;[17]
b. a regular relationship between singular and plural forms: e.g. *wifes*, *knifes*, instead of *wives*, *knives*;
c. the first person singular possessive pronoun is *mines*;
d. the demonstrative adjective *thae*, corresponding to *those*, competes with *them* in non-standard utterances; the typically northern three-way distinction in the system of demonstratives – which includes *this*, *that*, and *yon*, the last referring to objects remote from both speaker and listener (Hughes and Trudgill 1996: 32) – seems to apply to Scots, rather than SSE.

To these we may add the fact that, according to Aitken (1992c: 905), indefinite personal pronouns are generally formed with *-body*, rather than *-one*: this might relate to the formation of compounds with the previous form in Scots.

As regards syntax, Miller (1993) identifies the following phenomena:[18]

a. Plural subject nouns combine with singular verb forms (*is*, *was*): for instance, we may have *the windies wiz aw broken*; *wiz*, but not *is*, may occur with *we*, as in *we wiz aw asleep*.
b. In measure phrases with a numeral followed by a measure noun (*mile*, *stone*, *year*), the latter is generally singular: for instance, something may weigh *four stone*, or be *two foot high*. In addition to this, there is usually no preposition between the measure nouns *bit* and *drop* and the noun that follows them,[19] as in *a bit paper, a drop water*.
c. Relative clauses present particular constructions: the use of *that* + *possessive adjective* instead of *whose* seems very productive in spoken discourse. We also find that co-ordinate clauses may replace non-restrictive relative clauses. For instance, Miller (1993: 112) quotes the following example: *the boy I was talking to last night – and he actually works in the yard – was saying it's going to be closed down*. In addition to this, McClure (1994: 74) points out that in Scots a zero relative may also be employed as a subject, as in *Wha was the leddy gaed doun the road afore ye?*

---

17 In the latter case, Miller (1993: 106) finds that '*sellt* is simply *sell* + *ed*, *ed* being realised as *t* in Scottish English after *l* and *n* – cf. *killt* (= killed)'; a further example is *kent* (= knew).
18 Syntax is also discussed by Jones (2002); however, since this appeared after the manuscript of the present volume was submitted for publication, it has been impossible to include any extensive discussion of the points Jones makes.
19 According to Miller (1993: 110), this feature is typically Germanic (cf. *Ein Glas Bier* in German); however, he points out that this construction is less productive in Scots, where *A glass beer* is not possible.

d. Negation is possibly the area where the specificity of Scots and SSE appears to be closest. Following Miller's phrasing, 'in Scots, the verb in a sentence is negated by the independent words *no* and *not* (...) or by the dependent forms *nae* and *n't* (...). NO is most frequent with BE and next most frequent with *'ll* (...) (*she'll no be coming to the party*) and (...) the reduced forms of *have* and *has* (*I've no seen him the day, She's no phoned yet*). *Nae* is added to all the modal verbs and to DO: *He doesnae help in the house.* (...) In negative interrogatives (...) *n't* (...) is usually avoided and *not* is used.' This feature is also quite prominent in tag questions, e.g. *That's miles away is it no.* As regards negative sentences without auxiliary verbs, Broad Scots uses *never* with the past tense, as in *I could've got the job...but I telt them I couldnae leave till the end of May so I never got it*, although this use of the adverb is not emphatic; if it were, it would be *never ever*.

e. Linguists seem to agree on the fact that modal verbs in SSE are considerably different from StE. This is due to the fact that 'Broad Scots lacks SHALL,[20] MAY and OUGHT' (Miller 1993: 116). Consequently, the future is expressed by *will*, permission is expressed by *can, get to* and *get + gerund* (as in *the pupils get to come inside in rainy weather*, or *they got going to the match*), and *should* substitutes *ought*. Both *have to* and *need to* substitute *must*, which is only used to express conclusions (also in negative sentences, as in *this mustn't be the place*), and *need* behaves like a main verb. In fact, Miller (1993: 11) finds that it may even be more frequent in Scots than in other varieties. Obligation can also be expressed by *supposed to* or *meant to*. The latter may also be an equivalent of *It is said that*, as in *The new player is meant to be real fast*. As regards double modals, which are frequently pointed out as one of the most distinctive features of Broad Scots, we should stress the fact that they hardly ever occur in SSE.[21] What is certainly more interesting is the use of *maybe* in sentences where *may* would occur in StE, as in *You've maybe seen it*, instead of *You may have seen it*. In fact, Miller (1993: 120) finds that even *might* could be 'developing into an adverb, syntactically equivalent to *maybe*' in sentences like *They might could be working in the shop* or *She might can get away early*.

f. As we saw in the tables based on Aitken's and McClure's studies, aspect is also different in Scots and in SSE; thus, in Scots, progressive forms may be applied to verbs like *want, need* (Trudgill and Hannah 1985: 86), *like*, and *understand*. As far as the perfect is concerned, Miller (1993: 123)

---

20 McClure (1994: 71) claims that the loss of *shall*, or *sall*, is fairly recent; he refers to literary attestations that are said to be common until the beginning of the twentieth century and to conservative pronunciation, which retains the reduced form.

21 Indeed, no instances of double modals have been found to occur in the Miller-Brown Corpus of Scottish English (cf. Chapter 7).

identifies an interesting use of the *past progressive* + *there* — instead of *just* + *present perfect* — to express an event that took place recently but is now finished, as in *I was speaking to John there*. *There* obviously does not point to a place, and recalls a similar usage in the kind of self-portraiture described by Lass (see p. 27). *Want* and *need* are often followed by a past participle, as in *The car needs washed* (Hughes and Trudgill 1996: 16), or by a preposition, as in *The cat wants out*.

g. In interrogative forms, *how* and *what for* may replace *why*; *what* may be used instead of *which*; *about* may be added after *where* and *how* to introduce an idea of approximation, as in *Where does he stay about?*, or *How old was he about?* Tag questions, which have already been mentioned with reference to negative forms, have specific Scots forms in *e* and *e no?*, as in

- *we know him quite well by now e?*
- *it's no too dear e?*
- *you're taking her to the pictures e no?*

These forms may also occur in imperative sentences which function as requests (as in *put it down there e*), with the effect that they 'always reduce the sharpness' of the request, unlike StE *won't you*, which may in fact make the request stronger.

h. Another feature that is often stressed in descriptions of Scots and SSE (and which are found in the tables summarising present-day Scotticisms) is the use of the definite article with nouns denoting institutions (e.g. *church, school, college, hospital*), certain illnesses (e.g. *flu, measles, chickenpox*), certain periods of time and with quantifiers such as *both* and *all* (Miller 1993: 128). Many examples are quoted, the most widespread of which seem to be the ones concerning adverbs of time, i.e. *the day* = today, *the morn* = tomorrow, *the now* = now, and prepositions, i.e. *in the house*[22] = at home, *through the post* = by post, *over the phone* = by phone. Determiners may also be introduced in the form of possessive adjectives, as in *I'm off for my dinner*. Again, this is something that is regularly described as a Scotticism. Beal (1997: 362–363) refers to Tulloch (1980) and Macaulay (1991a) for a discussion of the use of determiners and she reminds us of the use of the definite article in time expressions that have become lexicalised: for instance, the years of the Jacobite rebellions, *the Fifteen* and *the Forty-five*.[23] To these, we can add the use of the article with languages, especially with *Gaelic*, as in *Do you have the Gaelic?*, meaning *Can you speak Gaelic?*

---

22 The analogy with the Scots phrase *ben the hoose* seems to point to a syntactic calque in SSE.

23 An example of this is to be found in Stevenson's *The Master of Ballantrae* (1889/1984: xx), where the phrase '[He] was out in the Forty-five' is a euphemism for 'He took part in the Jacobite rebellion'.

i. Prepositions and adverbs also feature quite prominently in the sum-
maries of Scottish features to which we have been referring. Although
Miller (1993: 131) reminds us that 'the prepositional system of Broad
Scots has yet to be studied in detail', certain elements may be worth
noting:

- in passive clauses *from, frae/fae, off* (= of) and *with* may replace *by*:
  e.g., *ah'm gonna get killt fae ma maw, I was very impressed with
  the way they dressed*;
- *off* may replace *from* expressing the source of something: e.g., *I got
  the book off Alec*;
- *by* is avoided in its location sense, and *at, beside, next to* or *past* are
  used instead: e.g., *they drove past the house on their way to the
  airport*;
- *in* and *out, up* and *down* do not need to be followed by *to* (or *of*)
  after verbs of movement; after verbs of location *up* and *down* do
  not require *at*: e.g., *They were up the town yesterday*; *outside*,
  instead, is usually followed by *of*, as in *outside of the school*.
- *bored / fed up* are usually followed by *of*, instead of *with*; this
  instance seems to fall in the same category as other prepositional
  phrases that have already been mentioned, such as *over the phone,
  through the post*, or verbs that become prepositional, such as *wait
  on someone, married on someone*.
- Other 'distinctively Scottish usages' identified by McClure (1994:
  87) include *among the snow, It's not for any use, Tell your father I
  was asking for him* (= asking after his health), *I'm for a drink, Did
  you get it in a present?, You'll be better of a rest, Shout on him to
  come in, He missed the bus with sleeping in, a fried egg to my tea, I
  got up through the night, Have you on your shoes?*. According to
  Trudgill and Hannah (1985: 86), 'The last phrase is attributable to
  the fact that SSE, like AmE, allows the adverbial particle in
  compound verbs to remain directly after the verb, as in *He turned
  out the light, They took off their coats*'. Moreover, according to
  their rather brief summary of ScotEng grammar, 'the full verb *have*
  behaves more like an auxiliary in ScotEng than in EngEng', which
  implies that it does not require a *do* auxiliary in questions and
  negative sentences (Trudgill and Hannah 1985: 86).

Scotticisms in discourse organisation

After morphology and syntax, the last aspect that Miller (1993) considers is
the organisation of discourse; this may prove especially important for the
definition of the specificity of SSE in relation to Scots. As the highest number of

non-standard features is perceivable in spoken language, discourse may provide important clues for our description of Scotticisms today.

The first strategy identified by Miller concerns the ways in which speakers announce a new topic by means of either the duplication of the theme, which is expressed both by a noun phrase and a pronoun (e.g., *The driver he's really friendly*, or *And there's one girl she's a real extrovert*), or a construction in which two clauses are used as an adjacent pair (e.g., *So what you had to do was you got a partner and you got a match*, or *But what you did in the evening you carried a sandwich or two*). According to Macaulay (1991a: 119), whose investigation focuses on social varieties,[24] theme duplication seems to occur most frequently. In this construction the noun phrase can be rather complex, as in *And the fermer that I was wi at that time he was bate oot of the ferm*.

Miller then underlines the frequency of cleft sentences, as in *Where is it he works again?* (1993: 134). Macaulay (1991a: 79) finds that *it*-clefting, as in *It was her that got them*, is not unlike what he calls *demonstrative focusing*: this construction, however, 'occurs either at the climax or the conclusion of a narrative or a reminiscence'. His definition is as follows:

> [Demonstrative focusing] consists of a demonstrative pronoun followed by a form of the verb *be* and the object form of a pronoun with a complement that can be either an adjective, a past participle, a present participle, or an adverbial clause:
>
> a. WL1474 that was *him* idle
> b. EL394 that was *you* shut in the house for a week
> c. WL2116 but that's *me* seen it
> d. WL1147 that's *us*
>   1148 going for another game
> e. HG583 and that was *you*
>   584 maybe slaving until eicht or nine at nicht
> f. WL1453 that was *you* till aboot six o'clock
> (1991a:121–122).

In this respect, Macaulay takes the discussion into the area of pragmatics; a similar highlighting strategy may be identified in the constructions of 'self-portraiture' which were described in the first chapter and to which reference was made in the paragraph on aspect. Miller (1993) and McClure (1994) do not mention this idiomatic feature of SSE syntax at all, while Aitken (1979: 108) seems to have been the first to comment on it, although he restricted his analysis to the degree of acceptability of this construction: 'Some but perhaps not all middle-class Scots would find acceptable (...) the idiom *that's me* or

---

24 Macaulay's study in 'discourse microsociolinguistics' (1991a: xiii) is based on interviews made in 1978–79 with Ayrshire dialect speakers from different social backgrounds; cf. also Macaulay (1985; 1995/96; 1997a; 1997b).

that's him etc. (doing or having to do something), as in *that's me humphing*, or *having to humph it away out to Blackhall* or *having to chum her right down to the station'*.

Other focusing devices are identified by Miller in the use of *see* and *ken* (which introduce themes, as in *ken this wee lassie comes in with tea towels*), *like* (which generally highlights explanations, as in *there's a wee kiddies' pool you know where my wee girl can swim you know she has her wings like – she jumps right in*), and *the thing is*, which may be expanded with an adjective and which introduces propositions or properties of the theme (as in *thing is he's watching the man*, or *the only thing wi Beth – Beth's mean – she'll no gie ye two haufs for a one*).

To the features that have been outlined so far we can add the use of diminutive forms, which, from the point of view of pragmatics, may cause the comparison between English and SSE to prove particularly fruitful, since scholars so far have pointed out the remarkable lack of diminutive forms in English, as opposed to more frequent occurrences in SSE and Australian English (AusE) (Dressler and Merlini Barbaresi 1994: 113).[25] Dorian (1993: 134) stresses the diffusion of diminutive forms in Northeast Scots and briefly investigates its possible connection with East Sutherland Gaelic, identifying 'a corresponding freedom of occurrence for diminutives which does not seem to exist in western dialects of Gaelic'.[26] She quotes one Mull speaker, according to whom 'the way ESG speakers attached diminutives liberally to body-part terms sounded childish to him, like a form of baby-talk'. As a matter of fact, linguists have identified the sound-iconism of [i], which is typically found in diminutive forms (as in It. *gattino*, Ger. *Mausi*, Sc. *beastie*), as an element that contributes to the emotional colouring of these. This colouring is typically associated with child-centred speech situations and is transferred to pet-centred and lover-centred speech situations.[27] On the other hand, diminutives may also occur in expressions of irony and even sarcasm. For instance, an insult may be strengthened by the presence of a diminutive, while on the surface it may seem attenuated. Bulloch (1921/1970: 146) finds that while 'the diminutive is

---

25 The pragmatic value of diminutives in SSE was discussed in greater detail in Dossena (1998b).

26 Dorian (1993: 134) reports that Gaelic speakers from the Isle of Mull do not use many diminutives in free conversation, nor do they produce them in elicitation contexts which had 'quite reliably produced them in East Sutherland'.

27 Dressler and Merlini Barbaresi (1994: 196) refer to 'Freud's assertions on the 'kindischen Gesten aller Verliebten' (i.e., the childlike gestures of all lovers). The parallelism is clearly exemplified in Bulloch (1921/1970: 140–142), in which the author quotes rhymes that express both smallness and endearment through the application of diminutives not only to the addressee, but also to other items that set the context: in the case of the child-centred speech situation Bulloch quotes the following lines: 'Dance to your daddie, My bonnie laddie. Dance to your daddie, my bonnie lamb! And ye'll get a fishie In a little dishie – Ye'll get a fishie when the boat comes hame (…)' (p. 140). For the lover-centred speech situation he quotes 'Come under my plaidie' (p. 142).

admirable for expressing the physical smallness of a child, and the child quality in the things we love, so it represents equally well all kinds of spiritual smallness and meanness'.[28]

The most productive diminutive suffix is certainly *-ie*; other Scots diminutive suffixes, such as *-ock, -kin* and *-ag* do not seem to occur in SSE. However, their usage is described in Aitken (1992a: 896) and *-ag* seems specially interesting because it typically occurs in the North, implying Gaelic influence on lexis. It also influences morphology, because *-ag* is the feminine diminutive suffix (the equivalent masculine suffix is *-an*), so 'nominal gender assignment gets an enormous boost in the dialect' (Dorian 1993: 134). Besides, suffixes may also co-occur, as in *lassockie*, and they may be reinforced through the use of an attributive adjective like *wee*.

An important aspect of the pragmatic value of diminutives is summarised in Bulloch's claim that 'the diminutive does for the Scot what the understatement does for the Englishman' (1921/1970: 147). As a matter of fact, the very high degree of co-operation between speaker and listener that is required in the comprehension of understatements allows us to draw a parallelism with diminutives, the use or avoidance of which helps participants classify themselves as insiders or outsiders. This may be specially applicable to forms which are restricted in their domain, thus being used in a kind of jargon. In the language of education, for instance, we find *maxie* (< *maximus error*) as the 'name given to the worst kind of mistakes in a Latin translation'. Tulloch (1997b: 391) associates it both with similar forms for lesser mistakes (*medie, majie*) and quotes an early twentieth-century rhyme that summarised the kind of punishment that students could expect in each case: 'Yae palmie for a minie, twa for a majie, an' three for a maxie'. *Palmie* obviously referred to a hit on the palm of the hand with a cane or a strap, so it could also be called *pandie*, both forms deriving from the formula *pande palmam*, which summoned learners to their punishment.

The role of diminutives in word-formation also seems quite productive in Scots: *gabsie* (= talkative person) joins a noun (*gab*) and a diminutive suffix with an intrusive consonant, thus producing an almost iconic new item; *grippie* (= avaricious) exploits the same strategy, applying it to a verb (*grip*); *gaffie* (= grandfather), instead, shows the kind of phonological simplification that might be expected in baby-talk, again providing an iconic counterpart of the word. Tulloch (1997b: 401) identifies the formation of adjectives from nouns and verbs, of nouns from verbs and other nouns. Suffixation is often accompanied by reduplication, clipping, or both: this is the case of *eeksie-peeksie* (= on an

---

28 This contemptuous use is allegedly epitomised in 'Wee German Lairdie', whose opening lines are 'Wha the de'il ha'e we gotten for a king But a wee, wee German lairdie?' (Bulloch 1921/1970: 148).

equality, much alike), which derives from *equal*. Clipping and suffixation, instead, are generally used for proper names and nouns.[29]

This mechanism may be integrated with phonological adjustments: thus, phonological rules concerning vowel length are at the basis of the intrusive <n> in *jannie* (< *janitor*) and of the substitution of the voiced fricative /v/ with its voiceless equivalent /f/ in *scaffie* (< *scavenger*). As a matter of fact, Scots seems to extend diminutives from proper names to nouns indicating jobs. Though this phenomenon is not discussed by Aitken (1984a and 1984b), Miller (1993) and McClure (1994), it is mentioned by McClure (1987a[30] and 1993), and by Milton (1992); but the most thorough description is offered by Tulloch (1997b). This feature is transferred to SSE, where we find *postie, gamie, fiddlie, pipie*, and many other similar entries.[31] Euphemistic nouns may also be formed from names, as in the case of s*hankie* (= lavatory), from the brand name of the product.

The importance of diminutive forms is also shown in their role in the formation of compounds: Tulloch (1997b: 409) refers to Macafee's study of Glaswegian (1994a) for the case of *midgie* (= refuse collection arrangements), which has become part of *midgie-man* (= dustman) and *midgie-motor* (= the dustman's lorry).

In the descriptions of Scots and SSE on which we have based this chapter the interaction of the two codes is constantly in the foreground and, as a matter of fact, according to Aitken (1992a: 895), the highest number of dialect isoglosses in the English-speaking world seems to appear in the Borders, i.e. the area between Scotland and northern England. This appropriately emphasises the close connection of the two languages, so that sociolinguistic considerations are inevitable when the selection of items from either end of the continuum is concerned. These will be considered further at a later stage in our study, when the development of SSE has been outlined in the framework of the numerous internal and external causes that contributed to the progressive convergence of Scots and English. This will also allow us to identify the historical roots of the

29 In everyday conversation diminutive forms like *Jamie, Dougie, Lizzie*, etc. occur; *Jimmie* has now become a familiar way of addressing a man, especially a stranger. Nicknames based on diminutive forms may also be applied to cities: the case of *Auld Reekie* (= Edinburgh) is perhaps the most famous one.

30 In his discussion of the features of Lallans and Doric in North-Eastern poetry McClure associates the 'use of the characteristic – even stereotypical – diminutive' to the latter (p. 218). As a matter of fact, numerous instances may be identified in Fenton (1995: *passim*): in this collection of stories written in the Buchan dialect the density of diminutive forms is certainly very high and occurrences do not only concern nouns (both with reference to childhood – e.g. *trykies*, p. 53 – and to endearment – e.g. *a blinkie o sin*, p.67), but also adverbial phrases, such as *a filie back* (= some time ago, p. 84) or *a bittie* (= a little, p. 74).

31 Among these, we may quote the case of *bluachie* (= bluish) as particularly interesting in its mixture of Gaelic and Scots suffixation on the English word *blue*, since the Scots suffix -*ie* is added to the typically Gaelic -*ach* suffix.

dualistic tendency that seems to have characterised Scottish discourse to the present day: an attempt to maintain tradition while striving to attain standardisation, with one objective being at times more powerful than the other.

CHAPTER THREE

Convergence and Distinctiveness

Methodological considerations

My study of the convergence between Scots and English, and of the attitudes towards specifically Scottish features from a socio-historical point of view, begins with the seventeenth century, as 1603, the year when James VI became James I of England and Scotland, is generally assumed to be one of the turning points in Scotland's linguistic history (the other being 1707, with the Union of Parliaments). As a matter of fact, the indication of any other date would be just as arbitrary, since it is always difficult to identify a precise point in time when language features (and the attitudes that speakers have towards their usage) actually change. The process is generally slow, complex and encompassing a period of time the borders of which are hardly definable. However, in this case a date may be seen as a turning point, because its historical incidence had inevitable consequences on linguistic issues and the way in which commentators have approached them. Before 1603 England and Scotland were two separate countries, so the linguistic physiognomy of either could be presented as independent, though philologically related. Once the court moved to London, the trend towards anglicisation accelerated considerably; on the other hand, this process was deeply rooted in the centuries preceding the Union of the Crowns, so it is certainly useful to be aware of the linguistic history in those times, in order to provide a framework for the explanation of subsequent phenomena.

From the methodological point of view, the study of these periods in Scotland's language history has received an impressive boost with the publication of the *Helsinki Corpus of Older Scots 1450–1700*[1] (Meurman-Solin 1993c and 1995). Although this collection is a supplement to the historical part of the *Helsinki Corpus of English Texts*, it can be used independently and it includes texts mainly from Central Scotland with a few documents from the Aberdeen area, for a total of about 850,000 words. The eighty texts in the corpus are subdivided in the following categories: law (burgh records), Bible, sermon, education, science, handbook, history, (auto)biography, travelogue, diary,

---

1 As far as earlier dialectology is concerned, some key elements of contemporary scholarly debate are presented by Laing and Williamson (1994). In the field of corpus linguistics, two new corpora are currently being compiled by Anneli Meurman-Solin: *A Corpus of Scottish Correspondence 1500–1800* and *A Corpus of Early Scottish Women's Writings (1540–1800)* (cf. Meurman-Solin 2001: 26).

private letter, official letter, trial, and pamphlet. However, only educational treatises are included in the subsection 1450–1500, and the 1500–1570 subsection presents a more limited selection of text types. The corpus includes 123 idiolects, but the geographical distribution of documents deserves greater attention. For this reason, a linguistic atlas of Older Scots is currently being compiled at the Institute for Historical Dialectology of Edinburgh University.[2]

Especially in recent times, many studies have been carried out on specific features of Older Scots.[3] An interesting point that emerges from these investigations is that the process of language standardisation was not uniquely in the direction of anglicisation,[4] but there were simultaneous trends of divergence of the two varieties, especially in the latter half of the sixteenth century.[5]

Among the conditioning factors that determined a lower or higher number of distinctively Scottish features in prose texts, we find that geographical distribution of texts, together with date, sex of the writer, genre and subject matter are identified as crucial by Meurman-Solin (1997c: 13–18); of course these variables are typically considered in sociolinguistic analyses, but their application, in association with the principles of corpus linguistics, to the investigation of historical varieties proves particularly fruitful. The outcome is a general overview of how Scottish and English variants appear to occur together in many texts, thus allowing Scots forms to be maintained longer, as in the case of *kirk* or *bairn* (Meurman-Solin 1997c: 21). While it may be unsurprising that scientific expository prose, such as Gilbert Skeyne's *Descriptioun of the Pest* (1568), is more Latinate,[6] and therefore closer to contemporary English texts

2 This is a continuation of the work that produced *A Linguistic Atlas of Late Medieval English* (1986); cf. Aitken (1991: 37), Williamson (1992/93 and forthcoming), Laing (1994), Meurman-Solin (1997b: 207; 1997c: 5 and 2000c: 227).

3 For instance, cf. Meurman-Solin (1993b, 1993c, 1997a, 1997b, 1997c) and, particularly, (2000a). While phonology has been investigated by Johnston (1997a), grammar and vocabulary in texts before 1700 have been discussed by Romaine (1984), Moessner (1997), King (1997), Macafee (1992/93 and 1997a) and Dossena (2001a and 2001b). As for the standardisation of written texts between 1520 and 1659, a relevant study is due to Devitt (1989).

4 The presence of a standard dialect in Middle Scots is also discussed by Agutter (1988b).

5 By divergence we mean the phenomenon through which a specifically Scottish regional norm became distinct from the Northern English dialect. When spelling is under discussion, however, attention ought to be paid to the kind of documents that are being examined, whether they are autographs or any kind of editorial intervention is to be accounted for; in the *Helsinki Corpus of Older Scots* the editor specifies that, leaving aside manuscripts, only texts available in early prints or edited texts where modernisation was not obvious were considered (Meurman-Solin 1993a: 76). On this point, see also Corbett (1997: 236-237). MacQueen (1983) also discusses aspects of anglicisation in grammar and spelling in the seventeenth century, though in a very brief study which provides relatively little terminological or methodological clarification. On the other hand, spelling is discussed at length by Kniezsa (1997a and 1997b).

6 Part of the text is quoted by Görlach (1991c: 365), although he quotes a different date from the ones provided by Williamson (1982: 56) and in the *Helsinki Corpus*; notice that Skeyne was aware that such a text ought, in fact, to have been written in Latin, but he justified his choice of language with an interest in being understood by the general public: 'Howbeit it become me

of the same genre, than, for instance, private letters, distinctions within the same genre may provide interesting insights, since variants in the texts may be related to the author's personal history in terms of education, place of residence, job, ideological beliefs, etc. As far as gender is concerned, Meurman-Solin (1997c: 18) finds that spelling in letters written by women between 1570 and 1640 is more conservative, although some women's phonetic spellings show them to be forerunners of phonological change.[7]

The variety of attitudes and of usage in the sixteenth century thus provides very valuable elements for the assessment of convergence between Scots and English. At the same time, close investigation shows that several patterns were incipient in the previous centuries, when Middle English was gaining prestige and literary achievements in that language were increasingly popular both north and south of the Border.

Older Scots and Middle Scots

These labels identify crucial stages in the history of English in Scotland, as they refer to periods when awareness of the distinction between Scots and English began to increase and influence stylistic choices at various levels. While the former is assumed to go from the twelfth century to 1700, the latter comprises the years from 1450 to 1700 (Aitken 1985/1996: xiii), and it is in these years that we find the identification of *Scottis* as the local variety,[8] as opposed to *Inglis* or *Southeron* or *Sudron*. The latter label, however, had a more marked connotation, meaning English (in the political sense), or Englishman,[9] and it is in this sense that it occurs in Blind Harry's *Wallace* (mid-fifteenth century) (McClure 1981a/1995: 50).

The degree of patriotic feeling that is reflected in literary texts is obviously related to the political history of the two kingdoms of England and Scotland.

---

rather (...) to had vrytin the samin in Latine, Zit vnderstanding sic interpryses had bene nothing profitable to the commoun and wulgar people, thocht expedient and neidfull to express the sam in sic langage as the vnlernit may be als weil satisfyit as Masteris of Clargie.' [Although it would have been preferable for me to write this same text in Latin, yet I could see that such an enterprise would have been of no use to the common people, so I thought it useful and necessary to express it in such language that both uneducated people and scholars may be satisfied.] The point of intelligibility is also made by the author of the *Complaynt of Scotland* (1550) when he says he used 'domestic scottis langage, maist intelligibil for the vlgare pepil'.

7 On this point, cf. also Meurman-Solin (1999).
8 Görlach (1988b/1990: 43) reminds us that this is the only variety ever to have achieved complete independence as a national language. The reference is obviously to the centuries before 1603. Bald (1928: 163) has pointed out that 'It was just before the Scots dialect entered on its period of decline that the term 'Scottis' was applied to it'.
9 Nowadays a similar effect is possibly achieved through the use of *Sasunnach*, derived from the Gaelic word meaning 'Saxon', though this item is also applied to non-Gaelic-speaking Low-landers, 'the Scots and English languages not being differentiated in Gaelic' (*CSD*). On this point, cf. also MacInnes (1989).

The official document in which the distinction between England and Scotland is possibly drawn most passionately is the Declaration of Arbroath.[10] This was a diplomatic letter dated 6 April 1320 addressed to the Pope for the achievement of peace:

> Hinc est, Reuerende Pater et Domine, quod sanctitatem vestram omni precum instancia genuflexis cordibus exoramus quatinus sincero corde Menteque pia recensentes quod apud eum cuius vices in terris geritis cum non sit Pondus nec distinccio Judei et greci, Scoti aut Anglici, tribulaciones et angustias nobis et Ecclesie dei illatas ab Anglicis paternis occulis intuentes, Regem Anglorum, cui sufficere debet quod possidet cum olim Anglia septem aut pluribus solebat sufficere Regibus, Monere et exhortari dignemini vt nos scotos, in exili degentes Scocia vltra quam habitacia non est nichilque nisi nostrum Cupientes, in pace dimittat.

> [Therefore it is, Reverend Father and Lord, that we beseech your Holiness with our most earnest prayers and suppliant hearts, inasmuch as you will in your sincerity and goodness consider all this, that, since with Him Whose vice-gerent on earth you are there is neither weighing nor distinction of Jew and Greek, Scotsman or Englishman, you will look with the eyes of a father on the troubles and privation brought by the English upon us and upon the Church of God. May it please you to admonish and exhort the King of the English, who ought to be satisfied with what belongs to him since England used once to be enough for seven kings or more, to leave us Scots in peace, who live in this poor little Scotland, beyond which there is no dwelling-place at all, and covet nothing but our own.]

At the same time, we find that scholars (Aitken 1979, Görlach 1985b and McClure 1984/1995) have often stressed the fact that the lack of any serious linguistic loyalty in the centuries preceding the Union of the Crowns (and, subsequently, of Parliaments) was the main reason why the process of anglicisation was comparatively fast and almost went unobserved.

The first recorded use of *Scottis* dates back to 1494, but this was not a clear sign of increasing linguistic awareness: even such strongly patriotic compositions as Blind Harry's *Wallace* used *Inglis* as the name for the poet's language (McClure 1994: 32) and Dunbar actually identified the languages as shared in an apostrophe to Chaucer in which he said 'Was thou noucht of oure Inglisch all the licht?' (*The Goldyn Targe*, 259 – quoted by McClure 1984/1995: 7).[11]

Gavin Douglas also showed attention to English and to 'venerabill Chaucer',

10 The text is available in Latin and present-day English from the website of Edinburgh University at the following Internet address: <http://www.geo.ed.ac.uk/home/scotland/arbroath.html>.

11 The influence of Chaucer, however, may have been overemphasised by modern commentators, who have often described Scottish *makaris* (= poets) as 'Scottish Chaucerians' (cf. Pollner 2000: 368, 371). These courtly poets flourished from about 1425 to 1550: Robert Henryson, William Dunbar, Gavin Douglas, and Sir David Lyndsay became the best-known authors. Although

whom he described as 'hevynly trumpat, orlege and reguler, in eloquens balmy, cundyt and dyall, mylky fontane, cleir strand and royß ryall, of fresh endyte, throu Albion iland braid' [heavenly trumpet, sundial and regulator, balmy in eloquence, leader and compass, milky fountain, clear strand and royal rose of fresh poetry through Albion's broad island].[12] On the other hand, it was the same Gavin Douglas who made a point of distinguishing the two varieties. The passage from the Introduction to his translation of Virgil's *Æneid* is often quoted as an example of the growing linguistic awareness in Scotland and, most famously, Douglas's declaration of intent has been singled out as the epitome of Scottish linguistic pride in the early sixteenth century:

> I set my bissy pane, as that I couth to mak it braid and plane, kepand na sudron bot our awyn langage, and spekis as I lernyt quhen I was page.
>
> [I took pains to make it broad and plain, using no English but our own language, and speak as I learnt when I was a page.]

At the same time, the text also contains remarks that confirm the delicate balance between the two varieties.[13] For instance, we find elements that point towards the use of English as a language that, alongside others, may be used to improve the translation and we even recognise Douglas' acknowledgement of his own mixed usage:

> Nor ʒit sa cleyn all sudron I refuß, bot sum word I pronounce as nyghtbouris doys: lyke as in Latyn beyn Grew termys sum, so me behufyt quhilum or than be dum sum bastard Latyn, French or Inglys oyß quhar scant was Scottis – I had nane other choys.
>
> [Nor do I refuse all English completely, but some words I pronounce like our neighbours; similarly, as Greek terms were borrowed into Latin, every now and again I had to use Latin, French or English where there was not a Scottish word for what I meant – I had no other choice.]

Douglas's observation that 'besyde Latyn our langage is imperfite' could apply both to Scots and to English, since the examples he provides, i.e. the difficult translation of *animal* and *homo*, is the same in the two varieties:

Chaucer was their acknowledged model, they used different styles for different types of poems, ranging from courtly aureate English, to mixtures of English and Scots, to the broadest Scots vernacular, as their subjects ranged from moral allegory to everyday realism or *flyting* (= abuse): cf. Watson (1984).

12 Gavin Douglas, Introduction to *Eneados* (1513). The text in this chapter is quoted from Görlach (1991c: 263–264).

13 Jack (1997: 243) reminds readers that Douglas was not 'a man usually given to Anglophobic pronouncements' and refers to his role as a negotiator for James V. Besides, he finds that Douglas's specific identification of language is not related to sociolinguistic considerations, which may have been superimposed by later critics, especially in the twentieth century, but by the kind of text he is writing, i.e. a translation, which could be justifiably compared with existing English versions.

vndyr animal beyn contenyt all mankynd, beist, byrd, fowll, fisch, serpent and all other sik thingis at lyfis and steris (...) And (...) Homo betakynnys baith a man and a woman, and we haue na term correspondent tharto, nor ȝit that signifyis baith twa in a term alanerly.

[animal includes mankind, beast, bird, fowl, fish, serpent and all such other things that live and move (...) and (...) Homo betokens both man and woman, and we have no corresponding term, nor any that signifies both in one term only.]

The practice of distinguishing *Scottis* and *Inglis* did not spread immediately, possibly because of the implicit acknowledgement of the common descent[14] of the two languages in spite of the perceptible differences. McClure (1981a/ 1995: 45) finds that the claim that *Scottis* actually meant Gaelic 'is much less well founded than the frequency with which it is made might suggest'; as a matter of fact, Gaelic was usually called *Irische* or *Ersche*.[15] The two languages are actually mentioned together in a suit quoted by McClure (1981a/1995: 47): the document, written by a notary named Mason and involving one Donald MacIlchattane from Arran, refers to 'interpretoris of the Scottis and Ireis toungis betwix the said Donnald and [the notary]', but its date is not provided.[16] *Irische* is the label that is also used in the Statutes of Iona (1609), and its association with 'barbaritie and incivilitie' points to traditional Lowland attitudes towards speakers of Gaelic, most famously and even hyperbolically represented in the *Flyting of Dunbar and Kennedy*, where the former poet attacks the latter on account of his speech, which was viewed as uncouth (Barisone 1989: 132; Jack 1997: 220). Speakers of 'Irish' are also scorned by the Crier in the anonymous early-sixteenth-century poem *The Manere of the Crying of ane Playe* (Parkinson 1995: 27–28), and this trend will even be continued in nineteenth-century literary texts, where the speech of Highlanders is represented through its phonological idiosyncrasies.[17]

14 Görlach's estimate (1990: 126) is that Scots and English 'must have shared more than 80% of their basic vocabulary (if phonological differences are neglected), even in the period of their greatest distance, say, in the sixteenth century'.

15 A more modern spelling was *Erse*. The identification of Scots Gaelic and Irish Gaelic was due to the fact that the former is a relatively recent offshoot of the latter. Introduced into Scotland about AD 500, it developed into a distinct dialect in the thirteenth century. Although a common Gaelic literary language was used in Ireland and Scotland until the fifteenth century, by that time the divergence between Scottish and Irish Gaelic had made mutual intelligibility quite difficult (cf. Chapter 1).

16 Hume Brown (1891: 27) quotes the report by Æneas Sylvius Piccolomini (who visited Scotland about 1435 as papal legate) according to which 'The Scots who live in the wooded region [i.e., the Highlands] speak a language of their own', but no label is provided. In general, though, Hume Brown's work is a valuable collection of extracts from twenty-four travelogues written by visitors who travelled in Scotland between 1295 and 1689.

17 Already in the seventeenth century observers commented on the coexistence of two languages in the Highlands: for instance, Thomas Tucker, who visited Scotland in 1655, claimed: 'The

As regards the distance between Scots and English, a very good chronological setting is given by the observations of foreign ambassadors. In 1498 Pedro de Ayala, from Spain, observed that the language of James IV was 'as different from English as Aragonese from Castilian' (quoted by McClure 1981a/1995: 48).[18] Although Ayala's competence in linguistic matters may be challenged,[19] even a cursory look at the correspondence between James VI and Elizabeth I shows differences that are bound to have been noticeable even two generations before (see, for instance, the texts in Görlach 1991c: 350–353, referring to the years 1586–88). On the other hand, Justus Scaligerus, who visited Holyrood in 1566 or 1567, stated that 'Les Escossois et Anglois parlent mesme langage Saxon, vieux Teutonique, ils se servent de mesme Bible, et ne different pas plus que le Parisien d'avec le Piccard' [The Scots and the English speak the same Saxon language, old Teutonic, use the same Bible and are no more different than a Parisian and a Piccardian] (Mitchell 1901: 462).

What is perhaps one of the earliest representations of spoken language appears in the account of Estienne Perlin, who visited Scotland in 1551–1552 and in 1558 published his *Description des Royaulmes d'Angleterre et d'Escosse*. In this book he complains of the difficulty in obtaining accommodation and states:

> If you say to an ordinary sort of man in Scotch, *Guede guednit goud maistre praie gui mi longini*, which is to say in our language, 'Good night, my master, I pray you to give me a lodging;' they will answer you haughtily in their tongue, *est est no bet*, which is to say, there is no bed. (Hume Brown 1891: 76)[20]

---

inhabitants beyond Murray land (except in the Orkneys) speake generally Ober garlickh, or Highlands, and the mixture of both in the town of Invernesse is such that one halfe of the people understand not one another' (Hume Brown 1891: 174). Thomas Kirke, whose account was published in 1679, reported that 'Erst' was unknown to most Lowlanders, 'except only in those places that border on [the Highlands], where they can speak both' (Hume Brown 1891: 262).

18 This passage had also been quoted by Hume Brown (1891: 39-40), who added: 'The king speaks, besides, the language of the savages who live in some parts of Scotland and on the islands', which is said to be 'as different from Scotch as Biscayan is from Castilian'. A footnote is added, according to which this is the latest statement regarding a king's knowledge of Gaelic.

19 As a matter of fact, the distance between Aragonese and Castilian at that time was possibly less dramatic than it was made out to be. Ayala's authority was followed in the account of the Venetian ambassador Andrea Trevisano, who did not visit Scotland, but met Ayala in London and then reported that 'The language of the Scotch is the same as that of the Irish, and very different from the English; but many of the Scotch people speak English extremely well, in consequence of the intercourse they have with each other on the borders' (Hume Brown 1891: 54).

20 Perlin's account was published in French and Hume Brown relies on the translation provided in the fourth volume of *The Antiquarian Repertory* (Hume Brown 1891: 71). Another sentence in Scots ('whea buyes sawer milk') appears in Kirke's account (Hume Brown 1891: 263).

Perlin's 'transcription' seems to emphasise Scots vowels, and though we may not be certain how reliable this representation may be assumed to be, the very fact that he actually tries to transcribe it for his readers points to its specificity in the perception of external observers.

In the advancement of anglicisation a crucial role was played by the introduction of printing to Scotland in 1508,[21] as printers frequently adapted Scots to English spelling and grammar[22] (Bald 1926a). Although this tool might have been extremely valuable for the preservation of Scots distinctive features, the fact that printers were often English or foreigners used to printing English texts (McClure 1994: 33) increased the view of Scots as a language that could be improved. On the other hand, Meurman-Solin (1997b: 206) claims that the degree of 'Scottishness' is not directly related to the text being printed or not: according to her findings, the type of addressee was a more important element for the decision of conscious anglicisation.[23] In this respect, Görlach (1997a: 7-8) stresses that James VI's *Basilikon Doron* (1595) was first printed in Edinburgh with anglicised spelling in spite of its being in Scots.[24] The samples he provides (Görlach 1991c: 310) show changes that mainly affect spelling, while some also involve syntax (for instance, in the use of the pronoun *other* instead of the repetition of *craftis*) and word-formation (cf. *skilledest* vs. *skilfullest*):

MS – Be in youre awin person ualkeryfe, diligent, and painfull, using the aduyce of thaime that are skilledest in the craft as ye man do in all craftis
1603 – Be in your owne person walkrife, diligent, and painfull; vsing the aduice of suche as are skilfullest in the craft, as ye must also doe in all other.

21 This is the year in which the first printed texts in Scotland were published by Walter Chepman and Andrew Myllar: among these, Dunbar's *Tretis of the Tua Marrit Wemen and the Wedo* (Barisone 1989: 9). In the following century, the ratio of books printed in Edinburgh with a higher or lower number of specifically Scottish features changed dramatically. Görlach (1991c: 18-19) reports figures that show a complete reversal of the trend between 1560 and 1625: in 1560, 18 Scots books were printed, and no English/anglicised ones, whereas in 1625 only two Scots books were printed, against 21 English ones. At the turn of the century the situation seemed quite balanced, with 10 Scots books and 13 English ones printed in 1590. However, already in 1600 the number of English books was more than double the number of Scots ones: 38, as opposed to 18. In addition to this, we ought to consider the role played by English books imported into Scotland, details of which are provided by Bald (1926b).

22 Henrie Charteris appears to have been an exception: Bald (1927: 181) describes him as 'something of a national champion'.

23 This point is also discussed by Aitken (1997) in a study in which the findings of Bald (1927) are re-assessed in the light of the relationship between encoder and addressee. In a recent analysis Meurman-Solin adds: 'Besides time and space, other conditioning factors such as social status, contacts with the court, education, and mobility may influence the choice of variants' (2000c: 233).

24 This phenomenon is also described in greater detail by Romaine (1982: 58–59), though different dates are provided for composition (1598) and for the first printed edition (for private circulation – 1599); an enlarged and revised edition was produced for a wider audience in 1603. Cf. also Blank (1996: 157–159).

At the same time, Kniezsa (1997b: 641) reminds us that Scottish men of letters might complete their education in Oxford[25] (where Balliol College, one of the earliest, was a Scottish foundation), so spelling conventions could be acquired fairly easily. Kniezsa also considers the works that James VI wrote while still in Scotland and she finds 'a considerable proportion of southern forms – 10% of all the tokens. [In fact,] his special Scottish spellings are not very considerably more numerous than what were found in John Knox's writings' (1997b: 647).

James VI's own views are also evident in the comments on linguistic features found in the manuscript text of *Basilikon Doron*, when James encourages the future king to use language that is

> plaine, honest naturall, cumlie, clene, shorte and sententiouse escheuing baith the extremities alsueill in not using *a rusticall corrupt leid*, nor yett booke langage and penne and inkorne termes, and least of all mignarde and æffeminate termis (text in Görlach 1991: 311, my italics).

The reference to a 'rusticall corrupt leid' might seem to point to Scots, *leid* having been the Scots word for 'language' since the late fourteenth century.[26] In fact, it is shown to refer to dialect in general when, further on, James states the 'yle of brittaine [is] allreaddie ioined in unitie of religion, and langage' (text in Görlach 1991c: 311).

On the other hand, the Statutes of Iona (1609), though following the Union of the Crowns, use rather obvious Scots features in spelling and morphology:

> Forasmekle as, the Kingis Majestie haveing a speciall care and regard that (...) the vulgar Inglishe toung be universallie plantit, and the Irishe language, whilk is one of the chief and principall causis of the continewance of barbaritie and incivilitie amongis the inhabitantis of the Ilis and Heylandis, may be abolisheit and removit (text in Görlach 1991c: 384).[27]

Scots was first 'branded' as a homely language soon after the Union of the Crowns: Aitken (1979: 89) refers to the works of Sir William Alexander, Earl

25 Though of course attendance at continental universities was also widespread.

26 Cf. the entry for *leed, lede* &c. in the *CSD* (p. 365). This usage is also attested in David Lyndsay's *The First Buke of the Monarchie* (1574); in the first paragraphs of 'Ane Exclamation to the Redar, Twiching the Wrytting of Vulgar, and Maternall Language' we find that the translation of the Scriptures into 'our toung vulgare' is advocated because 'euerie commoun may not be ane clerk Nor hes no Leid, except thair toung maternall' (text in Görlach 1991c: 381).

27 Note the use of *Inglische* and *Irische* as labels for Scots/English and Gaelic. On the other hand, the Dundonald School regulations (1640) refer to the teaching of 'reiding Scottish quhither print or writ' (text in Görlach 1991c: 388); Görlach claims that this implies that Scots was the medium of instruction in that context, but we find that the linguistic label may simply point to what the Statutes of Iona called *Inglische*; however, it is clear that teachers were bound to present a local variety, rather than a southern one, as may be gathered from the vocabulary and spelling in the text of the Regulations themselves. On the persistent interchangeability of the two terms, cf. Williamson (1982: 55–61) and Williamson (1983).

of Stirling, and he quotes the address 'To the Reader' of his *Darius* (1603), in which the author describes the language of the poem as 'mixt of the English and Scottish Dialects' and then goes on to beg his readers to bear with him, although this mixture 'perhaps may be unpleasant and irksome to some readers of both nations', because he has retained 'peculiar' words 'especially when (...) propre, and significant'. Yet, 'for the more parte [he used] the English phrase, as worthie to be preferred before our owne for the elegance and perfection thereof.'

As we can see, we are already quite far from Gavin Douglas's choice of language according to its suitability from the expressive point of view. Alexander explicitly flatters one variety and somehow lays the basis for subsequent denigration of Scottish elements in writing. Bald (1927 and 1928) has drawn a very neat outline of ways in which similarities and differences between Scots and English were described around the time of the Reformation, and she finds that in either case convergence seems to be the trend that was being set; those commentators who emphasised distinctiveness generally did so owing to their 'partisan bias' (Bald 1928: 166), whereas those who stressed resemblance paved the way for a process of anglicisation that appeared to be impossible to stop.

As we saw in Chapter 2, the first occurrence of that notorious item, *Scotticism*, appears to be earlier than the occurrences provided in the *OED*, since it goes back to 1678, instead of 1717. In the pamphlet *Ravillac Redivivus* the author claims to have moved to England to learn the language, and asks his reader to 'make remarks upon [his] Letters, and faithfully Admonish [him] of all the Scotticisms, or all the Words, and Phrases that are not current *English* therein' (text in Aitken 1979: 94-95).

This method of correction and improvement will also be applied in the eighteenth century, but this author has not yet reached the level of anxiety that will feature so prominently in other intellectuals' writings. In fact, he does 'confess (...) a great Veneration for our own and the Northern *English* Language, upon the account of the Anglo-Saxon'.[28] Besides, his interlocutor also appears to be Northern ('our own and the Northern *English* Language'), so not the perfect *arbiter* who will be sought in the following century, and the connection with Anglo-Saxon first points to a supposedly greater purity of the Northern variety that will also be emphasised at later stages in its history.

Bailey (1991: 71) has challenged Aitken's idea that this usage was a symptom of early linguistic self-consciousness on the basis that the author of the pamphlet was not a Scot, 'but an Anglo-Catholic Englishman, George Hickes (1642–1715), pretending to be a Scot in this anonymous pamphlet written for an English audience'.[29] However, whether the author was Scottish

---

28 Görlach (1987/1990: 125) reports that 'the conviction that Scots had remained more germanic than Southern English was a commonplace among sixteenth- and seventeenth-century scholars'.

29 On early stereotypical representations of Scots characters and their language in English texts, cf. Porter (1999).

or simply pretended to be, would not seem to be a crucial issue, since what appears to matter most is the kind of linguistic comment which is provided. Besides, it is hardly likely that Hickes would have expressed his view in these terms if it had been completely unimaginable for Scottish speakers.

Differences between northern and southern speech had already been pointed out in Chaucer's *The Reeve's Tale* and elsewhere: Bailey (1991: 67) quotes *Cursor Mundi, The Second Shepherd's Play*, the works of Ranulf Higden and of John Trevisa;[30] to these, he adds the case of a witness heard at a trial in York in 1364, who struck the court as untrustworthy because he 'often changed his way of speaking' (that is, he switched, or drifted, between English and Scots). The witness is said to have been a native of Peebles who had resided in Yorkshire since 1346, so this obviously accounts for his use of two dialects; what appears to be far more interesting is the kind of reaction that this type of code-mixing caused in his listeners, though it is difficult to imagine that this was an isolated case.

Görlach (1991c: 233–236) reports a few paragraphs from W. Harrison's *The Historie of Scotland* (1587). The title of this passage, *Of the Languages Spoken in this Iland*, exemplifies the perception of geographical variation in the late sixteenth century. Besides, the first paragraphs are not exempt from sociological considerations of a certain 'chauvinistic' kind when they refer to the time when, after the Norman conquest,

> euen the verie carters began to wax wearie of there mother toong, and laboured to speake French, which as then was counted no small token of gentilitie. And (...) euerie French rascall, when he came once hither, was taken for a gentleman, onelie bicause he was proud, and could vse his owne language.[31]

However, Harrison sketches the rise of Middle English and criticises those writers who, 'by fond affectation of forren and strange words', corrupt the language 'with externall termes of eloquence, and sound of manie syllables'. He finds that the 'excellencie of the English toong is found in ... the south', and again he has words of contempt for foreign speakers, 'especially the French men', who mispronounce English. As regards the other languages of sixteenth-century Britain, Harrison mentions Welsh and Cornish: he finds the two languages to be 'but a corrupted kind of British' and accounts for the differences saying that 'the British of Cornwall is (...) corrupted, sith the Welsh toong that is spoken in the north and south part of Wales, doth differ so much in it selfe, as the English vsed in Scotland dooth from that which is

---

30 Higden (c. 1280–1364) is remembered for his *Polychronicon* (c. 1385-87), a compilation of much of the knowledge of his age, based on about 40 sources, and several theological works. The *Polychronicon* was translated by John Trevisa.

31 These remarks sound very close to those that were voiced with reference to English when the loss of Scots as a prestige variety was openly regretted in the twentieth century.

spoken [in England]'. As a matter of fact, the case of Scotland is described in the following terms:

> The Scottish english hath beene much broader and lesse pleasant in vtterance than ours, because the nation hath not till of late indeuored to bring the same to any perfect order, and yet it was such in maner, as Englishmen themselues did speake for the most part beyond Trent, whither any great amendement of our language had not as then extended it selfe. Howbeit in our time the Scottish language endeuoreth to come neere, if not altogither to match our toong in finenesse of phrase, and copie of words, and this may in part appeare by an historie of the Apocrypha translated into Scottish verse by Hudson, dedicated to the king of that countrie, and conteining six books, except my memorie doo faile me (text in Görlach 1991c: 235).

First of all, what is worth observing in Harrison's remarks is his judgement on Scots, which is seen as much broader and less pleasant than southern English, though close to northern English, and the equation between these linguistic features and the 'backwardness' of a nation which, allegedly, had only recently begun to strive for the attainment of 'perfect order' in language. Together with this, Harrison's reference to an early translation of a history of the Apocrypha by Hudson is a sign of the way in which this practice on the part of Scottish writers was becoming increasingly pervasive and clearly perceptible outside Scotland.

The reference to Hudson's translation also highlights the attention that was being paid to the development of Scots in prose writings. McClure (1994: 31) focuses on the growing importance of the Lowland tongue after the royal capital was shifted from Perth to Edinburgh (in the fifteenth century) and when the Acts of Parliament began to be recorded in the vernacular instead of Latin after the return of James I in 1424. However, he admits that narrative and expository prose was late in emerging due to the pre-eminence of Latin and he mentions John Ireland's theological writings (1490) as early specimens of Scots scholarly prose. This point is also made by Williamson (1982: 56–57), who also acknowledges John Ireland's *Meroure of Wyssdome* as 'the earliest extant (partly) original prose work of scholarship in Scots', but then identifies the Reformation, with its use of an English Psalter and of English Bibles, as one of the reasons why 'a fully fledged 'high' Scots prose did not develop before the influence of Southern English began to bear'.

As a matter of fact, the influence of English had begun long before the Reformation. Although this is not the place to discuss the literary achievements of the fourteenth and fifteenth centuries – our focus being on linguistic developments, rather than genres – texts like Barbour's *The Bruce* (1377) certainly prove very relevant in any discussion of language issues in Scotland; for instance, Pantaleo (1997), underlines the linguistic complexity of this work by emphasising the multiplicity of lexical items used in warfare terminology and geographical names, which points to the multifarious aspect of Scotland's languages.

The connection between more or less anglicised forms and text types has been outlined in an accurate study by Görlach (1998b) and, as a matter of fact, the interaction of styles appears to be crucial in the works of William Dunbar. Barisone's monograph (1989) on the *Tretis of the Tua Marrit Wemen and the Wedo* sets this poem in the context of contemporary literary conventions, while Jack (1997) provides a summary of the most salient features in the stylistic choices of various authors. Among these, the 'Castalian Band' and James VI are often regarded as the epitome of change because of the extent to which their language became more anglicised after 1603. As regards the literary register, James I attempted a handbook for Scots: *The Reulis and cautelis to be obseruit and eschewit in Scottis Poesie* (1584). However, his own writings were anglicised by the printers (Görlach 1991c: 20), and the text that appears to be most anglicised is his *Counterblaste to Tobacco*, published in London after 1603.[32] As regards James's *Reulis and Cautelis*,[33] he provides two reasons for his work. One is the change that has taken place in stylistic considerations: 'lyke as tyme is changeit sensyne, sa is the ordour of Poesie changeit'. The other reason is that no such texts exist for Scots: 'albeit sindrie hes written of it in English, quhilk is lykest to our language, Zit we differ from thame in sindrie reulis of Poesie'. Consequently, James refers to the works of Du Bellay and others for the figures that are 'vsit in all languages', but reserves the right to discuss those that are allegedly specific to Scots.

Jack's claim (1997: 258) that Drummond of Hawthornden wrote a patriotic appeal in English – in *The Forth Feasting* (1617), written for James's return to Scotland – because, 'like all writers of this time, he thought of language choice decorously rather than politically', is certainly tenable. A glance at the linguistic (and literary) scene in England in those years shows what high standards were being set by poets and dramatists with names like Shakespeare and Donne. However, the political issue ought not to be disregarded altogether: it should perhaps be considered in a different sense than is commonly applied, since linguistic anglicisation could be perceived as a means towards enhancement of the connection between the two countries.[34]

---

32 Because it is so highly anglicised, any statistical analysis of the corpus material which includes this text ought to be assessed very carefully as it may distort the overall picture of Scots before 1700.

33 Quotations in this text are taken from 'The Preface to the Reader' (in Görlach 1991c: 308–310).

34 This view will also emerge after the Union of Parliaments in 1707, cf. Chapter 4.

Language and religion

Together with political issues, the importance of religious texts, and particularly of the Bible, in language history should not be underestimated, especially when the epoch under scrutiny was a time of controversy, reform and passionate debate such as there was in Scotland in the days of John Knox.[35]

As the foremost leader of the Scottish Reformation, Knox is generally regarded as one of the most influential anglicisers of Scots, and his education – together with his period of intermittent imprisonment and exile in England[36] and on the Continent (until 1559) – may have influenced his language. It is supposed that Knox trained for the priesthood under the scholar John Major, most probably at the University of St. Andrews. According to McClure (1981a/1995: 54), Major stated in his *History of Greater Britain* that English was 'spoken by the English and by the civilised Scots', and this kind of sociolinguistic consideration was possibly as widespread as the one that stressed the differences existing between the two varieties, since these could be made to suit ideological stances. McClure (1981a/1995: 53) reminds us that these remarks should not be overemphasised (since each opponent did, in fact, focus on arguments relating to doctrine, history and politics). But we cannot ignore them, because they shed some light on the kind of sociological framework within which the controversy was set. Among those that are quoted most frequently are two remarks directed at John Knox and the Calvinists, one by John Hamilton and another by Ninian Winzet:[37]

> Gif King James the fyft war alyue, quha hering ane of his subjectis knap suddrone, declarit him ane trateur: quhidder wald he declaire you triple traitours, quha not only knappis suddrone in your negative confession, but also hes causit it be imprentit at London in contempt of our native language?

> [If King James the Fifth were alive, who hearing one of his subjects speak English declared him a traitor, how couldn't he but declare you triple traitors, who not only speak English in your negative confession, but have also had it printed in London in contempt of our native language?]

> Gif ȝe, throw curiositie of novatiounis, has forȝet our ald plane Scottis quhilk ȝour mother lerit ȝou, in timis cuming I sall write to ȝou my mind in Latyn, for I am nocht acquent with ȝour Suddrone.

---

35 John Knox was born in Haddington (Lothian) c. 1514 and died in Edinburgh on November 24, 1572. His most important literary work is his *History of the Reformation in Scotland* (1566).

36 Jack (1997: 214–215) describes a similar case for James I, whose language was inevitably influenced by his imprisonment in England from 1406 to 1424.

37 Both are reported by McClure (1981a/1995: 53); the latter is also discussed by Aitken (1997: 18).

[If you, in your search for novelty, have forgotten our old plain Scots which your mother taught you, in the future I shall write to you in Latin, as I am not acquainted with your English.]

Both remarks are obviously sarcastic. However, it is interesting to note that both Hamilton and Winzet use *suddrone* as a disparaging label. It could also be argued that the use of *Scottis* as a patriotic badge increased after the English victory at Flodden (1513) (Barisone 1989: 133).

Setting aside considerations arising from the writings of propagandists and pamphleteers, the overall picture that emerges is one of basic relatedness (though not of complete identity) between the two varieties. As a matter of fact, early printed texts of the Scots Confession of 1560 also show unconcern for linguistic issues (Robinson 1983), as the point was not language, but doctrine, and this explains why a similar attitude was taken towards the importation of English Bibles.[38] Wright (1988b: 155) points out that Scottish reformers relied on English translations (Tyndale's Bible having reached Scotland by early 1527), and indeed the first reprinting of the Geneva Bible in Scotland in 1579[39] did not present 'the slightest attempt at adaptation in vocabulary or spelling for a Scots readership'. Wright's contribution proves particularly interesting in its attempt to compare different versions of sixteenth-century religious writings in Scots, since it provides insights into the proximity of the latter to English in that register. The texts that Wright includes are (i) by Murdoch Nisbet, who transcribed the New Testament into Scots around 1520; (ii) by John Gau (whose *The Richt Vay to the Kingdom of Heuine* (1533), a translation into Scots of a Danish treatise, appears to be strongly influenced by Danish and German); (iii) by John Hamilton, whose *Catechism* of 1552 is said to be 'in Inglis'; and (iv) by the compiler of the collection of *The Gude and Godlie Ballatis*.

Nisbet's text circulated in manuscript only and its Wycliffite roots are probably the reason why lexical choices are very close to the Latin Vulgate on which other Lollard versions were based.[40] Wright (1988b: 156) quotes a few specifically Scottish items that are preferred to more standard ones: for instance, *newk* instead of *cornere* or *tolbuth* instead of *moot halle*, whereas a Scotticism like *speir* (= ask) is absent. Even at this early stage, we see how flexible language was, and we can assume that certain choices had already become automatic.

---

38 Romaine (1982: 58) mentions a Scottish law of 1579 according to which 'every householder worth 300 *merkis* 'marks' was obliged to possess a Bible'.

39 This is known as the Bassandyne Bible, although it was finally produced by Alexander Arbuthnot, printer to James VI. Thomas Bassandyne, whose name appears on the title page, died in 1577 after preparing the New Testament (Wright 1988b: 161).

40 On the issue of the neutrality, or anglicising trend, of Nisbet's lexical choices, see also Pantaleo (1992a: 233). On the history of Bible translations in Scotland, cf. Tulloch (1989).

The text that Wright compares in the four versions is the Lord's Prayer, but he does not stop to analyse lexical or grammatical variation in any detail, preferring to move on to other aspects of the Reformation, such as the use of vernacular texts in preaching. However, it is worth resuming his comparison:

Nisbet	Gau	Hamilton	Ballatis
Our fader	Our fader	O our Father	Our Father
that art	thow quhilk is	quhilk is	that art
in heuenis,	in ye heuine	in Hevinnis	in heuin,
hallowit be	thy nayme mot	Thy name mot	hallowit be
thi name.	be hallowit	be hallowit	thy Name
Thi Kingdom	thi kingdom	Thy kyngdome	Thy kingdome
come to.	mot cum (to vsz)	mot cum.	cum.
Thi will	thi will mot	Thy wyll mot	Thy will
be done	be dwne	be done	be done
in erde,	in ye zeird	in erd,	in eirth
as	as it is	as it is	as it is
in heuen	in the heuine	in hevin.	in heuin
Gefe to vs	giff wsz	Geve us	Giue vs
this day	this day	this day	this day
our breid ouer	our dailie breid	our daylie breid.	our daylie breid.
vthir substance.			
And forgif	and forgiff	And forgyff	Forgiue
vs our dettis	wsz our dettis	us our dettis	us our trespassis
as we forgef	as we forgiff	as we forgyfe	as we forgiue
to our dettouris	our dettours	our dettouris	them that trespas
And leid vs	and leid vsz	And lede us	aganis vs.
nocht into	notht in	nocht in	And leid vs
temptatioun,	temptatione	temptatioun	not into
bot deliuer	bot deliuer	Bot delyver	temptatioun.
vs fra evile	vsz fra ewil	us fra evyl.	Bot deliuer
Amen	Amen	Sa be it.	vs from evill.
			For thine is
			the Kingdome
			the power, and
			the glorie for
			ever. Amen.

The text in the *Ballatis* collection appears to be closest to English; the main differences seem only to appear in spelling.[41] At the same time, we find variants in the use of relative pronouns (*quhilk* vs. *that*) and in the use of the modal *mot*

41 Some of these, however, reflect phonological differences: cf. *erd* vs *eirth*, *fader* vs. *father*; this phenomenon persists in the Shetlandic dialect, where the pronoun *thou* is realised as *du*.

(= must), which appears in Gau's and Hamilton's texts, but not in Nisbet's and in the *Ballatis*, thus showing the closer analogy between Nisbet's and southern versions. As regards the use of the definite article, Gau's is the only version in which it appears in the phrases *in ye/the heuine* and *in ye Zeird*, while Nisbet's, Gau's and Hamilton's consistently use the conjunction *and* to join 'give us this day our daily bread' and 'forgif us our dettis'; Nisbet's, however, is the only version in which 'our breid' is expanded into 'our breid ouer vthir substance'. Again on the lexical level, we see that Nisbet, Gau and Hamilton all use *dettis* instead of *trespassis*, which is used in the *Ballatis* text and in the Book of Common Prayer. Also the phrase 'For thine is the Kingdome the power, and the glorie for ever' is only appended in the *Ballatis* version before 'Amen' (which is rephrased as 'Sa be it' by Hamilton). In general, the degree of Scottishness in these four versions of the Lord's Prayer does not seem to vary significantly. Differences become perceptible upon close scrutiny, and it is very likely that sixteenth-century churchgoers acknowledged these texts as English.

Another instance from Nisbet's version of the New Testament could also be used to show that his language may have been simply an attempt to bring spelling and pronunciation closer together. Görlach (1997b: 212–213) provides Nisbet's text of the parable of the prodigal son (from Luke, 15. 11–32), which lends itself to comparison with numerous other versions. While it is certainly true that Northern peculiarities are very limited in Nisbet's text, at the same time Scottish uses and phrases appear alongside spelling forms which represent Scottish morphology (e.g., the suffix *-it* instead of *-ed* for the past participle, as in *destroyit* – cf. Görlach 1996b: 167-169) and phonology (e.g., *fader* instead of *father*). Among these uses we find the use of *sal*, instead of *will* in *18 I sal rise up and ga to my fadere*, or the use of *after* in the sense of *no sooner than*:[42] *30 Bot eftir that this thi sonn, that has destroyit his substance with huris com, thou has slayn to him a fat calf.* Thus, in Nisbet's work we identify early instances of the discrepancy between an increasingly anglicised written language and the distinctiveness of Scottish pronunciation:[43] a feature that would mark later stages of linguistic history in Scotland even to this day.

Early collections of dialect words

The history of Scottish lexicography runs parallel to the history of the convergence of Scots and southern varieties, since collections of Scottish lexical items were often works in which elements were singled out on account of their

---

42 As we saw in previous chapters, this use of *efter* could be related to the phrase *To be after doing sth.* (= to have just done sth.), which is generally associated with Irish English syntax, so it could be described as a Gaelic calque.

43 Alexander Hume (early seventeenth century), in his *Treates of the Orthographie and Congruitie of the Britan Tonge*, mentions 'dialectes of ane tong, differing in the sound of them' (McClure 1981a/1995: 55).

geographical distribution. Williamson (1995/96: 128) seems to have identified the earliest example of Scottish lexicography in Sir John Skene's *De verborum significatione*, 'a compilation of glosses to legal terms found in the *Regiam Majestatem, Quoniam Attachiamenta* and the Acts of Parliament', printed in Edinburgh in 1597. McClure (1981a/1995: 47) also refers to an interesting text of 1627, Sir Thomas Kelly's *Pallas Armata*, which could be taken to be an early dictionary of military technical words, since contents are described in the following way:

> In the columne upon the right hand, are contained the tearmes of command in our Scots Language; on the left the English.

As far as everyday usage is concerned, Bailey (1991: 71) mentions the journal of three Englishmen (Lowther *et al.* 1894) who visited Scotland in 1629, in which Scots forms and English equivalents are provided. However, the reliability of the list is perhaps questionable, and indeed Görlach (1987/1990: 134) and Aitken (1987a) also caution readers against the complete reliability of dictionaries for the assessment of the vitality of Scottish lexical items. On the other hand, works like John Ray's *Collection of Words not Generally Used* (1674, revised and augmented edition 1691) prove invaluable. Ray's appears to be the first attempt at a systematic description of English dialect vocabulary, but he makes no distinction between Scots and Northern English, marking items like *bairn, flyte, ken, thole* and *bannock* as 'north country'. This is possibly due to the fact that Scots and Northern English have always shared many features, making it difficult for lexicographers to discern a clear Scottish distinctiveness. However, there may be further considerations; for instance, Görlach finds that the limitations of these data make them less useful than might be expected, especially since this work might have provided 'evidence of a contemporary observer's attitudes on the status of the words in question'. In fact, the very lack of distinction between England and Scotland is symptomatic of the attitude of the author, who possibly showed the extent to which he believed in the unification of the two countries in this implicitly political statement as a lexicographer.

Ray's alleged aim in collecting dialect words is very similar to those declared by collectors of other non-standard varieties, especially by collectors of canting terms, who identified a utilitarian purpose in their work: as Elisha Coles put it, '[Some knowledge of cant] may chance to save your throat from being cut, or (at least) your Pocket from being pickt' (cf. Gotti 1996: 231). Similarly, Ray identifies novelty, usefulness and entertainment as the main considerations that encouraged him to publish his collection:

> I knew not of any thing that hath been already done in this kind. ... [it] may be of some use to them who shall have occasion to travel the Northern Counties, in helping them to understand the common language

there. ... [it] may also afford some diversion to the curious, and give them occasion of making many considerable remarks.

Unfortunately Ray does not explain what kind of 'considerable remarks' he expected his readers to make: whether they could relate to phonological or spelling variants, to lexical items or to definitions and examples. However, he appears to be right in claiming novelty for his work.

As far as northern and Scottish entries are concerned, dictionaries like Robert Cawdrey's *A Table Alphabeticall* (1604) and John Bullokar's *An English Expositor* (1616) had not included any of them. Peter Levins' *Manipulus Voca-bulorum* (1570) had listed words that he described as 'barbarous, straunge, or fallen out of vse' (cf. Gotti 1997), but none of these were labelled as Scottish or Northern, although some were obviously so (as in the case of *brambles, to flyte, hoggates, to kenne, kirk, mirke, myckil, a nooke, to thole, yool*). In Elisha Coles' *An English Dictionary* (1676) we find only a few items that are explicitly marked as 'Scottish': for instance, *anent, kirk, Angus*, and *law* (= hill). In Ray's collection, instead, among the entries marked as Scottish we find *anent, to greit, a lown/loon, to bourd, to breid/brade of* and *bleit/blate*. What appears to be specially interesting about the last three entries is that they are illustrated with proverbs, respectively:

> *Bourd [Jest] neither with me nor with my honor*
> *Ye breid of the Millers Dog, ye lick your mouth or the poke be ope* [= you are like the miller's dog: you lick your chops even before you know what's in the bag]
> *A toom purse makes a bleit merchant* [= an empty purse makes a shamefac'd merchant]

As a matter of fact, collections of proverbs and maxims had appeared since the sixteenth century, but it was only much later that they found their way into publication; for instance, the proverbs collected in 1598 by David Fergusson, minister at Dunfermline, were printed by Thomas Ruddiman in 1785. What is important is the fact that the interest in Scottish vocabulary and phraseology was increasing and that the specificity of this variety was beginning to be outlined from different points of view, such as we see in dictionaries, collections of proverbs and, later, grammar books. These trends, either more strictly lexicographic, or more focused on popular culture, would be taken up and expanded in the eighteenth century, when systematisation became the centre of attention following the changes in political life, scientific developments and new literary styles.

CHAPTER FOUR

The Heyday of Prescriptivism

Observations in the previous chapter have shown that language in Scotland was not really perceived as a significant issue till relatively late in the history of the country. The issue of progressive anglicisation certainly received far greater attention in the eighteenth century, when another political event, little more than a century after the Union of the Crowns, bound the destinies of England and Scotland even more closely together: the Union of Parliaments in 1707. This event had actually been anticipated in previous years as a consequence of the English Parliament's decision to choose a successor to Queen Anne and the need to have this choice accepted by the Scottish Parliament. To this were added strategic and economic considerations. The Act was finalised after long debates and less than clear operations on 16 January 1707 (Steel 1984: 149–164). Thus the Scots Parliament was ended and the Westminster Parliament increased by just 45 commoners and 16 peers representing Scotland.[1] On the other hand, Scotland benefited by gaining free trade with England and its colonies, by the grant of a money 'Equivalent' of the share of the English national debt that Scotland would assume, and by the explicit safeguarding of its national church and legal system.[2]

While it may seem that the importance of 1707 in the history of Scotland's languages has been overemphasised, in fact the value that it added to the prestige of the south was certainly considerable, since it put greater weight on the idea of politeness that was associated with the standard variety and the English accent. Having lost both its court and its political centre, Scotland found itself far from the centres of attraction of 'good society', hence the constant attempt, on the part of gentry and nobility, or anyway upwardly mobile classes, to imitate southern lifestyle and modes of expression. At the same time, the eighteenth century was also the age of the Scottish Enlightenment, which was distinctively European in its orientation. This was an outstanding period of intellectual activity and achievement exemplified in the works of David Hume, the philosopher and historian, and Adam Smith, the

1 An overall sense of loss on the part of Scotland is generally summarised in the comment of the Scottish Chancellor, Seafield, who is reported to have remarked: 'There's the end of ane auld sang' (Steel 1984: 164).
2 This explains why so many lexical items belonging to these fields have survived in Scottish English.

political economist. The architect Robert Adam designed buildings in Edinburgh and London and, with his brother James, revitalised Palladian Neoclassicism; Henry Home, Lord Kames, though a judge, was also an agriculturalist and a philosopher. Scientific studies proved increasingly important: Francis Home, Professor of Materia Medica at Edinburgh, studied bleaching processes and plant nutrition; James Watt, instrument maker to the University of Glasgow for a time, worked on the steam engine, which was to prove crucial for the Industrial Revolution. The oldest and largest English-language general encyclopaedia, the *Encyclopædia Britannica*, or *A Dictionary of Arts and Sciences*, conceived by two Scottish printers, Andrew Bell and Colin Macfarquhar, was printed and published in Edinburgh, beginning in 1768. In the humanities, the works of the historian William Robertson and of the rhetorician Hugh Blair contributed to the cultural flourishing that gave Edinburgh the special nickname of 'Athens of the North'; and Henry Raeburn exploited this Northern 'Athenian' cityscape as a background in many of his portraits.

In McClure's words (1994: 40), 'it is something of a paradox that the outstanding literary and intellectual achievements of eighteenth-century Scotland should so clearly manifest an almost pathological confusion, which has never been resolved, in the matter of language, arising from a still deeper confusion regarding the national identity'. The framework of cultural identity within which the linguistic quest of the Scottish Enlightenment is situated may be described as unstable – Scottish intellectuals were acutely aware of the importance of an identity within English cultural settings for the reception of their own views. However, they also felt excluded from such a context because of the very mark of their valued specific identity, i.e. their language.[3] This specific identity was only strengthened by the remarkable cultural setting of this period. As David Hume wrote in 1757 in a letter to Gilbert Elliot:

> Is it not strange that, at a time when we have lost our Princes, our Parliaments, our independent Government, even the presence of our chief Nobility, are unhappy, in our Accent and Pronunciation, speak a very corrupt Dialect of the Tongue which we make use of; is it not strange, I say, that, in these Circumstances, we shou'd really be the People most distinguish'd for Literature in Europe? (Greig 1932, 1: 255).

Basker (1993: 81) traces the efforts 'to purify and standardise the English language' to the Restoration, when, 'inspired by the example of the Académie Française, Dryden, Roscommon and others had urged the Royal Society of London ... to found an English academy of letters'. Though such an academy

---

3 On the other hand, this dichotomy was not perceived by external commentators: Carlo Deanina, for instance, praised the achievements of Scots scholars in various fields, adding that 'writing in the same language [as the English], [Scots scholars] suffer not to appear, if we may so express it, to the eyes of other nations, any diminution or decay in the studies of the fine arts' (1763: unnumbered pages).

was never founded, the aim to achieve a standardised form of English, the purity of which was to be pursued both in diction and in prose writing, was constantly in the foreground. The Regulations that were published by the Select Society of Edinburgh in 1761 seem particularly relevant. A short quotation from these may highlight their sociolinguistic focus:

> As the intercourse between this part of GREAT BRITAIN and the Capital daily increases, ... gentlemen educated in SCOTLAND have long been sensible of the disadvantages under which they labour, from their *imperfect knowledge* of the ENGLISH TONGUE, and the *impropriety* with which they speak it (quoted by Jones 1993a: 97; my italics).

Indeed, the Select Society for Promoting the Reading and Speaking of the English Language in Scotland had been established by such prominent figures as Hugh Blair (Professor of Rhetoric and Belles Lettres),[4] Adam Ferguson (Professor of Natural Philosophy), and William Robertson, as a follow-up to the elocution lessons that had been given to a large audience in Edinburgh in 1761 by Thomas Sheridan (1719–1788, father of the dramatist), notwithstanding the fact that he spoke with a broad Irish accent himself (Daiches 1964: 21).[5] In the following year Sheridan published his *Course of Lectures on Elocution*, including a *Dissertation on the State of Language in other Countries, But More Particularly in Our Own, and its Consequences*, and in later years he compiled a *General Dictionary of the English Language, One Main Object of Which is to Establish a Plain and Permanent Standard of Pronunciation* (1780). The key words in the Dictionary's subtitle are obviously *plain, permanent* and *standard*, since they emphasise both the clarity of the work (thus aimed at the presentation of comprehensible rules), and the correspondence to a widespread need for linguistic systematisation, a con-

---

4 Although this role made Hugh Blair a key figure in the intellectual setting of his time, his language did not escape critical assessment against the prestige model, and Boswell harshly stigmatised Blair's 'burring pronunciation and drawling manner with the Lothian tone' (Reed and Pottle 1977: 31).

5 Kenrick forcefully criticised Sheridan's and Buchanan's work in the Introduction to his *New Dictionary of the English Language* (1773), which was published in 1784 as *A Rhetorical Grammar of the English Language*: 'There seems indeed a most ridiculous absurdity in the pretensions of a native of Aberdeen or Tipperary, to teach the natives of London to speak and to read' (Kenrick 1784: i, also quoted by Pollner 1994: 294). The same view is adopted by Millar (1912: 179), who describes Sheridan's venture in the following terms: 'The ridiculous experiment ... of importing into Edinburgh an Irishman with an appalling brogue for the purpose of imparting to those who sought his assistance a pure English accent'. Already Johnson had challenged the idea when, during a conversation with Boswell and Alexander Macdonald on 28 March 1772, he asked: 'What entitles Sheridan to fix the pronunciation of English? He has in the first place the disadvantage of being an Irishman; and if he says he will fix it after the example of the best company, why, they differ among themselves' (Wimsatt and Pottle 1960: 322-323). However, John Stuart, Lord Bute, was impressed with Sheridan's scheme for a pronouncing dictionary and granted him a pension of £200 a year.

sequence of which would be 'a general improvement in civility and morality' through increased politeness (Bailey 1992: 184–185).

Sheridan's work had, in fact, been preceded (and was to be followed) by numerous works aimed at freeing the expression of Scottish speakers and writers of *Scotticisms*.[6] As far as orthography and phonology are concerned, we can mention the following works published in Scotland, which are presented in chronological order:

- James Robertson, *The Ladies Help to Spelling*, Glasgow 1722;[7]
- John Warden, *A Spelling Book*, Edinburgh 1753;
- James Buchanan, *Linguae Britannicae Vera Pronuntiatio* 1757;
- A. Masson, *An English Spelling Book*, Edinburgh 1761;
- James Dun, *The Best Method of Teaching to Read and Spell English Demonstrated in Eight Parts*, Edinburgh 1766;
- William Angus, *A New Spelling Book*, Paisley 1769;
- Cortez Telfair, *The Town and Country Spelling Book*, Edinburgh 1775;
- John Burn, *A Pronouncing Dictionary of the English Language*, Glasgow 1777;[8]
- Sylvester Douglas, *Treatise on the Provincial Dialect of Scotland*, Edinburgh 1779;

6 As mentioned in Chapter 3, the first occurrence of this word is earlier than the ones quoted by the *OED*, but these prove of a certain interest anyway, because three out of five of them have a clearly negative connotation:

1717 De Foe *Mem. Ch. Scot.* ii. 137 This is a Scoticism in Speech.

1759 W. Robertson *Hist. Scot.* viii. Wks. 1851 II. 323 Many of those vicious forms of speech, which are denominated Scotticisms, have been introduced by them [lawyers] into the language.

1772 Wesley *Jrnl.* 11 Dec. (1827) III. 470 The book is wrote with great accuracy of language, (allowing for a few Scotticisms).

1815 L. Hunt *Feast of Poets* Notes 62 His style in prose, setting aside it's Scotticisms, is very well where [etc.].

1892 B. Matthews *Americanisms and Briticisms* 16 The Scotticisms of the North Briton.

The quotation taken from Robertson's *History of Scotland* seems worth observing in greater detail: it refers to the specific usage of lawyers, who obviously 'had' to use Scottish lexical items because of the specificity of the Scottish legal system even after the Union of Parliaments. At the same time, Robertson was among the earliest scholars who attributed the 'vulgarisation' of Scots to the fact that Scotland no longer had a court and so 'no domestic standard of propriety and correctness of speech remained' (quoted by Craig 1961: 305).

7 This volume is aimed at providing guidance in the acquisition of 'proper English' on the part of women; to this end, long before the foundation of the Select Society, Scotland saw in 1719 the foundation of the Fair Intellectual Club for the self-improvement of Edinburgh young ladies. The issue of women's education is discussed by Jones (1997a: 277–278 and 1997b) and by Aitken (1979: 96).

8 This is claimed to be the first 'pocket dictionary' in the history of lexicography: although Burn refers to the works of Samuel Johnson, William Johnson, Buchanan, Kenrick and Walker, he presents his dictionary stating that 'a pocket Dictionary, ascertaining the orthography, the pronunciation, the accents, and the explanation of English words, was wanting' (Burn 1786: i–ii; reference is made to the second edition, as the first one only seems to have survived in a unique and very fragile copy at Marietta College).

- John Sinclair, *Observations on the Scottish Dialect*, London and Edinburgh 1782;
- James Adams, *The Pronunciation of the English Language*, Edinburgh 1799;
- Alexander Barrie, *A Spelling and Pronouncing Dictionary of the English Language*, Edinburgh 1799;
- William Angus, *A Pronouncing Vocabulary of the English Language*, Glasgow 1800.[9]

The list could be much longer,[10] so a selection is necessary whenever the subject is approached. The search for 'refined forms' affected phonology, vocabulary and, though seemingly to a lesser extent, syntax. While the first has been widely discussed (cf. Aitken and McArthur 1979; Jones 1991, 1995 and 1997a), vocabulary and syntax seem to have attracted less attention. For the purpose of this study, which aims at identifying ways in which specific Scottish features have been perceived and acknowledged or stigmatised through the centuries, I choose to discuss those in which the sociolinguistic perspective is most clear.

This kind of focus appears to be quite prominent and to have explicit political connotations in the work of James Buchanan, *An Essay towards Establishing a Standard for an Elegant and Uniform Pronunciation of the English Language, throughout the British Dominions as practised by the Most Learned and Polite Speakers* (1764). In his Preface he made specific reference to 'the inhabitants of North Britain' and connected the acquisition and teaching of 'a proper Pronunciation' with 'removing national prejudice, which has too long subsisted, and been chiefly fostered between the two kingdoms from their different forms of speech!' According to Buchanan's view, sharing linguistic features was expected to connect England and Scotland 'by much more benevolent and generous ties than that of political union' (quoted by Crowley 1991: 79). In his previous work, *Linguae Britannicae Vera Pronuntiatio*, Buchanan had even claimed that 'The people of North Britain seem, in general, to be almost at as great a loss for proper accent and just pronunciation as foreigners' (1757: xv).

The discrepancy between the written and the spoken modes of expression is emphasised by Buchanan (1757: xv) when he finds that

---

9 In this work the self-consciousness of the author appears in his response 'To those who, without examination, may object to this attempt, as being the production of a Native of North Britain', in which he states that his dictionary 'makes no innovation in English Pronunciation' (Angus 1800: 4).

10 An invaluable source of information is of course provided by Sundby, Bjørge and Haugland (1991). As regards Scotland in particular, Volker Mohr (unpubl. MS) is currently compiling a *Dictionary of Scottish English Normative Grammar*, which will certainly add a very useful collection of data. A brief introduction to this topic is provided by Frank (1994).

It would be surprising to find [Scots] writing English in the same manner, and some of them to as great perfection as any native of England, and yet pronouncing after a different, and for the most part unintelligible manner, did we not know, that they never had any proper guide or direction for that purpose.

Millar emphasises the amount of criticism expressed at the reception of Scottish writing on the part of English audiences when he asks: 'How were Scotsmen to write with credit to themselves – to write without incurring the ridicule of English critics?' (1912: 179). This shows that it was at this point that Scottish *literati* came to stress a difference between the two varieties that was possibly exaggerated: for instance, the idea of Scots and English as two distinct languages was also emphasised in 1748 by Alexander Carlyle, who complained: 'Since we began to affect speaking a foreign language, which the English dialect is to us, humour, it must be confessed, is less apparent in conversation' (also quoted by Hewitt 1987: 254). At the same time, lexical differences signalled cultural differences, not only concerning the kirk and the law, but also regarding measures: Smollett, for instance, thus commented on Home's *Experiments on Bleaching* (1756):

> The language in some places is a little uncouth. – We meet with some *Scottish* words and measures, which an *English* reader will be at a loss to understand. Such as *tramp* for treading under foot, *lint* for flax, *dreeper* for a dripping-stand, *bittling* for a beetling, *mutchkin* for a pint, *chopin* for a quart, *Scots pint* for two quarts, *Scots Gallon* for sixteen quarts, etc. (*The Critical Review*, 1: 114, also quoted by Basker 1993: 87).

In the age of prescriptivism, one of the most notable works was James Beattie's *Scoticisms, arranged in Alphabetical Order, designed to correct Improprieties of Speech and Writing* (1779, republished 1787); here we find one of the earliest distinctions between covert and overt Scotticisms when the author refers to 'those Scotch idioms, which, in this country, are liable to be mistaken for English'.[11] On the other hand, the relationship between Scots and English is made out to be more problematic elsewhere in the text; for instance, Millar (1912: 180) quotes Beattie as saying: 'We who live in Scotland are obliged to study English from books like a dead language. Accordingly, when we write we write it like a dead language, which we understand but cannot speak'. Of course this claim denies the actual contact between the two varieties that was the very basis of an increased linguistic awareness in Scotland: a kind of awareness that was constantly verging on self-consciousness, if, as Beattie claims further on, '[Scots] are continually afraid of making *gross* blunders, and

11 According to Hewitt (1987: 256), this may actually be seen as evidence of the rise of Scottish Standard English, which Beattie was trying to limit by promoting the use of 'proper', i.e. southern, English.

when an easy, familiar, idiomatical phrase occurs, dare not adopt it if we recollect no authority, for fear of Scotticisms'. The reference to 'authority' echoes Johnson's views on the subject of good usage and would seem to imply English authorship. This is confirmed when Beattie challenges the idea that 'Hume, Robertson, &c. write English better than the English themselves: than which in my judgment there cannot be a greater absurdity. I would as soon believe that Thuanus wrote better Latin than Cicero or Caesar' (Letter to Sylvester Douglas of 1778, quoted by Millar 1912: 180 and Hewitt 1987: 256). The emphasis placed on English authorities explains the tremendous popularity of the *Spectator* in Scotland in those years (Craig 1961: 46–47). At the same time, Beattie's words point in the direction of tolerance where he finds that 'To speak with the English, or with the Scotch, accent, is no more praiseworthy, or blameable, than to be born in England, or Scotland' (1788: 91–92), although in a letter to Robert Arbuthnot (26 November 1785) he had complained:

> Our language (I mean the English) is degenerating very fast; and many phrases, which I know to be Scottish idioms, have got into [English] of late years (quoted by Hewitt 1987: 255).

In fact, Beattie subsequently goes on to explain that not all provincial accents are equally good, because 'of accent, as well as of spelling, syntax, and idiom, there is a standard in every polite nation' – in the case of Britain, 'the language ... of the most learned and polite persons in London, and the neighbouring Universities of Oxford and Cambridge, ought to be accounted the standard of the English tongue, especially in accent and pronunciation: syntax, spelling, and idiom, having been ascertained by the practice of good authors, and the consent of former ages' (1788: 92).

Jones (1991: 101, 1993a: 100, 1995: 15–20 and 1997a) tells us that some commentators of the time identified a Scottish standard in the speech of Edinburgh polite society: among these was Alexander Scot who, in 1779, claimed:

> The Scottish dialect of this day is no more that of Allan Ramsay than of Gawin Douglas; but that the language of Edinburgh is not nearer the language of London than it was a century ago, whether in idiom or in utterance, will irrefragably appear from the following letter, which fairly paints the present Caledonian English of the college, the pulpit, and the bar (*The Contrast*, quoted by Jones 1993a: 102).

Scot explicitly refers to the language of professors, clergymen and lawyers, i.e. educated speakers, while the reference to Allan Ramsay, whose re-assessment of Scots vernacular in poetry is equated with Douglas's own use of the same medium, draws a line between the vernacular and the prestige variety, though the latter does not present southern features of phonology and vocabulary.

The 'overt class basis' of prescriptive works is highlighted by Barber (1993:

205) together with their regional bias. The issue is also taken up by Mugglestone (1995: 45) and by Beal (1996), who point out the demand, from the rising middle classes, for guides to correct usage that could help them disguise their 'vulgar' origins. The correction of Scotticisms as a piece of etiquette had already been noticed by John Sinclair, who, in 1782, had defined the Scots forms as 'uncouth, unintelligible, equally conspicuous, at the table, in the pulpit, and at the bar' (cf. Craig 1961: 57), thus highlighting the ambiguity that characterised the question of 'intelligibility', which was, in fact, one of 'politeness' (cf. Crowley 1991: 64). The pedagogical value of prescriptive works, instead, was stressed very early by Buchanan (1757: xv), when he recommended his work to 'all whose business is to speak in public,[12] and all teachers of youth [in North Britain]', so that his readers 'be no more distinguished by that rough and uncouth brogue which is so harsh and unpleasant to an English ear'.

Jones's views on the identification of an ancestor of Scottish Standard English may be confirmed by a comment expressed by John Ramsay of Ochtertyre (Craig 1961: 47), who remembered conversing with a member of the Union Parliament who spoke the old 'upper-class Scots'. Ramsay also mentioned that 'besides the colloquial Scotch spoken in good company, there was likewise the oratorical, which was used by judges, lawyers and clergymen, ... [and] such as wished to excel in their public appearances, strove to bring their speeches or sermons some degrees nearer pure English than their ordinary talk' (quoted by Hewitt 1987: 252).[13] On the other hand, Beattie described this variety as 'an affected, mixed, barbarous dialect, which is neither Scotch nor English, but a strange jumble of both' (letter to John Pinkerton of 1778, quoted by Hewitt 1987: 256). Earlier on in the century a sociolinguistic distinction had already been made by Sir Robert Sibbald in 1710, when he mentioned 'The Language of the Common People', or 'That Language we call Broad Scots, which is yet used by the Vulgar, ... the *Highlanders* Language, and the refined Language of the Gentry, which the more Polite People among us do use, and is made up of *Saxon, French* and *Latin* Words' (*The History of the Sheriffdoms of Fife and Kinross*, Edinburgh, 1710: 15–16, quoted by Aitken 1979: 93–94).

That the two varieties, Scots and 'refined Language', were considered to be two poles of a continuum is also shown by an extract of the Records of the Burgh of Stirling (vol. 2, 23 Aug. 1718 – quoted by Williamson 1982: 59), in which Scots and English are used interchangeably in the discussion of the

12 Buchanan obviously refers to clergymen and lawyers, as further on in the text he mentions 'excellent and rhetorical speeches delivered by the learned both from the pulpit and at the bar' (1757: xv).

13 This kind of linguistic 'antisyzygy' (or almost paradoxical contrast) in Scotland in the latter half of the eighteenth century is also described in Hume's biography (Hill Burton 1846: 450–451), where the philosopher's 'broad Scottish pronunciation' is discussed; according to the editor, 'provincial broadness of pronunciation in Scotland is far from being incompatible with a very pure and unprovincial style of language'.

situation of a 'Scots class' for which a different person is needed 'for teaching English'. Differences may have been perceived more acutely in cities: it is Williamson again who quotes Telfair's advertisement for his English classes (*Edinburgh Evening Courant*, 16 September 1712), in which it is stated that 'Great care is taken that no Scotch may be spoken' (1982: 67). On this issue the *Old Statistical Account*, compiled between 1791 and 1799 on a parish basis, is a good source of information on how Scots was viewed at the turn of the century:[14] in several cases the local language is described as 'neither English nor Scottish, but a mixture of both' (Dumfries), or 'a dialect of the Scottish and English blended together' (Banff); in Midlothian, the process of convergence of the two varieties is described as rapid, whereas in Ayrshire and Moray it is said to have been gradual (Williamson 1982: 67–68). What Williamson correctly emphasises here is the recognition of an interesting process according to which the two linguistic entities are seen to be merging, thus implying their former distinctiveness, although this distinctiveness was not very widely acknowledged at earlier stages. Consequently, the linguistic perceptions of speakers on their variety and the way it had developed seems to have been shaped by the influence of prescriptive works and the adoption of a teaching standard.

Famous instances of linguistic concern: David Hume and James Boswell

The aspiration to conform to a southern standard of English was important for many educated Scots, with the possible exception of Adam Smith (the author of *The Wealth of Nations*), who believed that 'someone born north of the Tweed could yet attain 'a correct and even elegant style" (quoted by Rogers 1991: 59). Even Robert Burns, whose popularity was mainly based on a perception of the poet as a 'rustic bard', was in fact very careful in his linguistic choices.[15]

Other very famous instances of Scots who aspired to a southern standard were the philosopher David Hume and James Boswell: the latter strenuously attempted to overcome his provincial elocution (Rogers 1991: 56–71; Basker 1993: 85–86), while the former was so preoccupied with the standardisation of his written language that he drew up a list of Scotticisms to be avoided. The list, though apparently meant for private use only (Rogers 1991: 58), appeared

---

14 More attention was possibly given to place-names: in the *First Circular Letter to the Clergy of the Church of Scotland*, of 25 May 1790 (reported by Broadie 1997: 566), Sinclair included the following questions in section IV 'Miscellaneous questions':

    117. Has the parish any peculiar advantages or disadvantages?

    118. What language is principally spoken in it?

    119. From what language do the names of places in the parish seem to be derived?

    120. What are the most remarkable instances of such derivations?

15 An analysis of Burns' correspondence throws some light on this theme, as we shall see in Chapter 5.

in some copies of the 1752 edition of his *Political Discourses*,[16] then was reprinted in the *Scots Magazine* in 1760, and four years later the same periodical published a letter signed 'Philologus'[17] that criticised Hume's omissions and mistakes.[18] Hume's list thus found itself to be possibly the first of a series of prescriptive works which continued to be published well into the nineteenth century, both in Scotland and elsewhere. In general, these lists included lexical items that were either specifically Scottish and for which English equivalents were suggested, or usage variants, the latter also referring to grammatical patterns (for instance, in the use of prepositions).

Hume's list of Scotticisms

The 1752 edition of David Hume's *Political Discourses* included an appendix in which about 100 Scotticisms were listed together with their English counterparts. In this list we find a variety of items: 33 verbs, 18 nouns and noun phrases, 14 prepositions and prepositional phrases, 12 adverbs and adverbial phrases, 12 adjectives and adjectival phrases, four pronouns, one conjunction and one idiom, together with notes on word order and modality. The arrangement does not seem to follow any system, whether grammatical, semantic or pragmatic, since items of vocabulary and grammatical features are included in apparently random order.

Although this list is generally mentioned in studies of the sociolinguistic situation in eighteenth-century Scotland, it does not seem to have attracted much scholarly attention from the point of view of its linguistic, rather than sociolinguistic, value; however, Dossena (1997a) showed that it contains elements worth discussing in greater detail. An earlier study that had meant to

16 In the 1964 reprint of the 1882 London edition of the *Essays* we find an interesting note: 'This *List of Scotticisms*, printed from the Edinburgh edition of 1826, is said to occur in some copies of the 'Political Discourses', Edition H. The present editor has not found it in any Edition published during Hume's life-time' (Green and Grose, 1882, II: 461). The copy of the 1752 edition of the *Political Discourses* owned by the National Library of Scotland, however, does include the list, and it is on this that our study is based; this is also important because the book was printed before Hume's death in 1776. Greig, the editor of Hume's letters, seems to challenge Hume's actual authorship of the list itself, because he mentions a list of Scotticisms, 'believed to be of his compiling', 'bound up with some copies of the *Political Discourses*, 1752' (Greig 1932/1: 205). The same suggestion is made by McKnight (1968: 405). In his overview of the attention given to language in eighteenth-century Edinburgh he actually attributes the list to Elphinston; cf. also Basker (1993: 84).

17 Pollner (1994: 290) takes up Rohlfing's view that this pseudonym may conceal James Elphinston; cf. also Pollner and Rohlfing (1986: 128).

18 Both texts are reprinted in the Appendix to James Elphinston's *Animadversions Upon 'Elements of Criticism'* (1771: 113–122), which, in turn, includes a chapter called 'Scoticism, and other mixture' (1771: 84–92); the definition of Scotticism provided by Elphinston is the following: 'A species of old english, but english no more, ... and this whether in term or phraseology. For Scoticism consists chiefly in the different application or construction of english word' (1771: 84–85).

classify Hume's Scotticisms (Pollner 1994) was very valuable in its attempt to trace them in dictionaries; but it did not, in fact, consider all the items and subdivided them into four very broad categories (lexical items, morphological forms/word formation, prepositional use, and idiomatic phrases/order of items) without actually identifying the degree of overlapping in these categories. For instance, different prepositional uses may be the basis of different idiomatic expressions, as in the case of English *with child by a man* as opposed to Scottish *with child to a man*.

Below, Hume's list has been subdivided in the following tables,[19] so that it may be easier to assess the attention given to different parts of speech and linguistic features.

SCOTTICISMS

Will, in the first person, as *I will walk, we will walk*, expresses the intention or resolution of the person, along with the future event: In the second and third person, as, *you will, he will, they will*, it expresses the future action or event, without comprehending or excluding the volition.

Shall, in the first person, whether singular or plural, expresses the future action or event, without excluding or comprehending the intention or resolution: But in the *second* or *third* person, it marks a necessity, and commonly a necessity proceeding from the person who speaks; as, *he shall walk, you shall repent it*.

These variations seem to have proceeded from a politeness in the *English*, who, in speaking to the others, or of others, made use of the term *will*, which implies volition, even where the event may be the subject of necessity and constraint. And in speaking of themselves, made use of the term *shall*, which implies constraint, even though the event may be the object of choice.

Wou'd and *shou'd* are conjunctive moods, subject to the same rule; only, we may observe, that in a sentence, where there is a condition exprest, and a consequence of that condition, the former always requires *shou'd*, and the latter *wou'd*, in the second and third persons; as, *if he shou'd fall, he wou'd break his leg*, etc.

These is the plural of *this*; *those* of *that*. The former therefore expresses what is near: the latter what is more remote. As, in these lines of the Duke of Buckingham.

> 'Philosophers and poets vainly strove,
> In ev'ry age, the lumpish mass to move.
> But THOSE were pedants if compar'd with THESE,
> Who knew not only to instruct but please.'

Where a relative is to follow, and the subject has not been mention'd

---

19 The entries are ordered alphabetically; the italics are mine. In the original list the two varieties are called *Scotch* and *English*.

immediately before, *those* is always required. *Those observations which he made. Those kingdoms which Alexander conquer'd.*

In the verbs, which end in *t*, or *te*, we frequently omit *ed* in the preterperfect and in the participle; as, *he operate, it was cultivate. Milton* says, *In thought more elevate*, but he is the only author, who uses that expression.

Notice should not be used as a verb. The proper phrase is *take notice.* Yet I find Lord Shaftesbury uses *notic'd*, the participle: And *unnotic'd* is very common.

Hinder to do is *Scotch*. The *English* phrase is *hinder from doing.* Yet Milton says, *Hindered not Satan to pervert the mind.* Book IX.

Hume's Scotticisms	English equivalents (as proposed by Hume)
Verbs (33 entries)	
adduce a proof	produce a proof
advert to	attend to
cause him do it	cause him to do it
compete	enter into competition
cry him	call him
cut out his hair	cut off his hair
deduce	deduct
denuded	divested
drunk, run[20]	drank, ran
effectuate	effect
evite	avoid
exeemed	exempted
incarcerate	imprison
learn	teach
maltreat	abuse
mind it	remember it
misgive	fail
part with child	miscarry
pled[21]	pleaded
prejudge	hurt
proven, improven, approven[22]	prov'd, improv'd, approv'd
rebuted	discouraged by repulses
think shame	asham'd
to condescend upon	to specify
to crave	to dun, to ask payment

20 In this case, the difference is on the morphological level, rather than on the lexical one.
21 Cf. n. 20.
22 Cf. n. 20.

to depone	to depose
to discharge	to forbid
to extinguish an obligation	to cancel an obligation
to open up	to open or lay open
to remeed	to remedy
to send an errand	to send off an errand
to take off a new coat[23]	to make up a new suit
to want it	to be without a thing

Nouns and noun phrases
(18 entries)

a chimney	a grate
a compliment	a present
a park	an enclosure
a wright	a carpenter
annualrent	interest
bankier	banker
common soldiers	private men
debitor	debtor
discretion	civility
dubiety	doubtfulness
for my share	for my part
forfaulture	forfeiture
friends and acquaintances	friends and acquaintance
in no event	in no case
superplus	surplus
Thucydide, Herodot, Sueton	Thucydides, Herodotus, Suetonius
to get a stomach	to get an appetite
vacance	vacation

Prepositions and prepositional phrases
(14 entries)

alongst	along
anent	with regard to
come in to the fire	come near the fire
contented himself to do	contented himself with doing
in favours of	in favour of
lookt over the window[24]	lookt out at the window
marry upon	marry to
notwithstanding of that	notwithstanding that

23 This entry might have been grouped with nouns; however, the verb appears to be more prominent, since the recommended usage avoids the semantic ambiguity of *take off*.

24 I preferred not to classify this entry together with verbs because Hume apparently stresses the difference in usage of the prepositions; the same applies to *marry upon*.

rather chuse to buy as sell   rather chuse to buy than sell
tear to pieces   tear in pieces
to be angry at a man   to be angry with a man
to furnish goods to him[25]   to furnish him with goods
to inquire at a man   to inquire of a man
with child to a man   with child by a man

Adjectives and adjectival phrases
(12 entries)

amissing[26]   missing
big coat[27]   great coat
big with a man   great with a man
bygone   past
conform to   conformable to
defunct   deceast
fresh weather   open weather
heritable   hereditary
notour   notorious
tender   sickly
tenible argument   good argument
to be difficulted   to be puzzled

Adverbs and adverbial phrases
(12 entries)

allenarly   solely
alwise   always
evenly   even
for ordinary   usually
in the long run   at long run
in time coming   in time to come
on a sudden   of a sudden
out of hand   presently
readily   probably
simply impossible   absolutely impossible
there, where   thither, whither
yesternight   last night

25 In this case the use of a different preposition is also connected with modified word order.
26 Cf. n. 20.
27 This item was placed in this category because it is the adjective that changes in the two varieties; however, if we consider *great coat* to be a collocation, then it could be classified together with nouns.

Word order
(5 entries)

a pretty enough girl	a pretty girl enough
as ever I saw	as I ever saw
butter and bread	bread and butter
paper, pen, and ink	pen, ink, and paper
pepper and vinegar	vinegar and pepper

Pronouns
(4 entries)

'tis a week since he left this	'tis a week since he left this place
nothing else	no other thing
severals	several
some better	something better

Conjunctions
(1 entry)

'tis a question if	'tis a question whether

Idioms
(1 entry)

as I shall answer	I protest or declare

As we see, verbs are the most numerous category, whereas nouns, prepositions and adjectives (together with the phrases that are based on them) are given almost equal prominence. The main aim of our tables is to arrange the items according to a sufficiently systematic criterion. However, this is often hindered by the extreme fuzziness in the list itself, which, as we mentioned, includes lexical items together with idioms, morphological differences and differences in usage. Some items in the list are also annotated as follows:

- '*alongst*. Yet the *English* say both amid and amidst, among and amongst
- *cause him do it*. Yet 'tis good *English* to say, make him do it
- *effectuate*. This word in *English* means to effect with pains and difficulty
- *a wright*. Yet 'tis good *English* to say a wheelwright, etc.'

The list itself is preceded by some paragraphs on *will, shall, wou'd* and *shou'd*;[28] these, however, seem to be meant to remind Hume of rules of usage, since they do not include any explicit reference to Scottish patterns to avoid. The same may apply to the very brief note on *these* and *those*; the first comparison between English and Scottish usage appears in the notes on verbs, where Hume observes that 'we [Scots] frequently omit *ed* in the preterperfect and in the participle'. He identifies the same feature in Milton, yet he discards

---

28 The extent to which modals were an actual touchstone of proper usage is discussed by Tieken-Boon van Ostade (1985) and Arnovick (1997); they are also discussed in similar terms in nineteenth-century grammars, as shown by Macbain (1882: 17).

this example, since he claims that 'he is the only author, who uses that expression'. Milton's authority is also referred to in the discussion of *hinder to do*, which is described as '*Scotch*. The *English* phrase is *hinder from doing*. Yet Milton says, *Hindered not Satan to pervert the mind*. Book IX'.

The reference to authority in linguistic matters is also prominent in Hume's correspondence. In several cases Hume asks or thanks for advice on how to avoid a Scotticism, or he provides advice himself. Among his interlocutors on these issues we find David Mallet,[29] John Clephane, Andrew Millar, William Robertson and Hume's own nephew Joseph. As we might expect, Hume's concern with appropriateness is expressed most warmly in his letters to his nephew[30] and to those who had asked for his opinion on their works, but Hume also paid great attention to his correspondents' views of his own usage; in various cases he eagerly asks for lists of Scotticisms for future reference (Greig 1932/1: 233, 235–236, 369).

In a letter to David Mallet of 8 November 1762 (Greig 1932/1: 369) Hume defines Scotticisms as 'Negligences of Style' and 'Vices of Expression'. His preoccupation with proper language is also reflected in his comments on specifically Scottish words. For instance, his letter to his nephew Joseph, of 12 May 1771, opens with an apology for his delay in answering. referring to 'the occupation which proceeds from flitting, or as ... Englishmen call it, removing' (Hunter 1960: 130). According to Klibansky and Mossner (1954: 212), an undatable letter to Colonel Edmonstone also includes playful use of a Scotticism, as Hume writes about 'timeous or rather timely Information'.

Hume was clearly aware of his own accent and of the contrast between this and his aim of purity in writing: in his letter to John Wilkes of 16 October 1754 (Greig 1932/1: 205) he wrote:

> Notwithstanding all the Pains, which I have taken in the study of the English Language, I am still jealous of my Pen. As to my Tongue, you have seen that I regard it as totally desperate and irreclaimable.

The letters do not include many references to the Scotticisms in the 1752 list. Of these, only *hinder to do, maltreat* and *conform* are discussed with his correspondents: *conform* is pointed out as a Scotticism as early as 1747 in a letter to

---

29 Rogers (1991: 65) quotes Giuseppe Baretti as saying: 'Mallet wrote good English, and I remember that Richardson ... used to say that Mallet was the only Scotchman who never confused 'shall' and 'will' in the future tense'. Mallet's attempt to anglicise his language had even caused him to change his Scottish name, which originally was Malloch (cf. Basker 1993: 86). As for the other interlocutors, Rogers finds it emblematic of the sociolinguistic climate if David Hume, 'the luminary of half of the civilised world, could seek the advice of undistinguished English scribblers' (1991: 68).

30 In a letter of 12 May 1771 Hume wrote to his nephew: 'I believe all the officers of your Regiment consist of Englishmen or Scotchmen thoroughly naturalised; so that you have a good opportunity of learning the pronunciation exactly; and I beseech you not to neglect it. ... I was too negligent in this particular when I was of your age' (Hunter 1960: 131).

Henry Home (Klibansky and Mossner 1954: 27); then, in February 1763, he corrects Thomas Reid for writing '*hinder to do*, instead of *hinder from doing*, which is the English [phrase]' (Greig 1932/1: 376); finally, in a letter written to William Robertson in November or December 1768, Hume states that '*Maltreat* is a Scotticism which occurs once' (in Robertson's work) (Greig 1932/2: 194).

Hume also comments on items not included in the 1752 list:

- *enough – enow* (letter to John Clephane, 8 December 1753, in Greig 1932/1: 182). Hume suspects the distinct pronunciations to be 'a mere Scotticism' and urges his correspondent to ask his English friends for clarification;[31]
- *circumstantiate*, which 'wou'd also be better supply'd by *circumstantial*' (letter to Andrew Stuart, 4 February 1773, in Greig 1932/2: 271);[32]
- *expiscate; prestations* (letter to Robert Wallace, early 1753, in Klibansky and Mossner 1954: 31);
- *interference; whole nobles* (letter to William Robertson, 8 February 1759, in Klibansky and Mossner 1954: 45).

James Boswell

Boswell has been identified as the epitome of the Scot striving to gain access to London society in spite of his own cultural (and linguistic) background (cf. Basker 1993: 85; Rogers 1991: 62-63). He attended Sheridan's lectures in Edinburgh and became a member of the Select Society. Later on he was always wary of his strong Scottish accent, though also reluctant to accept complete anglicisation. This ambivalent attitude appears in his diaries, where we find references to projected works that have a clear linguistic focus. Apart from the Scots dictionary, which will be discussed shortly, he also wrote 'Proposals for a periodical paper in the Scots dialect' (cf. Pottle, Abbott and Pottle 1993: 106). The paper was to be named *The Sutiman* because 'it was the best titil for a periodical Paper to be published in *Auld Reekie*'. On the issue of Scotticisms, instead, while he found that it was unnatural for a Scot to acquire perfect English, he and Henry Erskine agreed 'to give each other a copy of every one of our printed [legal] papers, and each was to be censor on the other. For every ungrammatical expression and every Scotticism except technical phrases, a shilling was to be incurred' (Ryskamp and Pottle 1963: 124–129).

31 It is interesting to see that Hume also suggests the method by which this clarification should be obtained: not asking directly, but engaging the interlocutor 'to employ the expression about which we are in doubt'; besides, he recommends consulting the ladies, because 'they have a more delicate sense of the propriety of expressions': almost a reference to the sociolinguistic attitude to prestige forms that has been described in detail by twentieth-century linguists.
32 Stuart replied that 'a very eminent Critick' had selected the Scotticisms that appeared in the letters and could get him 'a compleat list of them'; Hume, although disbelieving this claim, wished this list to be sent to him, since he supposed the 'great English Critic' to be Johnson (letter to A. Stuart, 22 March 1773, in Klibansky and Mossner 1954: 201).

Boswell is inevitably associated with the lexicographer Samuel Johnson; through their linguistic interests, they were deeply aware of the developments that were taking place in Scotland, and indeed their observations in the journals of their tour of Scotland in 1773 cast some interesting light on their own views, since these also take into consideration Gaelic (or Erse) forms and mention the dramatic changes that had been taking place in the Highland lifestyle after the failure of the last Jacobite rising in 1745. For example, Gaelic was being supplanted directly by English, with hardly any development of Scots forms (except in areas where contact with the Lowlands was more frequent). This explains why we find evidence of what today is called 'Highland English' in Johnson's entry for Anoch, 'a village in Glenmollison', in terms that mark the distinction between Highland speech and a Lowland accent:[33]

> I found that my host's diction had nothing peculiar. Those Highlanders that can speak English, commonly speak it well, with few of the words, and little of the tone by which a Scotchman is distinguished' (Johnson 1775/1996: 30).

Johnson was aware of the fact that it was probably too late to observe the classic forms of Highland society,[34] yet his interest is certainly genuine.[35] In 1769 he had even encouraged Boswell to compile a dictionary of Scotticisms,[36] but the project never went beyond a short specimen,[37] because Boswell had

33 Before Johnson another traveller, Thomas Pennant, who had visited the Highlands in 1769, had remarked in his *Tour of Scotland* (1771): 'Of the ten parishes in Cathness, only the four that lie South-East speak *Erse*; all the others speak *English*, and that in greater purity than most parts of North Britain' (cf. Youngson 1974: 150).

34 Johnson observed: 'We came thither too late to see what we expected, ... a system of antiquated life. The clans retain little now of their original character ... Of what they had before the late conquest of their country, there remain only their language and their poverty. Their language is attacked on every side' (1775/1996: 49–50). Cf. also Drescher (1968).

35 As regards Gaelic, for instance, Johnson says he heard it for the first time in Nairn, then he heard it sung in Raasay, and compared its intriguing sound to that of Italian opera: 'After supper the ladies sung *Erse* songs, to which I listened as an *English* audience to an *Italian* opera, delighted with the sound of words which I did not understand' (1775/1996: 51). The tour gave rise to a host of parody and satire, and for this reason it will be discussed at greater length in the next chapter, together with other travellers' accounts.

36 Görlach (1995b: 84) finds a contradictory attitude in Johnson's recommendation to Boswell, while he had, in fact, 'excluded Scots lexis' from his own work. As we shall see later in this chapter, Johnson did not exclude Scots altogether, but included what Görlach himself later defines 'regional standard'. As a matter of fact, an earlier study of Görlach's (1987: 135) had used this suggestion to Boswell as evidence that Johnson considered Scots an independent language. Johnson's actual words as reported by Boswell, however, seem to point to an antiquarian interest, rather than a sociolinguistic one.

37 Rogers (1991: 62) reports that a manuscript of Boswell's projected dictionary was sold from his son's library in 1825. According to Pottle (1929: 302) 'the manuscript ... was sold for 16 shillings as lot 3172 of the sale of James Boswell the Younger, 1825', but he says he is 'unaware of its present whereabouts', and although it is mentioned in the *Catalogue of the Papers of James Boswell at Yale University* (Pottle, Abbott and Pottle 1993), no copy seems to have been traced: see also Pottle (1966: 493).

doubts as to its usefulness. Certainly Johnson's suggestion that Boswell should compile 'a Dictionary of words peculiar to Scotland' cannot have been intended as a means to promote Scots and is to be seen in the same antiquarian context as his other recommendation to compile 'a work on the antiquities of Scotland', as his reference to Ray's work on northern dialects makes clear. The exchange is reported in the *Life of Johnson* (19 October 1769):

> He advised me to complete a Dictionary of words peculiar to Scotland, of which I shewed him a specimen. 'Sir, (said he), Ray has made a collection of north-country words. By collecting those of your country, you will do a useful thing towards the history of the language.' He bade me also go on with collections I was making upon the antiquities of Scotland. 'Make a large book; a folio.' BOSWELL 'But of what use will it be, Sir? JOHNSON 'Never mind the use; do it.' (II, 91–92)

Boswell had been considering the idea of a dictionary of Scottish words since 1764,[38] but not with an antiquarian interest, and Rogers (1991: 62) even claims that Boswell saw 'distinctive Scottish vocabulary as a racial marker'. It is undeniable that the fear of Scotticisms was often the cause of hypercorrection and extreme fastidiousness in the scrutiny of writings: for instance, Basker (1993: 87) mentions the case of Tobias Smollett,[39] who identified Hume's Scotticism *adduce* in *An Essay on the Writings and Genius of Pope* and cited it in his review of the anonymous work. In fact, this had not been written by a Scotsman, but by Joseph Warton, a scholar educated at Oxford. Persistent linguistic uncertainty in the latter part of the century thus expressed itself through acute wariness of 'impolite' forms. At the same time, political and sociological issues were constantly in the background, since the anti-Bute[40] agitation of the 1760s was also a factor in the negative view of Scotland that followed the failure of the Jacobite risings.

Scotticisms in eighteenth-century dictionaries

When Samuel Johnson published the first edition of his *Dictionary* in 1755, Scotland was experiencing a kind of linguistic 'witch-hunt' against Scotticisms. However, it was not only in Scotland, where the issue was felt with special keenness. In England the ideal of making language more polite, accurate and

---

38 The project is outlined in Boswell's Journal entry for 24 February 1764: 'I am writing a dictionary myself! ... It is a Scots dictionary. ... We have not a single Scots dictionary. Really, that is amazing' (Pottle 1952: 103-104).

39 Smollett parodied the situation in his novels *The Adventures of Roderick Random* (1748) and *The Expedition of Humphry Clinker* (1771).

40 John Stuart, 3rd Earl of Bute (1713–1792) was the Prime Minister (1762–63) who negotiated the peace ending the Seven Years' War (1756–63) with France, but he failed to create a stable administration; on the climate of anti-Scottish feeling in England in the latter part of the eighteenth century, cf. Rogers (1995: 192–215).

stable was a key element of scholarly thought. The most famous instance was Swift's publication, in 1712, of *A Proposal for Correcting, Improving and Ascertaining the English Tongue*; for the same purpose, Addison planned a dictionary with quotations, and four 'identical dictionaries' were published in 1735, 1737, 1739 and 1741 'design'd for the use of Gentlemen, Ladies, Foreigners, Artificers, Tradesmen; and All who desire to Speak or Write English in its present Purity and Perfection' (Starnes De Witt and Noyes 1946/ 1991: 139). At the same time, the perception of the important sociolinguistic changes taking place in Scotland was quite different south of the border, where fewer scholars actually considered describing a variety that was fast becoming obsolete. The prescriptive aim was obviously less of interest, so very few dictionaries included non-standard forms, and in those that did northern lexical items were not awarded any privileged prominence.

Pollner (1994) starts from Hume's 1752 list of Scotticisms to see how many of these items are included in general English dictionaries before Johnson, and he examines the following:

- Robert Cawdrey, 1604, *A Table Alphabeticall*;
- John Bullokar, 1616, *An English Expositor*;
- Elisha Coles, 1676, *An English Dictionary*;
- John Ray, 1691, *A Collection of English Words Not Generally Used*;
- Nathan Bailey, 1721, *A Universal Etymological Dictionary*.

If we exclude the dictionaries dating back to the seventeenth century, which were discussed in the previous chapter, we find that Bailey identifies *kirk* as a North Country word, but also includes Scottish entries such as *barn/bearn* (= child), *loon*, and *maiden*, the ancestor of the guillotine. An encyclopaedic approach is apparent, though in a rather episodic way: as if certain items belonged to some kind of linguistic *Wunderkammer*, collected like exotic artefacts from distant countries and put on display as curios.

Scottish entries in Johnson's Dictionary[41]

Dossena (forthcoming) shows that Johnson's *Dictionary* includes about 200 'Scottish' items, although dialectal variations are not discussed in the *Plan of a Dictionary* (1747) or in the *Preface*. We may assume that Johnson meant to

---

41 In the following paragraphs are quotations from the electronic edition of Johnson's *Dictionary* (McDermott 1996). Each entry is preceded by *I* or *IV*, depending on whether it appears in the first or fourth edition; when there are no differences between the two editions, only the first one is quoted. If an entry has more than one meaning, we report the one referring to the Scottish context, leaving the number it has in the original sequence of meanings. The quotations are only included when explicit reference is made to them in the definitions, since these are the actual focus of our analysis. Görlach (1987: 135) points out that Todd's revision of 1818 treats regional and obsolete forms in a rather different way, 'apparently as a consequence of the reviser's antiquarian and dialect interests'.

exclude them in the same way as he had meant to exclude 'fugitive cant'. Yet, the appearance of unexpected Gaelic or Scots entries provides fascinating insights into this lexicographer's approach to language. Given the purpose of his work, his treatment of Scottish forms is obviously not thorough and systematic; we may, however, recognise some interesting patterns. The first important thing to note is the fact that these entries do not only represent obsolete or 'incorrect' expressions (in the tradition of 'words-to-avoid lists'), but also refer to specific aspects of Scottish culture, such as had been glimpsed in previous dictionaries, although this time with greater accuracy in the attribution of geographical distribution. We may therefore identify a dual interest in Johnson's entries: on the one hand, a philological approach to the etymological forms of lexical items that were being imported into English, and which Johnson had traced in the authors from whose works he had taken his quotations; on the other, an encyclopaedic interest in a distant culture.[42] According to Basker (1993: 82–86), Johnson 'seems to have included a Scottish word or usage ... simply to single it out and stigmatise it as a Scotticism'.[43] However, our study of the way in which entries relating to Scottish life and culture are presented does not seem to point to a strictly prescriptive approach.

The first edition of the *Dictionary* (1755) includes several entries on specific features of Highland life, and many etymologies or cognate forms are marked *Erse* or *Earse*.[44] As regards words relating to the Highlands, we find that their reference to a peripheral cultural system is clearly specified, but their usage is not actually stigmatised; only the quotations may have a disparaging value, as in the case of *dirk*,[45] in which two lines provide a portrait of the stereotypical Highlander:[46]

I **DIRK**. n.s. [an Earse word.] A kind of dagger used in the Highlands of Scotland.
In vain thy hungry mountaineers
Come forth in all their warlike geers,

---

42 This kind of dual interest is mentioned in Hayashi (1978: 92–93). Also Nagashima (1988: 18–25) highlights Johnson's attention to linguistic phenomena and language descriptions.

43 The issue of Johnson's opinions on Scotland and the Scots has also been discussed by Brunner (1949: 184–190), who points out that 'There are hardly any references to any antagonism against Scotland and the Scottish in any of Johnson's works' (p. 185). In a more recent study, Rogers (1995: 203) reminds us that, according to Arthur Murphy's *Essay on the Life and Genius of Dr Johnson* (1792), '[Johnson] scorned to enter Scotland as a spy... He went into Scotland to survey men and manners'.

44 Almost immediately, however, critics perceived that many of these etymologies were rather inaccurate, especially the Celtic ones: cf. Nagashima (1988: 149). Others were the object of more or less explicit correction at various scholarly levels: cf. Iamartino (1995).

45 We may note that, according to the *OED*, the spelling *dirk*, instead of *durk*, was introduced by Johnson without authority, probably reflecting the merging of the two separate sounds represented by <-ir-> and <-ur-> into one.

46 However, the lack of references to Scotland in the definitions of *highlander* and *bagpipe* would seem to point to an attitude that goes beyond mere stereotypes.

The shield, the pistol, dirk, and dagger,
In which they daily wont to swagger.
Tickell.

We also find many other entries referring to Highland weaponry and warfare, possibly as a reminiscence of the Jacobite fear that had spread across England only a short time before the *Dictionary* was actually started; for instance, *firecross, skean, morglay* and *portglave*:

I **FI'RECROSS**. n.s.[fire and cross.] A token in Scotland for the nation to take arms: the ends thereof burnt black, and in some parts smeared with blood. It is carried like lightning from one place to another. Upon refusal to send it forward, or to rise, the last person who has it shoots the other dead.
I **SKEAN**. n.s. [Irish and Erse; sagene, Saxon.] A short sword; a knife.
I **MORGLA'Y**. n.s. A deadly weapon. Ains. Glaive and morte, French, and glay môhr, Erse, a two-handed broad-sword, which some centuries ago was the highlander's weapon.
I **PO'RTGLAVE**. n.s. [porter and glaive, Fr. and Erse.] A sword bearer. Ainsworth.

On the other hand, we also find entries that almost point in the direction of the idealised picture of Scotland that was to be developed in the nineteenth century: scenery, wildlife, legends, and whisky:

I **GLEN**. n.s. [gleann, Erse.] A valley; a dale; a depression between two hills.
I **GLYN**. n.s. [Irish; gleann, glyn, plur. Erse; glenn, Scottish.] A hollow between two mountains.
I **LOCH**. n.s. A lake. Scottish.
I **SE'COND Sight**. n.s. The power of seeing things future, or things distant: supposed inherent in some of the Scottish islanders.
As he was going out to steal a sheep, he was seized with a fit of second sight: the face of the country presented him with a wide prospect of new scenes, which he had never seen before.
Addison's Freeholder.[47]
I **USQUEBA'UGH**. n.s. [An Irish and Erse word, which signifies the water of life.]
It is a compounded distilled spirit, being drawn on aromaticks; and the Irish sort is particularly distinguished for its pleasant and mild flavour. The Highland sort is somewhat hotter; and, by corruption, in Scottish they call it whisky.

---

47 As in the case of *dirk*, it is the quotation, not the definition, that has a negative connotation. The issue of Johnson's presumed animosity against Scotland was discussed in two letters to the editor of the *Times Literary Supplement* (Wimsatt 1946 and Hudson 1946) which drew attention to the selection of quotations for the dictionary entries. While the former emphasised the fact that a large number of quotations were drawn from John Cleveland's poem *The Rebel*

While the inclusion of some entries may be unsurprising when we consider how topical the Highlands had been in England only a matter of a decade before the *Dictionary* was published, such entries as *usquebaugh*, actually recorded with seemingly accurate Gaelic spelling, and the intriguing phenomenon of *second sight*,[48] seem to point to the author's interest in features of Scottish life and culture, expressions and products that were becoming common in English life.

Johnson was also aware of the specificity of Scottish culture in terms of differences in the school and university system, the legal system and the church. In the 1755 edition of the *Dictionary* 23 entries refer to these contexts, and most of them are presented in a fairly neutral way. As expected, we find *kirk* and *laird*, and also several entries relating to university and cultural life, such as *humanist, humanity, laureation* and *lere*. A larger number of entries refers to the Scottish legal system, such as *deacon, holograph, incarcerate*,[49] and *fabricate*. A fairly lengthy entry concerns one typical aspect of Scottish church life: the 'cutty stool', or *stool of repentance*, the function of which is described in detail, once more revealing an encyclopaedic feature of the *Dictionary*, which not only provides definitions, but also expands these through accurate explanations on usage and custom.

Johnson's *Dictionary* also includes a large number of items described as dialectal or obsolete. Also in this case, however, the actual stigma attached to some morphological or lexical variance is not always obvious. What is much more apparent is the selection of items, many of which have a negative connotation; for instance, this is the case with insults like *lag, loon, scambler,*

Scot, the latter reminded readers that, in fact, 'Cleveland's works were for a long period the *locus classicus* of gibes against both Scot and Puritan'. As regards the 'Second Sight', Johnson probably became interested in it on reading Martin Martin's *Description of the Western Islands of Scotland* (1703): a book with which he had been familiar since his youth and which he took on his own journey to Scotland with Boswell.

48 Both entries reappear without changes in the fourth edition; moreover, Johnson's *Journey to the Western Islands of Scotland* also included a fairly long paragraph on the superstitious beliefs relating to second sight, and the Gaelic word *Taisch* was discussed in the following terms:

In the *Earse* [the Second Sight] is called *Taisch*; which signifies likewise a spectre, or a vision. I know not, nor is it likely that the Highlanders ever examined, whether by *Taisch*, used for *Second Sight*, they mean the power of seeing, or the thing seen. (Johnson 1775/ 1996: 95)

This kind of linguistic interest was also related to the controversy over Macpherson's (*Ossian*) poems, which Johnson perceived as a forgery; in spite of the negative publicity that this attitude gave to Johnson in Scotland, his interest in Gaelic is also shown to be genuine in his subscription to William Shaw's *Galic and English and English and Galic Dictionary* (1780), and, even before then, in the Proposals that he wrote for the same author's *An Analysis of the Scotch Celtick Language* (cf. Nagashima 1988: 22). Shaw himself acknowledges: 'To the advice and encouragement of Dr. Johnson, the friend of letters and humanity, the Public is indebted for these sheets' (Shaw 1778: xxiii). The lexicographer's support of Shaw's studies is also discussed by Curley (1987).

49 This verb had been identified as a Scotticism (to be substituted with *imprison*) in Hume's list.

or *redshank*, which 'seems to be a contemptuous appellation for some of the people of Scotland', or such offensive feminine epithets as *jilt, giglet, fren* or *drotchel*. It is possibly the obvious impact such entries have on the recipient that has partially hidden the other numerous entries in which Johnson simply observes the sociolinguistic evolution of English, making notes of obsolete or low forms, depending on whether his focus is on a social variety, or on changing vocabulary.

Among entries in which the focus appears to be primarily on changing morphology and syntax we find *algates, ever* and *eye*. Further on in the *Dictionary* occurs an entry in which the Scottish participial suffix *-and* is commented on (*glitterand*) and one in which it is exemplified, but not explained (*gloarand*). Finally, the Scottish use of the suffix *-ful* in *hopeful* is actually approved, because it supports Johnson's concept of good usage, which is based on the works of 'good writers':

> I HO'PEFUL. adj.[hope and full.] 2. Full of hope; full of expectation of success. This sense is now almost confined to Scotland, though it is analogical, and found in good writers.

As regards pronunciation, the only remark to be found in the *Dictionary* concerns the guttural fricative /x/, which is described in the entry for *H*, and where we find another reference to older usage compared with Scottish phonology. Lexical items are awarded far more attention: among these, we may identify entries related to their French origin, such as *chopin, cibol* and *scelerat*. In the second item is also a remark on pronunciation, whereas in the third we recognise Johnson's typical attitude towards French borrowings.[50] Then, of course, we find such overt Scotticisms as *auld, bonny, loch* and *wee*, and also *bannock* and *oats*:

> I OATS. n.s. [aten, Saxon.] A grain, which in England is generally given to horses, but in Scotland supports the people.

The latter is often quoted as the epitome of Johnsonian antipathy toward Scottish lifestyle and vocabulary. However, in Boswell's account of his tour of Scotland with Johnson we find that this entry is referred to as 'a joke' (Boswell 1786/1996: 395).[51] In other instances no disparaging attitude is evident: indeed,

---

50 Johnson's hostility to French borrowings is stated in very strong terms in the *Preface*: 'If an academy should be established for the cultivation of our style, ... let them ... endeavour, with all their influence, to stop the licence of translators, whose idleness and ignorance, if it be suffered to proceed, will reduce us to babble a dialect of *France*' (Johnson 1755/1824: 11). Interestingly, Jones reports a letter that appeared in *The Weekly Magazine* in 1772, in which it is claimed that ' many ... Scotticisms, are strictly speaking, Gallicisms, or literal translations from the French' (1995: 255).

51 In Pottle, Abbott and Pottle (1993: C1450) we find a reference to Lord Hailes' remarks on this, since apparently he quoted 'a passage from John Major's *Historia Majoris Britanniae*, Edinburgh, 1740, to show that the Scots had long been teased about being eaters of oatmeal'.

we even come across a Scots proverb and a complete dialectal phrase in the entries for *leverook* and *luff* :

> I **LEVEROOK**. n.s. [lafere, Saxon.] This word is retained in Scotland, and denotes the lark.
> If the lufft faa 'twill smoore aw the leverooks. Scotch Prov.[52]
> I **LUFF**. n.s. [in Scotland.] The palm of the hand; as, clap me arles in my luff.[53]
> IV LUFF. n.s. [In Scotland.] The palm of the hand.

In general, we see that hardly any of the stigmatising labels identified by scholars in Johnson's *Dictionary* (cf. Nagashima 1988: 128–129; Hayashi 1978: 102) appear in association with Scottish entries. Instead, we find a very high number of occurrences of 'still', as in 'still used', 'still retained', implying the continuation of older forms; most importantly, we find no occurrences of 'Scotticism', the eighteenth-century proscribing label *par excellence*.

Comparing the two editions, we see that the attention given to Scottish forms is more or less equivalent. In some cases the Scottish remarks are omitted, but many entries are expanded to include explanations (as is the case with *humblebee* and *thrapple*). As regards the entries on Highland dress, it may be interesting to note that one entry (*caddis*) is made more accurate in definition and in geographical specificity, while in the other (*plaid*) we no longer find the reference to the Act of Parliament of 1746 that forbade the use of Highland garb:

> I **CA'DDIS**. n.s. 1. A kind of tape or ribbon.
> 2. A kind of worm or grub found in a case of straw.
> IV CA'DDIS. n.s.[This word is used in Erse for the variegated cloaths of the Highlanders.]
> I **PLAID**. n.s. A striped or variegated cloth; an outer loose weed worn much by the highlanders in Scotland: there is a particular kind worn too by the women; but both these modes seem now nearly extirpated among them; the one by act of parliament, and the other by adopting the English dresses of the sex.
> IV PLAID. n.s. a striped or variegated cloth; an outer loose weed worn much by the highlanders in Scotland: there is a particular kind worn too by the women.

These entries, like many others, highlight Johnson's interest in changing

---

Besides, the entry on 'oats' and other entries on grains have been shown to be condensations of similar entries in Philipp Miller's *The Gardener's Dictionary* (London, 1752): cf. Cooper (1936: 785-802).

52 This is one of the very few instances of broad Scots in the *Dictionary*; it may be translated as 'if the sky falls, it will smother all the larks'.

53 This phrase, which was omitted in the fourth edition, could be translated as 'put my earnest money in my hand'.

vocabulary: the fact that Scottish usage corresponds to an obsolete southern form implies a comparison with southern English, revealing the northern variety as being static. Consequently, this supports Pollner's claim that southern English dictionary compilers felt it 'quite unnecessary to itemise Scottish words in any systematic way' because Scots had lost its status (1994: 295).

Though Dr Johnson claimed he was 'not answerable for all the words in [his] Dictionary' (Boswell 1786/1996: 367), we know from other sources (Reddick 1990: 98-99; Pollner 1994: 293-294) that he himself selected the Scottish items which had been suggested,[54] and, in spite of his stated purpose to include only the best examples, entries that had a clearly limited geographical distribution were also admitted.

Elements of counterpoint

It has been alleged that in the period we have been considering 'Scots was rightly considered a different language' (Görlach 1995b: 91). However, extensive analysis of texts in which the opinions of intellectuals on linguistic issues are expressed either directly or through their linguistic choices shows that the status of Scots in the eighteenth century was, at best, controversial. From the phonological point of view, a distinct Scottish accent was increasingly considered to be 'provincial, vulgar, uncouth, conspicuous' (to name but a few of the adjectives that were used to describe it). At the same time, a fairly unobtrusive presence of Scots phonological features was the mark of an accepted variety used by the upper/professional classes of Scottish society. Thus, by the end of the century, James Adams could even claim that a 'tempered medium', 'the manly eloquence of the Scotch bar', actually 'affords a singular pleasure to the candid English hearer, and gives merit and dignity to the noble speakers who retain so much of their own dialect'. Indeed, 'total similarity of sounds would not be desirable, and dissonance itself has characteristic merit'. As a matter of fact, Adams' *The Pronunciation of the English Language Vindicated* (1799), from which these remarks are taken, is possibly the most powerful defence of Scottish forms: the author, an Englishman who had lived in France until the French Revolution and then had settled in Edinburgh and Musselburgh, may thus be seen as possibly the first theorist of the reassessment of the vernacular subsequent to the important literary developments of the latter half of the century.[55]

54 In this respect, we should mention the fact that five of his six amanuenses (Francis Stewart, Alexander Macbean, William Macbean, Robert Shiels and Mr Maitland) were Scots (cf. Reddick 1990: 37), so they may have suggested notes on usage, which were nonetheless filtered by Johnson (cf. Reddick 1990: 191; 218).

55 These developments related mainly to the works of Ramsay, Fergusson and Burns – whom Adams (1799: 157) actually mentions – and, somewhat later, of Scott; our analysis of this interaction between poetic diction and polite usage and of Adams' role in making it explicit will continue in Chapter 5.

As regards grammar and vocabulary, we saw that even the greatest minds of the time took pains to 'improve' their use of English. With the exception of vocabulary relating to the legal system, church and education, practically no concessions were made to Scots grammatical features in discourse and, in general, in non-literary texts. However, poetic expression was seen to be different, and typical Scots usage was allowed. According to McClure (1995: 57), this is epitomised in the words of John Pinkerton: in 1786 he published a selection of poetry from the Maitland Manuscripts with the title *Ancient Scotish Poems, never before in print*, and in the Preface he wrote:

> None can more sincerely wish a total extinction of the Scotish *colloquial* dialect than I do, for there are few *modern* Scoticisms which are not barbarisms... Yet, I believe, no man of either kingdom would wish an extinction of the Scotish dialect in poetry. (1786: 1/xvii)

At the same time, increased interest in popular forms of expression, such as proverbs, ancient lore and tradition, was to prove crucial in the construction of Scots as a 'Language'. A variety that was mainly regarded as a lower variety of English, and which might actually have lost its status completely if this trend had continued, found new vitality and acceptability through its association with poetry. We may therefore conclude that the eighteenth century laid the basis for the dichotomy of usage between Scots and English that was to regard the former 'the language of the heart', while the latter was defined as 'the language of the head' (Daiches 1964; Murison 1969). In spite of the obvious simplification behind these labels, they were to prove so pervasive that even contemporary usage is influenced by them; for this reason, the way in which they developed will be the subject of the next chapter.

CHAPTER FIVE

New Status for the Vernacular

The previous chapter focused on a widespread attitude of linguistic prescriptivism, on the basis of which Scots was considered to have inferior status, and English modes of expression were preferred on account of their prestige: hence the plethora of dictionaries, grammar books, spelling books and lists of proscribed Scotticisms that appeared in a few decades. At the same time, a different attitude was gaining ground, that accepted and even encouraged the use of Scots in poetry. The eighteenth century marked one of the brightest periods in Scottish literature, its influence continuing down to the present day. The idea of Scots as a literary medium, but not as an accepted medium in everyday formal communication – already expressed by Pinkerton – was to prove persistent: even after the success of Scott's novels had brought Scots back into the spotlight, Thomas Aird,[1] in his paragraphs 'Lyric Poetry – Scottish Poetry' in *The Old Bachelor in the Old Scottish Village* (1845), did not view the use of Scots as a hindrance to poetic expression – quite the opposite. But he acknowledged that the days of Scots as a medium for everyday communication were over.

This trend of linguistic reappraisal on the basis of literary production has often been labelled 'vernacular revival', but I agree with McClure (1994: 41) that this may not be the most appropriate definition, because the vernacular had never actually fallen out of use as a literary medium. Poems in Scots had been collected and published by James Watson as early as 1706: his *Choice Collection of Comic and Serious Scottish Poems* was published in three parts, the last two in 1709 and 1711, and the inclusion of both adjectives, 'comic' and 'serious', in the title shows the aim to use Scots in all literary registers. What may have contributed to restrict the use of Scots to comic and satiric production was the success of Robert Sempill's mock-elegy *The Life and Death of Habbie Simpson, the Piper of Kilbarchan* (1640), from which the six-line stanza form labelled 'Habbie stanza'[2] was to stem. Then, the works of Allan

---

1 Thomas Aird (1802-1876) contributed occasionally to *Blackwood's Magazine* and later became the editor of the *Dumfries Herald*; in 1845 he published *The Old Bachelor in the Old Scottish Village*, a collection of tales and sketches of Scottish scenery, character, and life.

2 Sempill (c. 1595–c. 1665) was the son of the poet Sir James Sempill of Beltrees. His humorous poem was included by James Watson in his *Choice Collection* (1706), and its fame was assured when Allan Ramsay called its metre 'Standard Habbie'; later this form became known as 'the Burns stanza'.

Ramsay[3] and Robert Fergusson, mainly written in a similar tone and code, prepared the way for the enthusiastic reception of masterpieces by Robert Burns. Consequently, it was not a case of 'reviving' Scots, but of reassigning it some of the status that it had lost in the eyes of educated opinion. To this end the contribution of literature was crucial, and other factors also added to the shaping of a different taste: the controversy over the authenticity of Macpherson's Ossian poems, for instance, but also the sense of loss that accompanied the Jacobite defeat and the aftermath of the 'Forty-five, the comments of travellers in the Highlands and the Hebrides, and, in general, an increased interest in popular culture that was also apparent in collections of vernacular proverbs and folk traditions.

Changing attitudes and the role of literature

The idea of 'improvement' that influenced the linguistic choices of eighteenth-century Scottish speakers and writers was to produce an intriguing medium for poetic expression through the contact between English and local varieties: a medium that, according to Hewitt (1987: 254), 'did not previously exist in either English or Scottish literature'. The use of English spelling to express Scots sounds and the adoption of Scots vocabulary in otherwise English sentences extended the expressive range for writers. At the same time, the style of the Bible continued to exert crucial influence on prose writings: Burns himself quoted (and misquoted) the Scripture, in his correspondence, though less frequently in his poetry (Roy 1988).

Forceful vindication of the vernacular in poetry was expressed by Alexander Ross (1699–1784) in the introduction to his pastoral epic *Helenore* (1768), when the muse, appropriately called Scota, invokes:

> Speak my ain leed, 'tis gueed auld Scots I mean;
> Your Southren gnaps I count not worth a preen.
> (also quoted by Hewitt 1987: 254)

The use of *Southren* in a disparaging sense echoes earlier remarks of a similar kind (cf. Chapter 3). It also modifies a noun, *gnaps*, that summarises the perception of the variety belonging to those who strive to attain pure English as 'Neither gueed fish nor flesh, nor yet sa't herrin'. The same negative connotation appeared when Burns collocated *Suthron* with *foes* in his poem *The Vision*.

The contrast between English and Scots thus continued along emotional lines. In the meantime, poets had reintroduced the Latin term *Caledonia* to

---

3 Romaine (1982: 61) attributes the role of reviving Scots poetry to Ramsay, but she points out that 'his lyrics and short poems were explicitly colloquial and informal', thus restricting the range of vernacular usage. On Watson's role as a 'patriotic publisher', however, cf. Ross and Scobie (1974) and Rendall (1978). An interesting overview is also provided by Harvie Wood (1977/1991).

describe what had now become North Britain[4] and to reassign it its historical dignity, as if to signal that the Union was perhaps not so thoroughly accomplished as some might have expected. From the linguistic point of view, the situation was extremely fluid and the issue of standards was as topical as ever. A concept of 'good English' had been developing that led to acceptance of what was later acknowledged as Scottish Standard English. Boswell himself commented on this in 1772, after Johnson had described his pronunciation as 'not offensive':

> Let me give my countrymen of North-Britain an advice not to aim at absolute perfection in this respect; not to speak *High English*, as we are apt to call what is far removed from the *Scotch*, but which is by no means *good English*, and makes 'the fools who use it', truly ridiculous. Good English is plain, easy, smooth in the mouth of an unaffected English Gentleman. A studied and factitious pronunciation, which requires perpetual attention, and imposes personal constraint, is exceedingly disgusting. A small intermixture of provincial peculiarities may, perhaps, have an agreeable effect, as the notes of different birds concur in the harmony of the grove, and please more than if they were exactly alike.
> (Quoted by Rogers 1991: 65)

The value of this passage as a description of a changing attitude does not seem to have been emphasised. In fact, Boswell's words appear to be very close to the distinction that James Adams was to make almost thirty years later in his *Vindication of the Scottish Dialect*[5] between broad 'Scoto-Saxon-English' and the 'tempered medium, generally used by the polished class of society' (1799: 156–157). In addition to this, Adams' text was to prove one of the most interesting documents that marked the transition between strict prescriptivism and a more lenient attitude towards dialect.

James Adams

As regards terminology, Adams' work refers to a previous one, in which the label 'Scoto-Saxon' had been used: Alexander Geddes' *Three Scottish Poems, with a Previous Dissertation on the Scoto-Saxon Dialect*, published in 1792. This was an aggressive attempt to justify the use of Scots on the basis of its alleged integrity in relation to English, which, instead, was described as a mixture of idioms (Jones 1997a: 275). Obviously philology was still too young to show how Scots itself owed its 'richness, energy and harmony' to the

---

4 J. Adam Smith (1970: 115) also associates this name with New Caledonia and Darien colonists as representative of a patriotic moment in Scottish history.

5 This was in fact an appendix to his work of 1799, *The Pronunciation of the English Language*; the full title is *Appendix on the Dialects of All Languages; and Vindication of that of Scotland* (pp. 131–164).

interplay of various languages, and the supposedly greater proximity to original Germanic languages was to become one of the strongholds of defenders of Scots.

On the other hand, the view that English was a politer language was also founded on pseudo-historical presuppositions. McClure (1985a/1995: 58) explains why 'Pinkerton had a low opinion of Fergusson, and a much lower one of Ramsay':

> Believing that the Picts had spoken a Gothic (i.e. Germanic) language which later gave rise to Scots and seeing 'a steady progress of refinement from the South', he imagined that Provençal had exerted a civilising influence on French, French on English and English on Scots.

Adams, however, challenged this view. In his opinion the Picts had 'disturbed the peace of the original Scots ... and formed an alliance with the powerful and encroaching Saxons' (1799: 148). Instead, he associated Welsh (and therefore all Celtic languages) with Hebrew, thus attributing to them high prestige (1799: 138). This claim of original purity was then extended from Gaelic to Scots when Adams disclaimed that 'the present Scotch dialect is our old English speech and pronunciation, even as near our times as 300 years back' (1799: 148) and underlined that Scots preserves 'the Saxon original in spite of the attempts of the Norman invaders and tyrants, who endeavoured totally to extirpate its antient form'.[6]

According to Jones (1997a: 276), Adams 'is one of the very few commentators in the eighteenth century who actively argues against the abandonment of provincial speech habits in favour of some metropolitan standard' and concludes that this may signal 'his consciousness of the existence of a prestigious form of Scots itself', the 'tempered medium' that has already been mentioned.[7] Of course this analysis appears to be correct, since Adams' own words do add elements that signal the cultural changes that had been taking place in the second half of the century. When Adams defends local varieties of speech, he associates them with other symbols of national identity, such as the kilt.[8] At the time Adams was writing, the law forbidding the use of the Highland dress had

---

6 This may be read as an attack on France, from which Adams had fled because of the Revolution. We also find similar *tirades*: French is described as a 'corrupt source' of vocabulary (1799: 150; 154; 159) and 'the unsoftened accent', i.e. Scots, is praised 'in the mouths of the sons of Mars' (1799: 160); after a series of rhetorical questions comes a warning to 'modern Giants' not to dare assail 'our united coast, our beloved home, our British Jove, our terrestrial heaven'. In addition to this, Voltaire is openly insulted as 'the obscene scoffer of religion, their mortalised Patriarch, deluding Buffoon, and self-confuted' because, 'as confidently and vauntingly, as falsely, [he] boasted that Adam was not the first father of the Americans' (1799: 140).

7 Crawford (1992: 24) mentions an earlier 'vindication', on the basis of which 'lectures on the Scottish language' had been delivered, but this clearly focused on Scots as a poetic medium and on an antiquarian interest in 'some of the first pieces of poetry that can adorn any language'.

8 Tulloch (1997b: 384-385) discusses the way in which this and other items relating to Highland culture got into English and Scots vocabulary, but he does not seem to associate this process with the Jacobite uprisings and their aftermath; he simply states that 'The eighteenth century

been repealed – indeed, this had become a uniform for Highland regiments (Trevor-Roper 1983/1987: 28–29) – and the kind of outlandish features that had once been both feared and derided had somehow become 'domesticated' and accepted:

> The sight of the Highland kelt, the flowing plaid, the buskin'd leg, provokes my antagonist to laugh! Is this dress ridiculous in the eyes of reason and common sense? No: nor is the dialect of speech: both are characteristic and national distinctions. National character and distinction are respectable. Then is the adopted mode of oral language sanctioned by peculiar reasons, and is not the result of chance, contemptible vulgarity, mere ignorance and rustic habit. (1799: 157)

Moreover, Jones himself acknowledges that Adams' position is 'primarily based on patriotic feeling and some sentimentality' (1997a: 277), and this emerges from Adams' reference to poetic usage as an appropriate means by which to vindicate dialect:

> Dunbar and Dunkeld, Douglas in *Virgilian* strains, and later poets, Ramsay, Ferguson, and Burns, awake from your graves, you have already immortalised the Scotch dialect in raptured melody! Lend me your golden target and well pointed spear, that I may victoriously pursue to the extremity of South Britain, reproachful Ignorance and Scorn still lurking there: let impartial Candor seize their usurped throne. (1799: 157–158)

The rhetorical structure of this paragraph and of the ones that precede it also shows Adams' own indebtedness to Ossian: passionate apostrophes, rhetorical questions, personification of concepts, marked lexical choices, metaphors relating to warfare and the call upon heroes to rise from the dead in order to assist contemporary warriors are clearly reminiscent of Macpherson's work. And Adams actually refers to Ossian's poems as the 'monuments of ancient speech' (1799: 148):

> I enter the lists in Tartan dress and armour, and throw down the gauntlet to the most prejudiced antagonist. How weak is prejudice! ... The arguments of general vindication rise powerful before my sight, like Highland Bands in full array. A louder strain of apologetic speech swells my words. What if it should rise high as the unconquered summits of Scotia's hills, and call back, with voice sweet as Caledonian song, the days of antient Scotish heroes. (1799: 157)

Inevitably, a vindication of the Scottish dialect was bound to include an attack on Johnson, whom Adams calls 'the Cinic Scotomastic' (1799: 150). This,

---

saw an awakening of interest by Lowlanders in the culture of the Highlands. The Highlanders' very different clothing and arms were of particular interest'.

however, does not seem to be too harsh, although reference is made both to the Dictionary and to Johnson's journey to Scotland: the context is a discussion of Scottish idiomatic usage which places itself in a more general account of Scots grammar and vocabulary. As a matter of fact, Adams' *Vindication* does not only appeal to the reader on an emotional basis, but also attempts to account for vernacular features in a scientific way.

Consequently, at the beginning of his analysis Adams adopts a historical perspective, one point of which is particularly interesting: in order to emphasise the difference between Scots and English, Adams refers to Barbour, supposedly analogous to Chaucer in his linguistic choices, and to ministerial correspondence in Elizabethan times. He grants that 'the lettered Scotch wrote, and do write classical English ... and that foreign ministers, as the Scotch then were, would not use a particular national dialect in writing to the court', but then he draws attention to Hamilton's Catechism as a sample of independent Scots forms and even claims that

> If the reader will consult some old acts of Parliament anterior to Barbour and Chaucer, he will find a formal act, and a severe mulct ordained against introducing the current English into Scotland. (1799: 149)

Unfortunately, I have not been able to identify the Act to which Adams refers, nor is it mentioned anywhere else in bibliographical sources, so the authenticity of this claim may be doubted, but it certainly throws light on how powerfully the issue was presented, to the point where it was associated with a past in which even the law was allegedly called upon to preserve linguistic purity.

With reference to contemporary usage, Adams begins his description of Scots with an account of its phonology (1799: 151–154), summarised in the following terms: '*The Scotch Alphabet*, to the eye, resembles our own: to the ear, it presents a mixture of Celtic, Gothic, Frankic, Saxon, Danish, German, Italian, French, and English sounds' (1799: 152). As regards lexical items, Adams selects 'a few, the form of which is English, ... very expressive, and occasionally found in our etymology and poetry'. Indeed, he finds that 'Many seem well suited to enrich our own stock, without running to the corrupt source of French'. He thus appears to present a list of recommended words, in complete contrast with the fashion for lists of proscribed Scotticisms. Adams' own list includes the following 45 entries, of which the author also provides the translation (my italics, except for *naif*):

> *Awn*, ear of corn; *aiven*, old horse; *antercast*, mischance; *atry*, angry; *blate*, bashful; *bonny*, more than simply good; *brae*, declivity; *braik*, harrow; *burn*, rivulet; *byre*, cow lodge; *birkie*, a stout youth; *ben*, within; *bumbazed*, astonished; *bent*, field of rough grass; *brander*, gridiron. *Canny*, skilful; *carl*, stout old man; *carlin*, stout old woman; *canty*, brisk; *cappit*, heady; *couth*, *couthy*, social; *clour*, tumor, rising of a bruise; *coof*,

stupid; *cosy*, snug; *chuffy*, plump-faced; *coble*, small boat; *cushet*, wood-pigeon; *daft*, merry; *fawsont*, decent; *glowr*, stare; *gusty*, tasteful; *havered*, half-witted; *hornie*, the devil; *ingle*, fire-place; *lear*, learning; *lum*, chimney; *mavis*, the thrush; *muckle*, great, noteless, unknown; to *pech*, breathe short; *prie*, to taste; *primsie*, precise; *sonsie*, one of engaging look; *naif*, genuine &c; *syne*, since. (1799: 154)

In the list we recognise items made popular by Burns' poems, but also one, *lear*, that had appeared in Johnson's Dictionary. To these, Adams adds '*Lyn*; watery places, hence Lincolnshire, &c.; *whilly*, cheat, thence whilly in the wisp, deluding meteor, like a blazing wisp of straw' (my italics) and a 'Remark on Kail and Whusle' (1799: 155). Of these two items, the former is an opportunity for a quite mild attack on Johnson ('it would have done honour to Dr Johnson to have mentioned it in his Dictionary, with grateful remembrance of what we know he experienced in the Highlands'), because the expression *kail the pot* is described as a term of hospitality; the latter, instead, provides Adams with reason to stigmatise ignorance and prejudice in those who laugh at the expression '*whisle, whasle, or whusle me a guinea*', because he explains it is based on a German word, meaning 'to change'. Etymology is also appealed to in a very brief paragraph on 'Compound Words' (1799: 156): 'Many shew a true Danish origin, as for poverty, rarity, kingdom, ugly &c. puretith, raretith, kunrick, ugsom; and *wun* or *wan* for *un* privative'. Word-formation is given a little more attention in the paragraph on 'Scotch Diminutives', a feature that previous lists of Scotticisms do not appear to have described. According to Adams, 'They express what we often want in English, and is so abundant in Italian and Scotch, and has sometimes a pretty effect, formed by ie expletive: *Bardie, bookie, doggie, ladie, lassie, manie*, &c. *Bardie* is a poor little poet, poetaster, a little book, dog, lad, lass, man, &c.' (1799: 155)

The favourable characteristics of Scots are thus highlighted throughout the text. In the paragraph on 'Scotch Phraseology' (1799: 156), the author asks his readers: 'If the Scotch differ from us occasionally in the application of words, and they understand one another, what is that to us?'. When mutual intelligibility is at stake, instead, 'both parties have equal right to laugh, and to continue laughing till an explanation takes place. But if they profess to write pure English, and mix their phraseology, then indeed we may censure the author, and laugh alone. Thus Dr Priestly has corrected Hume'. Adams seems to invite speakers to be aware of geographical varieties and to accept them without affecting or expecting unattainable 'perfection': indeed, he concludes that 'mere local dialectic sound *never should, never will, never can be* totally removed; the effort would be as vain, and the prejudice is as unjust, as to attempt to change the green colour of the eye in the natives of the Orknies' (1799: 161). It is an extraordinarily modern and powerful conclusion, made memorable by a skilful use of modality and an emphatic repetition of the negative adverb. Moreover, Adams himself inserts a Scots phrase in his account of how he formed an idea of his subject:

> A modern Baucis and Philemon, with whom I spent the summer-recess, taught me, with *their sonsie crack*, to form a just idea of this subject of my vindication: 'The honest peasant, the venerable villager, lose nothing of native worth, by the manly roughness of their dialect. Its disuse would expose the homely trader to the suspicion of lost probity; the English visitor would decline the commerce of those whom he suspects to have bartered away, by artful condescension of oral resemblance, the original characteristic and mark of a Scotchman,' said they in other words. (1799: 160)

Although Adams does rephrase his hosts' words, his use of *sonsie crack* (= pleasant talk) gives authenticity to the paragraph.[9] Finally, we find a *post-scriptum* (1799: 163–164) aimed at countering any possible accusation of 'pillaging Mr Sheridan': the author claims 'he had not read that Writer, till he had finished his work' and indeed he finds fault with his dictionary and grammar. Besides, Adams' work adopts an altogether different plan from Sheridan's, since his attempt to vindicate Scots manifests itself through a describing, rather than proscribing or prescribing, text: hence his seeming modernity. Nonetheless, throughout his work we find references to Greek mythology (as in the reference to the hospitable couple Baucis and Philemon) that point to the author's indebtedness to Classical culture and to stylistic traits that had their roots in much earlier times.

Allan Ramsay

While the works of Allan Ramsay (1685–1758) did shed new light on Scots, on its literary tradition and, consequently, on its dignity as a contemporary literary language, the very success of his works may have contributed to the restrictive view of Scots as a language for bucolic expression.

A wigmaker by trade, in 1712 he helped found the Easy Club, a Jacobite literary society, the aim of which was 'Mutual improvement in Conversation' and which therefore seems to precede associations like the Select Society.[10] In the Club everybody used pseudonyms, and Ramsay's pen names – first Isaac Bickerstaff and later Gawin Douglas – appear to suggest both Augustan English and medieval Scottish influences (Jack 1994: 152). By collecting and publishing poems by Robert Henryson, William Dunbar, and other late

---

9 The phrase is italicised in the original, thus signalling that Adams is evoking his hosts' actual speech.

10 A similar aim would also be shared by the Tarbolton Bachelors' Club, founded later by Burns (Daiches 1964: 23). On the rise and development of clubs and societies in eighteenth-century Scotland, cf., among others, Daiches (1986/1996: 35–39).

medieval Scottish writers, Ramsay contributed to their survival. In 1721 he published a subscriber's edition of his own poems, including several in mock-elegy style, and renderings in Scots of Horace's *Odes*; a second volume appeared in 1728 (cf. Kinghorn and Law 1972). An original pastoral comedy, *The Gentle Shepherd* (1725), gained much of its effect from the use of Scots (Buffoni 1992). *The Tea-table Miscellany* (1724–37), *The Ever Green* (1724), and a collection of Scots proverbs (1737) also present an outstanding collection of songs and traditional lore. After publication of the 1721 *Poems*, Ramsay became a bookseller, and founded Britain's first circulating library (1726). His interest in the theatre was also prominent, but what is possibly of the greatest interest for the purpose of our study is the statement he made in the 1721 preface about the role of Scottish features in poetry:

> The *Scotticisms*, which perhaps may offend some over-nice Ear, give new Life and Grace to the Poetry, and become their Place as well as the *Doric* dialect of *Theocritus*, so much admired by the best Judges.[11]

Daiches (1964: 25) has selected this quotation to show the ambiguity in Ramsay's attitude towards Scots, both defensive and assertive, 'as though he was presenting a provincial vernacular for the amusement of the educated' and wished 'to gain the indulgence of a genteel audience'. To some extent this is confirmed by the studiousness with which he edited and provided a glossary for his poems and his collection of proverbs. However, even his idea of 'improvement' helped maintain a tradition that was on its way to being lost; for instance, he made the poems in the Bannatyne Manuscript[12] available to a wider public, sanctioned the role of the vernacular in poetic expression and introduced veiled patriotic remarks, in spite of his attention to southern models.[13] A similar ambiguity also affected Burns' and his critics' attitude to Scots and English, and Daiches (1964: 28) himself correctly associates this phenomenon with a more general cultural dualism in eighteenth-century Scotland. Besides, this did not only affect North and South Britain: it also concerned the cultural differences that still existed between the Lowlands and the Highlands. Indeed, a more decisive contribution to Scottish literary tradition possibly came from the Ossianic fashion that swept Europe some years later and, though this may seem paradoxical, from the final Jacobite defeat in 1746.

In any case, as McClure (1987b/1995: 161) points out, it would be too simplistic to base a discussion of Ramsay's language on the binary opposition

---

11 This claim was taken up by other poets and critics, if as late as 1809 John Hodgson could stigmatise 'the coarseness and vulgarity of the Scotch dialect (of late so ridiculously compared to the soft and sweetest Doric of Theocritus)' (Low 1974/1995: 215).

12 This was an anthology of Scottish poetry collected by George Bannatyne in 1568.

13 This is the case with the preface to *The Ever Green*, in which he writes about 'imported ... foreign Embroidery in our Writings', comparing older, more authentic poetry with modern fashion.

between Scots and English. Not only do his works present a characteristic continuum that ranges from English to 'Full Scots' via 'Anglicised Scots' and 'Thin Scots',[14] but they also show how complex the interplay of these varieties may become. For instance, when written texts are read aloud, the phonological component is 'audibly Scottish' even in the poems classed as 'English'. Besides, different registers seem to draw on different linguistic resources in a rather inconsistent way, as when associating English with patriotic themes possibly 'not because of any conscious or unconscious assumption that Scots is unworthy of such noble sentiments, but to enlighten an English audience regarding the grounds of a Scotsman's patriotic pride' (McClure 1987b/1995: 167). Consequently, Ramsay appears to have chosen one variety instead of the others in relation to register variation, depending on expressiveness and on the models that were available. These were Dryden and Pope for 'serious' poetry (hence the use English or Anglicised Scots), whereas he relied on his more expressive vernacular for satire and farce.

Ossian

As Daiches (1964: 34–35) suggests, 'once the [Jacobite] cause was well and truly hopeless ... the appeal of a lost cause could be combined with a nostalgic sense of a dwindled nationhood'. Hence, a kind of duality seemed to emerge in literary language and even in the arrangement of traditional Scottish airs: an attempt to revive the native tradition while aiming at gentility and 'politeness'. At the same time, new light was being shed upon Highland culture. Finally, the cultural gaps that had been dramatically obvious in the days of the Jacobite uprisings began to be filled with an approach to the Highlands that aimed, more or less explicitly, at acquiring those symbols of antique nationhood the visibility of which had been diminishing in the Lowlands.[15]

14 The four levels are defined as follows by McClure (1987b/1995: 161):
- English: containing no marked Scots features at all;
- Anglicised Scots: containing rhymes which require a Scots pronunciation – English spellings, perhaps, notwithstanding – but no Scots features of grammar or vocabulary;
- Thin Scots: containing some, even if only a few, Scots features of grammar as well as phonology and an occasional Scots word;
- Full Scots: making frequent, if not necessarily consistent, use of Scots features on all three levels.

15 The metamorphosis of the Highlander 'from rebel to hero' is the object of a careful study by Clyde (1995), which had been preceded by a thorough investigation of the relationship between literature, the Stuart myth and national identity carried out by Pittock (1991 and 1994). In particular, the extent to which linguistic choices could be an index of potential political value is mentioned by Pittock (1991: 56), when, referring to Ramsay's 'Tartana', he points out that 'Although this poem may appear Jacobite, we should note that it is written in 'correct' English, which may partly neutralise its implicit aggression'. The progressive 'Highlandisation' of Scottish culture has also been investigated by Cameron (1998); Finlay (1998a), instead, relates this phenomenon to a more accurate analysis of the concept of 'North Britain' and the reasons why it was never very successful.

James Macpherson (1736–1796) did in fact provide genuine contributions to Gaelic studies, but the Ossian controversy somehow obscured this. He published *Fragments of ancient poetry ... translated from the Gallic or Erse language* (1760), *Fingal* (1762), and *Temora* (1763), claiming that much of their content was based on a third-century Gaelic poet Ossian. The support of the rhetorician Hugh Blair was crucial for the public's acceptance of what was, in fact, a forgery, though David Hume was sceptical about its authenticity. Samuel Johnson, instead, openly denied it, and this led to a series of fiery exchanges between Macpherson and Johnson (Rogers 1995: 205–208; Watson 1984: 188) that might even have ended in a duel.

The originals were only published after Macpherson's death. In the meantime these poems had set a backdrop against which an idealised, highly Romantic view of Highland culture and of its ancient original tradition would be formed (cf. Logan 1831/1843). Shaw (1778: xi) mentioned Fingal alongside Caesar and Alexander in the introduction to his description of Gaelic. Moreover, his execration of 'the policy of usurping invaders' and regret for the Gaels' lost culture, 'suppressed and obliterated by the policy of a neighbouring monarch', show an anti-English bias which casts a shadow on an otherwise correct historical analysis.[16] On the other hand, reference to post-Forty-five legislation (1778: xvi–xvii) justifies Shaw's attitude. His point of view is clearly set in the context of important socio-historical considerations, to which he adds a hearty appeal for the translation of the Scriptures into Gaelic: 'Is there no Bishop Bedel, no Robert Boyle in our days, and is the Society for propagating Christian Knowledge only a name?' (1778: xviii)[17]

On the linguistic level, Shaw mentions the *Introduction to the History of Great Britain and Ireland* by 'the ingenious Macpherson' as one of the basic sources for the presentation of Gaelic's importance in the past and attacks those ministers who do not write their discourses in their own tongue, although 'there are several ambitious to be reputed the translators of a few lines of Galic poetry' (1778: xvi). Further on, he maintains that 'An acquaintance with the Galic, being the mother-tongue of all the languages in the west, seems necessary to every Antiquary who would study the affinity of languages ... Antiquity being the taste of the age, some acquaintance with the Galic begins justly to be deemed a part of the *Belles Lettres*. The language that boasts of the finished character of Fingal, must richly reward the curiosity of whoever studies it' (1778: xxiii).[18] Finally, he mentions the case of Sir James Foulis, who

---

16 On the influence of Ossian on eighteenth-century historiography, cf. Kidd (1993).

17 Although Robert Boyle (1627–1691) is certainly more famous as a scientist, he actually took a deep interest in religion and provided financial help for the translation of the New Testament into Irish made by Bedel.

18 This kind of interest is also shown in John Cleland's *The Way to Things by Words, and to Words by Things; being a sketch of an attempt at the retrieval of the Antient Celtic, or, primitive language of Europe ...*, published anonymously in London in 1766.

has learned to read and write Gaelic 'and now drinks of the Pierian spring untainted, by reading fragments of poetry in Fingal's own language' (1778: xxiii–xxiv).

It is puzzling, however, to reflect on the distance that still appeared to exist between the general public and genuine Gaelic poetry (Colgan 1987: 347; Rogers 1995: 223). The eighteenth century also presented the works of poets like Alasdair MacMhaighstir Alasdair,[19] Duncan Bàn Macintyre and William Ross (Watson 1984: 192–216). Their range of themes varied from Jacobite poems to love, satire and natural descriptions, often influenced by the trend set by Thomson's *Seasons*, thus showing the liveliness of a language that could still be adapted to suit lyrical needs according to contemporary fashion, although prose writing was mainly restricted to religious tracts and pamphlets. The discrepancy between scant interest in actual Gaelic poetry and the Ossianic fashion may be explained by the latter's exact correspondence to the literary taste of the reading public,[20] thus highlighting the close connection between the audience's expectations, linguistic choices and literary production that was so obvious in the case of Robert Fergusson and Robert Burns. Besides, the Ossianic fashion was clearly associated with the taste for the sublime and the picturesque that took many travellers to the Highlands. Its linguistic legacy may be traced in the kind of hyperbolic rhetoric that we have already perceived in Adams' text, but it hardly seems to have affected vocabulary: for instance, Burns was apparently unique in using *duan* in his poem *The Vision* (Tulloch 1997b: 385) and he explained its meaning and origin in a footnote:

> *Duan,* a term of Ossian's for the different divisions of a digressive poem. See his *Cath-Loda,* vol. ii of M'Pherson's translation. (in Currie 1846: 108)[21]

Robert Fergusson

Fergusson's short life[22] and the aura of romantic (though often stigmatised) bohemian attitude that surrounded it in many of his readers' minds left a very deep mark on the history of Scottish poetry and on the destiny of Scots as a literary medium. J. Adam Smith (1970: 116) reports Thomas Ruddiman's[23] own comment to this effect, quoting it from the preface to the 1779 edition of

---

19 Many of his poems, however, were banned as Jacobite propaganda (Watson 1984: 189).
20 On this point see, among others, Dwyer (1998: 140ff).
21 This, however, has been claimed to be a statement of patriotism on the part of the author: cf. Murphy (1998: 73).
22 Born in 1750, Fergusson died in the Edinburgh Bedlam at the age of 24. He had been educated at St. Andrews University and became a copying clerk in a lawyer's office in Edinburgh; then, in 1771, he began to contribute poems to Ruddiman's *Weekly Magazine*. Their popularity was immediate, and a collected volume was published in 1773.
23 Thomas Ruddiman (1674–1757) was a printer and bookseller in Edinburgh; his 1710 edition of Douglas's *Aeneid* included what was possibly the first glossary of Scots words.

Fergusson's *Poems*: 'Had he enjoyed life and health to a maturer age, it is probable he would have revived our ancient Caledonian Poetry, of late so much neglected or despised'. As a matter of fact, Fergusson did provide a crucial contribution to the reassessment of Scots poetry, possibly not least because of the patriotic attitude that is often so explicit in his works and that is summed up in the lines:

> Black be the day that e'er to England's ground
> Scotland was eikit by the UNION's bond
>
> (The Ghaists: A Kirk-yard Eclogue)

To those who felt that the Union was not proving so advantageous as had been hoped, who regretted the Jacobite defeat, and who idealised a heroic independent past, this was the kind of writing that was bound to inspire the works not only of Robert Burns, who openly supported the French Revolution and equated it with the Scots' victory at Bannockburn in 1314,[24] but also of Scott and Stevenson, whose 'Jacobite' novels are tinged with a romantic hue that overshadows historical reality.[25]

Still, Fergusson was quite capable of using Augustan English and even twisted it into a parody of itself in one of his satires on Johnson's tour of Scotland published in the *Weekly Magazine* on 21 October 1773, even before the tour itself was completed (cf. Boulton 1974/1995: 231–233). The poem was 'To Dr Samuel Johnson: Food for a new Edition of his Dictionary'. The aim was to ridicule Johnson's style and highlight those entries in the Dictionary that had been most painful for Scottish readers, like the notorious entry on 'oats'; apart from the obvious reference to food in the subtitle, the theme is resumed in the following lines:

> Welcome, thou verbal potentate and prince!
> To hills and vallies, where emerging oats
> From earth assurge our pauperty to bay ....

References to Johnson's experience of the Highlands are also made ('Have you apply'd / The kelt aerian to your Anglian thighs, ...?') and the poem ends on a strong patriotic note that evokes the Jacobites' march into England:

> Then hie you home,
> And be a malcontent, that naked hinds,
> On lentils fed, can make your kingdom quake,
> And tremulate Old England libertiz'd.

---

24 J. Adam Smith (1970: 121) associates these themes with the composition of *Scots wha hae*, the poem in which Burns recalls Bruce's apostrophe to his army before the battle.

25 In other authors, however, it turned into a more 'couthy' attitude that expressed itself in the 'kailyard school'.

Fergusson's adoption of a 'mock-Augustan' style, rich in nonce Johnsonian-sounding formations of adjectives like *Scoticanian, Loch-lomondian,* and *usquebalian,* contrasts with the more homely tone of his poem 'To the Principal and Professors of the University of St Andrews, on their superb treat to Dr Samuel Johnson'; this is in Scots and Fergusson calls his addressees 'my winsome billy boys' or 'lads', while Johnson is 'Sam, the lying loun'. Again he takes up the issue of the entry on oats, but this time he rephrases it in the local language:

> Aits in England are a feast
> To cow an' horse, an' sican beast,
> While in Scots ground this growth was common
> To gust the gab o' Man an' Woman.

However, the jocular tone of the composition is made explicit at the end, when the author turns to those of his readers who might take offence at his remarks and offers an invitation 'ne'er ... o'er an empty bicker [to] blink', for 'what weets the wisen an' the wyme, / will mend your prose and heal my rhyme'. The simultaneous use of Scots and English for stylistic purposes, that is the use of an extended language, which some critics have defined as an Anglo-Scottish hybrid (Buffoni 1992: 127), became more refined in the works of Robert Burns. In the words of J. Adam Smith (1970: 122) Burns 'moves from Scots to English as he moves from the area of personal and local experience to that of general ideas': meaning and choice of vocabulary thus become associated, as if Burns switched between registers of the same language, rather than between languages – a suggestion that inevitably highlights deep awareness of stylistic ranges on the part of the poet, and which is worth investigating in greater detail.

Robert Burns

The appropriateness of Scots for poetic expression is often discussed by Burns himself. In his correspondence – studied in Dossena (1997b), but cf. also Strauss (1998) – we find very accurate appreciations of the linguistic changes that were taking place in Scotland, and especially in the letters to George Thomson (who was collecting popular tunes for his *Select Scottish Airs*)[26] numerous remarks underline this awareness of the linguistic potential of Scots, as opposed to English, in different contexts. On 26 January 1793 he claimed that:

26 A similar enterprise had been started some time before by James Johnson, who published *The Scots Musical Museum* in six volumes between 1787 and 1803. In both cases Burns' co-operation was enthusiastic and his correspondence with Thomson, begun in 1792, continued into the latter part of his life: the last letter is dated 12 July 1796, only ten days before the poet's death. The fashion for native Scottish airs was very popular throughout the century. As early as 1725 the first printed collection of airs for the voice was published as *Orpheus Caledonius,* and already in the seventeenth century there had been numerous anthologies of arrangements for various instruments. On this topic, cf. also Portier (1999).

There is a *naivete*, a pastoral simplicity, in a slight intermixture of Scots words and phraseology, which is more in unison (at least to my taste, and I will add, to every genuine Caledonian taste), with the simple pathos, or rustic sprightliness of our native music, than any English verses whatever (quoted by Currie 1846: 195).

On the other hand, Burns seems to have been very attentive to the socio-linguistic value of careful usage and provided a word-list in his *Poems, chiefly in the Scottish Dialect*, thus implicitly acknowledging the exotic character of his texts (Low 1974/1995: 14).

In the early days of his success he was being constantly advised to 'deal more sparingly for the future in the provincial dialect' (Dr. Moore's[27] letter of 23 May 1787, quoted by Currie 1846: 17), since 'the Scottish dialect is now becoming obsolete, and thereby the elegance and beauties of your poems are in a great measure lost to far the greater part of the community' (John Hutchinson's letter of 14 June 1787, quoted by Currie 1846: 17). Nonetheless, even this kind of advice was not without contradictions. Dr Moore himself, in another letter of 10 June 1789, allowed 'a sprinkling of Scots' ('for what poet would not prefer *gloaming* to *twilight*?') while still recommending 'that in your future productions you should abandon the Scottish stanza and dialect, and adopt the measure and language of modern English poetry' (quoted by Currie 1846: 46-47). Dr Moore was to repeat this recommendation almost verbatim in 1791, when he wrote:

In your future compositions, I wish you would use the modern English. You have shown your powers in Scottish sufficiently. Although in certain subjects it gives additional zest to the humour, yet it is lost to the English; and why should you write only for a part of the island, when you can command the admiration of the whole (quoted by Currie 1846: 65).[28]

However, in the very same letter he had just praised a passage from *Tam O'Shanter* ('the twenty-two lines from "Coffins stood round like open presses"') saying that, in his opinion, they were 'equal to the ingredients of Shakespeare's cauldron in *Macbeth*'. Again, this appears to be typical of what has already been identified as 'the Pinkerton syndrome' (McClure 1985a/1995). An early-nineteenth century reviewer quoted by Low (1974/1995: 25) expressed a similarly ambiguous attitude, but he could not help stressing the 'negative' phonological aspects of Scots lexis and indeed included a chauvinistic remark which is possibly even more offensive than the ones attributed to Johnson:

---

27 Currie (1846: xxvii) describes Dr Moore as 'well known for his *Views of Society and Manners on the Continent of Europe*, for his *Zeluco*, and various other works'.
28 On this issue, cf. also McGuirk (1985/1997: 67), in which the relationship between Scots verse and refined taste is discussed in the context of Burns' reception by the Edinburgh *literati*.

It is true, indeed, that many of the Highland words, having something of simplicity, and occasionally even of strength, are sometimes more expressive of pastoral imagery, than the more refined dialect of the English. The terminations ... having fewer consonants, are better adapted to the music of poetry. Such are the words 'brae' ..., 'burnie', and many others of the same kind, terminating with the soft vowels *i* and *e*. But this observation cannot be extended to all, for surely some of these words, such as 'grounche', 'gutter', 'gowk', and 'gryse', are such as the muse of poetry would not be very pleased to adopt, and which none but a Scotsman could undertake to utter.

Burns' request for 'an English dictionary – Johnson's, I suppose, is best' (letter to Mr Hill of 2 April 1789, quoted by Currie 1846: 43) seems to testify to a constant will to approach a standard of good English. It would seem that, in spite of popular tradition, Burns, after all, was not so distant from his contemporaries in assigning Scots a privileged place in songs and poetry, while acknowledging an increasing appeal of the English language as an accomplishment.[29] As Simpson (1993: 210) observes, Burns' remarkable range of voices may be ascribed to various reasons: the linguistic duality that was also experienced by his contemporaries, his dramatic talent, and his 'acute sense of displacement, both in his native Ayrshire and in fashionable Edinburgh society': a sense of displacement that was reflected and externalised in his linguistic choices.

Ramsay and Fergusson have been singled out as Burns' closest predecessors (Buffoni 1992; Simpson 1998; Connor 1998), not only from a chronological point of view, but also from a philosophical one. Fergusson showed such a high degree of mastery in both languages that it is almost inevitable to look to him as Burns' closest model. Nonetheless, Fergusson has often been described as a city poet, in contrast to Burns' rural origins, so it is all the more interesting to investigate the latter's use of language and the perceptions of his style on the part of the critics, because of the association of dialect with 'rusticity'. Indeed, Burns felt very close to Fergusson, and felt that he could take up his spiritual legacy, since an inscription in Burns' copy of Fergusson's *Poems* defines him as 'my elder brother in misfortune / By far my elder brother in the muse'.[30]

29 As a matter of fact, only one letter written by Burns in Scots has survived, which may indicate how unusual the use of this medium was in his private correspondence. The letter is addressed to Mr William Nicol, a very close friend, and its tone is clearly jocular (cf. Scott Douglas 1887/ 4: 243-245).

30 Poetic kinship with the precursor Fergusson was later to be acknowledged by Robert Louis Stevenson and, in the twentieth century, by the Edinburgh poet Robert Garioch. In 1787 Burns had a stone put up to mark Fergusson's grave in the Canongate Kirkyard in Edinburgh. The inscription is revealing:

> No sculptured marble here, nor pompous lay
> No storied urn nor animated bust;
> This simple stone directs pale Scotia's way
> To pour her sorrows o'er her poet's dust.

Critics appreciated and encouraged Burns, assuming that they had actually found the poet who could authenticate the theories on primitivism so fashionable at the time (Low 1974/1995: 4). Currie himself (1846: lxxix) pointed out how distant Burns' work was from 'modern' poetry when he commented that:

> His rhymes ... are frequently incorrect, while the measure in which many of the poems are written has little of the pomp or harmony of modern versification, and is indeed, to an English ear, strange and uncouth. The greater part of his earlier poems are written in the dialect of his country, which is obscure, if not unintelligible to Englishmen.

A very similar remark had appeared in an unsigned notice in the *Critical Review* in 1787: 'It is to be regretted, that the Scottish dialect, in which these poems are written, must obscure the native beauties with which they appear to abound, and renders the sense often unintelligible to an English reader' (Low 1974/1995: 80). In the same year, the English poet William Cowper wrote to Samuel Rose stressing the value of Burns' poems, but regretting the difficulty of his language and hoping that he would discard his 'uncouth dialect', 'divest himself of barbarism, and content himself with writing pure English, in which he appears perfectly qualified to excel' (Low 1974/1995: 91). Even admiring readers thus emphasised the sociolinguistic connotation carried by Burns' vocabulary, and some even challenged his choice of themes, considering them to be too parochial to be appreciated; among these is a letter of 1796 ascribed to Thomas Duncan:

> It is one misfortune – and a radical one – that the most beautiful of his poems are composed in a dialect which is little understood beyond the boundaries of his native kingdom ... [and] which, even there, is daily getting more and more into disuse among those who are most capable of reaping pleasure from the sentiments they contain. ... for the sake of our Southern neighbors, we certainly ought to regret that some of these poems are full of allusions to, and others are actually founded on local superstitions and local customs. Such poems cannot be so exquisitely

---

A few decades later Stevenson thought of having Fergusson's gravestone repaired, since he claimed: 'I had always a great sense of kinship with poor Robert Fergusson ..., as I always felt rather by express intimation than from evidence, so like myself. ... It is very odd, it really looks like transmigration of souls – I feel that I must do something for Fergusson' (letter to Charles Baxter, 18 May 1894; in Booth and Mehew, 1995: 8/290). Garioch, instead, expressed his 'spiritual' proximity with the two eighteenth-century poets in his poem of 1962, *At Robert Fergusson's Grave*, the final lines of which are as follows:

Aweill, we staund bareheidit in the haar,
murnin a man that gaed back til the pool
twa-hunner year afore our time. The glaur
that haps his banes glowres back. Strang, present dool
ruggs at my hairt. Lichtlie this gin ye daur
here Robert Burns knelt and kissed the mool. (1983: 86)

pleasing to strangers as to those who have witnessed such customs and observed the effects of such superstitions – nor can their interest be so much excited in perusing them. (quoted by Low 1974/1995: 114–116)

Although Currie, the presumed addressee of the above letter, was allegedly responsible for taking a simplified view of Burns into the nineteenth century[31] (Low 1974/1995: 23), the first critic to whom we owe Burns' description as a 'heaven-taught ploughman' is Henry Mackenzie, author of *The Man of Feeling*. In an article published in *The Lounger* of 9 December 1786 (in Cochrane 1897: 278–280), he praised Burns as 'a genius of no ordinary rank', although the title, *Extraordinary Account of Robert Burns, the Ayrshire Ploughman*, obviously emphasised the unexpectedness of this talent in a country lad. Mackenzie was aware of this, since he wrote:

In mentioning the circumstances of his humble station, I mean not to rest his pretensions solely on that title, or to urge the merits of his poetry when considered in relation to the lowness of his birth, and the little opportunity of improvement which his education could afford. (1786/1897: 278)

However, he certainly stressed Burns' 'humble and unlettered station' to explain his choice of language:

One bar, indeed, his birth and education have opposed to his fame – the language in which most of his poems are written. Even in Scotland, the provincial dialect which Ramsay and he have used is now read with a difficulty which greatly damps the pleasure of the reader: in England it cannot be read at all, without such a constant reference to a glossary, as nearly to destroy that pleasure. Some of his productions, however, especially those of the grave style, are almost English. (1786/1897: 278)

In spite of popular belief that Robert Burns was indeed just the simple ploughman that some of his contemporaries made him out to be, and that his posing as an unlettered peasant[32] in the Preface to the Kilmarnock edition of

---

31 James Currie (1756–1805) prepared the first collected edition of Burns' works (published in Liverpool in 1800) as a charity task on behalf of the poet's family. His 'Introductory Remarks on the Character and Condition of the Scottish Peasantry' and 'Life of Burns' were also reprinted in subsequent editions.

32 Burns' self-representation is also skilfully crafted in similar terms in another document sent to Mr Riddell. His claim is that 'on rummaging over some old papers, I lightened on a MS of my early years, in which I had determined to write myself out. ... It sets off thus: *Observations, Hints, Songs, Scraps of Poetry, &c. by R. B.* – a man who had little art in making money, and still less in keeping it. ... As he was but little indebted to scholastic education, and bred at the plough-tail, his performances must be strongly tinctured with his unpolished rustic way of life; but as I believe they are really his *own*, it may be some entertainment to a curious observer of human nature, to see how a ploughman thinks and feels, ...' (quoted by Currie 1846: 4). Low (1974/1995: 9) quotes a contemporary of Burns who actually describes this attitude as 'part of the machinery, as [Burns] called it, of his poetical character'.

his poems had encouraged, his education had included 'a thorough grounding in English' (Daiches 1996: 1). Among the authors whom Burns read, Shakespeare, Milton, Dryden, Pope, Richardson, Fielding and Smollett are quoted. Burns also knew the historical works of David Hume and William Robertson, and Daiches ascribes his 'rhetorical sentimentality', adequate to the 'genteel literary fashion' of those days, to his readings of Thomas Gray, James Thomson and William Shenstone.[33] Sterne and Mackenzie were also influential: in Burns' own letter to Dr Moore (1787), it is stated that *Tristram Shandy* and *The Man of Feeling* – were [his] bosom favourites' (quoted by Currie 1846: xxxi). The letter is a fairly lengthy account of Burns' development as a poet, and it is supported by evidence provided in letters by Gilbert Burns (the poet's brother – cf. Currie 1846: xxxiv–xxxviii) and Mr Murdoch (his preceptor – cf. Currie 1846: xl–xlii). In the latter text (a letter of 1799, addressed to Joseph Cooper Walker) it may be interesting to observe that Murdoch also describes Burns' father's speech, and associates it with the boys' cognitive development:

> He spoke the English language with more propriety (both with respect to diction and pronunciation) than any man I ever knew with no greater advantages. This had a very good effect on the boys, who began to talk, and reason like men, much sooner than their neighbours (quoted by Currie 1846: xlii).

However, Burns also had an 'informal education' based on the oral folk tradition,[34] an awareness of the older Scottish literary tradition, and Fergusson's poems in Scots. His works were to mirror these two sides of his education in a very intriguing way: not only as far as contents were concerned, but also, and most interestingly, on a linguistic level. As Daiches (1964: 87–88) has put it: 'His language varied from conventional eighteenth-century English parnassian to a Scots in which his native dialect was enlarged by words from other regions and even occasionally from older Scottish literature; his most successful idiom was often an English tipped with Scots'. Although it is not obvious whether 'successful' refers to readers' reception or to critical assessment, it is certainly true that Burns' language is notable for a deliberately subtle use of both codes

---

33 Indeed, in a letter of 15th January 1783 to John Murdoch, Burns had stated: 'My favourite authors are of the sentimental kind, such as *Shenstone*, particularly his *Elegies*; *Thomson*; *Man of Feeling*, a book I prize next to the Bible; *Man of the World*; *Sterne*, especially his *Sentimental Journey*; *Macpherson's Ossian*, &c. These are the glorious models after which I endeavour to form my conduct' (quoted by Currie 1846: 3).

34 In his letter of 1787 to Dr Moore (quoted by Currie 1846: xxviii), Burns said: 'In my infant and boyish days, too, I owed much to an old woman who resided in the family, remarkable for her ignorance, credulity, and superstition. She had, I suppose, the largest collection in the country of tales and songs concerning devils, ghosts, fairies, brownies, witches, warlocks, spunkies, kelpies, elf-candles, deadlights, wraiths, apparitions, cantraips, giants, enchanted towers, dragons, and other trumpery'.

to suit lyrical needs.[35] Smith (1996: 171) has analysed Burns' use of Scots and English in rhyming patterns and challenged traditional views of Burns' Augustan English as 'false' (cf. Wittig 1958: 203), since the poet's attention to the interplay of Scots and English may demonstrate his sophisticated linguistic competence in what Smith calls 'the incipient Scottish Standard English of the eighteenth century' (1996: 173). From our point of view, the adjective 'incipient' seems particularly significant – at this point, the co-existence of Scots and English appears to be developing into a standard variety the prestige of which was already beginning to be acknowledged.

As Tieken-Boon van Ostade (1996: 331) has remarked, 'The eighteenth century is an interesting period from the point of view of social network theory'. As far as Burns is concerned, the social and geographical mobility that characterised his life and that had him interact with Scottish people of all classes and from various districts may lead us to identify him as the subject who potentially qualifies as a linguistic innovator. As a matter of fact, according to Currie (1846: xxiv), Burns

> Had less of the Scottish dialect than Hume …; or perhaps than Robertson …; and if he had been in other respects fitted to take a lead in the British House of Commons, his pronunciation would neither have fettered his eloquence, nor deprived it of its due effect.

Dugald Stewart[36] also describes Burns' linguistic self-monitoring in similar terms:

> Nothing, perhaps, was more remarkable among his various attainments, than the fluency, and precision, and originality of his language, when he spoke in company; more particularly as he aimed at purity in his turn of expression, and avoided more successfully than most Scotchmen, the peculiarities of Scottish phraseology (quoted by Currie 1846: li).

Burns thus appeared to master two codes which represented two worlds. His popularity may also be connected with the way in which he adapted Jacobite songs and ballads and transformed them into lyrical pieces. As a result he contributed to a fashion that was to continue in the following century, and which is related to a sentimental discovery of Scotland on the part of English and continental visitors.

---

35 Burns' awareness of his own potentialities also emerges in the comment quoted by Ramsay of Ochtertyre on the *literati*'s suggestions: 'When [Ramsay] asked him whether the Edinburgh *literati* had mended his poems by their criticisms – 'See, said he, those gentlemen remind me of some spinsters in my own country, who spin their thread so fine that it is neither fit for weft nor woof' (reported in Fyfe 1942: 199).

36 Dugald Stewart was Professor of Moral Philosophy at the University of Edinburgh when Burns first visited the city in November 1786.

Travelogues

Accounts of the linguistic situation in Scotland appear as early as the seventeenth century, when phonological features are observed and discussed. Thomas Morer, who visited Scotland in 1689, remarked on the 'unhappy tone, which the gentry and nobles cannot overcome, tho' educated in our schools, or never so conversant with us'; however, he conceded that 'our Northern and remote English have the same imperfection' (quoted by Hume Brown 1891: 272–273).

As we saw, the peculiarity of the Lowlanders' accent had also been implicitly compared with the Highlanders' 'purer' pronunciation by Johnson. Although his *Journey to the Western Islands of Scotland* (1775) was published anonymously, it was immediately ascribed to the lexicographer, and it caused the outraged reaction of many Scottish critics.[37] Among their texts, the most aggressive one was possibly written by Donald McNicol, who may also have been helped by Macpherson (Boulton 1974/1995: 7). The very title page of McNicol's work, published in London in 1779, implicitly attacks Johnson, presenting the following quotation from Ray's Proverbs: 'Old Men and Travellers LIE by authority', while the title makes explicit reference to Johnson and provides important keywords that foretell the positive connotation that will be attached to Highland culture: *Remarks on Dr Samuel Johnson's Journey to the Hebrides; in which are contained, observations on the antiquities, language, genius, and manners of the Highlanders of Scotland*. Less forceful attacks appeared in Mary Ann Hanway's *A Journey to the Highlands of Scotland With occasional remarks on Dr Johnson's Tour by a Lady* (London, 1776), while Gaelic songs were written in the flyting style already made famous by Dunbar and Kennedy (Boulton 1974/1995: 240–241).

Not all of Johnson's observations, however, were as horribly chauvinistic as they were made out to be. In fact, a number of positive remarks are scattered in the text. For instance, Johnson observes that 'civility seems part of the national character of Highlanders' (1775/1996: 24). and though 'no man is so abstemious as to refuse the morning dram, which they call a *skalk*', 'they are not a drunken race' (1775/1996: 48). Besides, in the Islands, Johnson states: 'I did not meet with the inquisitiveness of which I have read, and suspect the judgement to have been rashly made' (1775/1996: 91). Most sympathy appears to be expressed concerning the consequences of the Disarming Act:

---

37 In England, instead, reviews were very favourable (cf. Boulton 1974/1995: 6; 28). For instance, in the *Monthly Review* of January–February 1775 Griffiths commented that 'Dr. Johnson's book may be regarded as a valuable supplement to Mr. Pennant's two accounts of his northern expeditions [*A Tour in Scotland*, of 1771, and *A Tour in Scotland and Voyage to the Hebrides*, of 1774-6] ... Mr. Pennant travels, chiefly, in the character of the naturalist and antiquary; Dr. Johnson in that of the moralist and observer of men and manners'. He then concluded by expressing 'thanks for the pleasure we have received in the perusal of his animated and instructive narration' (quoted by Boulton 1974/1995: 235).

Their pride has been crushed by the heavy hand of a vindictive conqueror, whose severities have been followed by laws, which, though they cannot be called cruel, ... operate upon the surface of life, and make every eye bear witness to subjection. ... That dignity which they derived from an opinion of their military importance, the law, which disarmed them, has abated. ... The loyal clans murmured, with some appearance of justice, that after having defended the King, they were forbidden for the future to defend themselves; ... These Islands might be wasted with fire and sword before their sovereign would know their distress. ... Laws that place the subjects in such a state, ... exact obedience, and yield no protection. ... In the beginning of the present century ... every man was a soldier, who partook of national confidence, and interested himself in national honour. To lose this spirit, is to lose what no small advantage will compensate (1775/1996: 78–80).

Johnson also showed interest in the roles of *bards* and *senachies*, or storytellers (1775/1996: 98–99), apparently in his quest for information concerning the reliability of Macpherson's claims, so frequent remarks appear concerning Gaelic and interviews he had on the alleged existence of the manuscripts (1775/1996: 101–104). As regards Scots, he observes that 'The great, the learned, the ambitious, and the vain, all cultivate the *English* phrase, and the *English* pronunciation, and in splendid companies *Scotch* is not much heard, except now and then from an old Lady' (1775/1996: 143). In one sentence we find what is perhaps the most precise description of the sociolinguistic context in which 'improvement' was sought in late eighteenth-century Scotland.

On his part, Boswell published his notes in 1786, two years after Johnson's death, with the title *The Journal of a Tour to the Hebrides with Samuel Johnson, LL.D.* Even here we find the author's obsession with Scotticisms; in a footnote he points out a phrase in a letter to Dr Beattie: 'We shall not be long of being at Marischal College. – This, I find, is a Scotticism. I should have said, "It will not be long before we shall be at Marischal College"' (1786/1996: 165). His remarks as a traveller also include references to legends, the Jacobite rebellion, and Ossian, so he was inevitably involved in the attacks on Johnson, and indeed satire also was directed at him.[38] Still, both travellers' interest was certainly genuine. Johnson had been looking forward to this tour since he had read Martin Martin's *A Description of the Western Islands of Scotland* (1703) in his early youth. Martin referred to a journey made in 1695,[39] i.e. before the

38 Most famously, this appeared in Thomas Rowlandson's caricatures *The Picturesque Beauties of Boswell* (London, 1786). The title may be a parody of *The Beauties of Johnson*, a collection of maxims the first volume of which appeared in 1781 (Boulton 1974/1995: 14). Johnson and Boswell's route was then followed by James Bailey, who published *Journey into Scotland with sketches of some picturesque ruins in that interesting country* in 1787.

39 In 1618, another English traveller, John Taylor, had actually walked to Scotland and subsequently published his notes with the intriguing title of *The Pennyless Pilgrimage, or the*

rebellions whose defeat changed the social order in the Highlands, and Johnson actually acknowledges that his 'are the thoughts of one who has seen but little' (1775/1996: 145).

Critics, however, overlooked these points, and McNicol even challenged the travellers' complaints about the climate, which in fact were quite understandable and inevitable, considering that the tour took place between 14 August and 22 November.[40] Another element that may have contributed to the difficult relationship between Johnson and the Scottish general public was his dislike of Calvinism, but perhaps the negative elements in Johnson's *Journey* have been overemphasised. Actually, it may seem surprising to see how badly the Scots reacted to Johnson's notes, when they themselves took the south as a model, and some comments seem to have originated with Scottish informants:

> What the Romans did to other nations, was in a great degree done by Cromwell to the Scots; he civilised them by conquest ... I was told at *Aberdeen* that the people learned from Cromwell's soldiers to make shoes and to plant kail (Johnson 1775/1996: 22).

Besides, a Scotophobic attitude was to become much more obvious in William Cobbett's *Tour in Scotland* (1831), in which Johnson was exploited for the presentation of racier prejudice (Rogers 1995: 213; Green 1984: 142), though Cobbett himself explained that it was an attitude inspired 'by the scoundrelly 'feelosofers', who preached up a doctrine tending to cause the people of England to be treated like cattle' (Green 1984: 60–61).

Special attention to the situation in the Highlands and Islands had also been given in important works of the Scottish Enlightenment: Adam Ferguson's *Essay on the History of Civil Society* (1767) and Adam Smith's *An Inquiry into the Nature and Causes of the Wealth of Nations* (1776). The former is regarded as one of the earliest works in modern sociology, while the latter is acknowledged as one of the landmarks in modern economic thought, and although it includes a reference to the nutritional value of oats that echoes Johnson's most notorious entry, this has never become an instance of offensiveness, possibly thanks to a subsequent 'egalitarian' remark that concerns 'the people of fashion' both in England and in Scotland:

> In some parts of Lancashire it is pretended, I have been told, that bread of oatmeal is a heartier food for labouring people than wheaten bread, and I have frequently heard the same doctrine held in Scotland. I am, however, somewhat doubtful of the truth of it. The common people in Scotland,

---

Moneyless Perambulation of John Taylor, alias, the King's Majesty's water-poet: how he travailed on foot from London to Edenborough in Scotland, not carrying any money to or fro, neither begging, borrowing, or asking meate, drinke, or lodging (Jackson Young 1997).

40 The date had been selected in accordance with the recess of the Law Courts, which began in August (Brunner 1949: 189).

who are fed with oatmeal, are in general neither so strong, nor so handsome as the same rank of people in England who are fed on wheaten bread. They neither work so well, nor look so well; and as there is not the same difference between the people of fashion in the two countries, experience would seem to show that the food of the common people in Scotland is not so suitable to the human constitution as that of their neighbours of the same rank in England (Smith 1776/1986: 265).

So far travellers had been observers; their role as a source of linguistic improvement appears in a remark made by the minister of Peterhead in 1795 for the *Statistical Account of Scotland*:[41]

The language spoken in this parish is the broad Buchan dialect of the English ... and stands much in need of reformation, which it is hoped will soon happen, from the frequent resort of polite people to the town in summer (quoted by Aitken 1979: 97).

By the end of the century travel in the Highlands had increased dramatically owing to the Ossian cult[42] and the taste for the Sublime in landscape (Leneman 1987; Andrews 1989; Glendening 1997; Fenyö 2000). At the same time, there was increasing attention to local accents. Beattie (1788: 90) thus criticises Sheridan's attempt to describe the differences between English, Irish and Scottish intonation:

[Sheridan] observed, that towards the end of the [interrogatory] sentence an Englishman lets his voice fall, an Irishman raises his, and a Scotchman makes his voice first fall and then rise. The remark is well founded; but it is difficult to express in unexceptionable terms a matter of so great nicety. I shall only add, that what is here said of the Scotch accent, though it may hold true of the more southerly provinces, it is by no means applicable to the dialects that prevail in Aberdeenshire, and other parts of the north: where the voice of the common people, in concluding a clause or a sentence, rises into a very shrill and sharp tone without any previous fall. 'You bark in your speech', says a man of Edinburgh to one of Aberdeen: 'And you growl and grumble in yours,' replies the Aberdonian. In Inverness-shire, and the western parts of Moray, the accents become totally different, and resemble the tones and aspirations of the Erse.

41 Linguistic comments in the *Statistical Accounts* have also been investigated by McColl Millar (2000 and 2003).

42 Willis (1897: 66) discusses the Ossian controversy and concludes: 'Of the poems of Ossian, I have made many enquiries, and believe, as is usual, in all controversies, that all are right, and all are wrong. Many songs, or odes, attributed to Ossian, are sung by the Highlanders; ... Macpherson has strung those pearls together, and formed something like an Epic poem; as to the manuscripts he talks of, they never, I believe, had an existence, for men begin to sing long before they begin to write, and as to Fingal himself, it is now doubted whether he was a Scotchman or an Irishman'.

This passage does not only show keen observation and awareness of local varieties, but it also challenges the 'purity' of Highland English[43] and highlights ways in which Gaelic may have influenced it.[44]

Proverbs and ideas of improvement at the turn of the century

In England collections of epigrams, sayings, proverbs and maxims had been fashionable for a long time and many were published throughout the sixteenth and seventeenth centuries.[45] As regards Scotland, one of the earliest specimens of this genre was written in the second half of the sixteenth century or early decades of the seventeenth century, but it was only published in 1957 by M. L. Anderson as the *James Carmichaell Collection of Proverbs in Scots* from the original manuscript in the Edinburgh University Library. This collection is interspersed with Latin adages and was compiled by James Carmichaell (1543?– 1628),[46] including numerous rhymed proverbs that had appeared in the Bannatyne Manuscript of 1568, fol. 134b (Scottish Text Society ed., III, 8ff.).

Motherwell (in Henderson 1832: xxx–xxxiii) transcribed the latter in his preface to Henderson's collection and he also referred to a collection in the Maitland Manuscript, later re-edited by Craigie (1919), but did not provide any instances from it; he then transcribed 232 'Resownes and proverbs' written in 1586 by John Maxwell Younger of Southbar.

Several of the Bannatyne / Maitland proverbs appear to be quite prominent in their moral character, a feature not uncommon in collections of proverbs; for instance, we find the following 'maxims' in a seventeenth-century collection by Andrew Melville, 'doctor and master in the song school of Aberdeen 1621–1640' (Rae Smith 1899):

- Ill company bringes a man to the gallows
- Cartis and dyce ar better givin ovir then usit
- Be the day nevir so long at last comes the evin song

---

43 On the other hand, Dorothy Wordsworth had thus described a man met in the neighbourhood of 'Loch Ketterine': 'He was a complete Highlander in dress, figure, and face, ... He spoke ... sufficiently well for our purpose, and very distinctly, as all the Highlanders do who learn English as a foreign language; but in a long conversation they want words' (1894/1974: 87).

44 Although Beattie here refers only to phonology, later on in his work he identifies a use of pronouns that might be related to Gaelic influence, since Gaelic does not have a neuter personal pronoun; Beattie claims: 'The common people of Scotland, when expressing the sea by a pronoun, often call it *She*, but I think never *He*: "Let us go and look at the sea; they say *she* is very rough to-day"' (1788: 139). Note that the Gaelic word for 'sea', *muir*, is feminine.

45 Motherwell (in Henderson 1832: xlviii–lii) mentions Florio's, Camden's, Davies' and Lord Bacon's. On collections of *sententiae* and commonplace books in Renaissance England, see also Anderson (1996).

46 Carmichaell was minister of Haddington parish; he also published a Latin grammar designed for use in Scottish schools (*Scoticae Juventuti*), printed in Cambridge.

This collection is also specially valuable because its geographical provenance allows us to gain some insight into the different degree of convergence with English presented by the northern variety of Scots.[47] However, what appears to be one of the earliest and most influential collections of Scottish proverbs was compiled by David Fergusson in the late sixteenth century, though according to Hislop (1868: i) the earliest work on the subject was drawn up by Beaton, Archbishop of Glasgow, 'about the time of the Reformation'. In any case, 'the definite information which we have of this work is so very slight ... that it has been of little or no value to subsequent collectors and writers on the subject.'[48]

The botanist John Ray reprinted Fergusson's collection in 1670, then in 1710 Palmer published his *Moral Essays on some of the most significant Proverbs, English, Scottish, and Foreign,* and in 1732 Thomas Fuller published *Aphorisms of Wisdom, or a complete collection of the most celebrated Proverbs in the English, Scotch, French, Spanish, Italian, and other languages, ancient and modern* (Motherwell, in Henderson 1832: liii). Note that in this last collection Scots is considered on a par with other European languages, not as a dialect of English.[49]

Fergusson's collection was subsequently republished in Edinburgh by Thomas Ruddiman in 1785[50] together with several other pieces of vernacular writing.[51] The title of the work is *A Select Collection of Scots Poems chiefly in the broad Buchan dialect to which is added a collection of Scots Proverbs by the Reverend Mr David Fergusson some time minister at Dunfermline,* and in the table of contents it is described as 'A Collection of Scottish Proverbs, The

---

47 On this point, see Meurman-Solin (1997c: 11-12).

48 It is possible that Hislop based his own comment on Motherwell's reference to Mackenzie, who ascribes 'The Scots Proverbs, in 12mo. 1614, and in divers other years' to this prelate; it is the same Motherwell, however, who underlines Mackenzie's lack of accuracy when he points out that in a previous paragraph he had quoted 1610 as the date of the oldest edition (Motherwell, in Henderson 1832: xii-xiii).

49 Dialect, however, was presented in such collections as the one included in *The Praise of Yorkshire Ale* (1685, 1697) (Motherwell, in Henderson 1832: liii) and Motherwell even presents nine proverbs in the Creole language of the black population of Demerara: the first one, for instance, says *Hungry dogs nam ra carn* (= Hungry dogs will eat raw corn) (Motherwell, in Henderson 1832: lvi-lviii).

50 In this same year a collection of Gaelic proverbs was also edited by Donald Macintosh (Motherwell, in Henderson 1832: xliv) – possibly an attempt to rediscover antiquity as a result of the Ossian fashion and the interest in older Celtic languages and traditions, such as the Welsh one, to which the prestige of greater antiquity than Greek was ascribed (Adams 1799: 138).

51 These are: 'Ajax's Speech to the Grecian Knabbs – in broad Buchans – from Ovid's Metamorphoses', 'Ulysses' Answer to Ajax's Speech, in the same dialect; never before published', 'A journal from London to Portsmouth, in the same dialect', 'A shop-Bill, by Robert Forbes, in the same dialect', 'A Glossary, or Explanation of the hard words contained in the foregoing Poems', 'The Dominie Depos'd', by William Forbes, MA late Schoolmaster at Petercoulter', 'Polemo-Middinia inter Vitarvam et Nebernam by William Drummond of Hawthornden Esq.', and 'Praelium Gillicrankianum. Cantilena'.

greatest part of which were at first gathered together by Mr David Fergusson, some time Minister at Dunfermline: And put into an Alphabetical Order after he departed this life, anno 1598'.[52] Ruddiman as 'the Publisher', but also as the editor, reappears at the beginning of the collection, where he echoes Fergusson's earliest printer, who had stated, somewhat apologetically: 'And wheras there are some old Scottish words, not now in use, they must be borne with, because, if you alter these words, the Proverb will have no grace'. This justification, together with the context in which the collection is set (mainly comic poetry in the vernacular) presents the collection as a curiosity, in which both antiquity and lexical quaintness are emphasised for the benefit of a public obviously unaccustomed to dialect (as is also shown by the glossary of hard words contained in the Buchan poems).

Before Ruddiman's reprint of Fergusson, two very important collections had appeared in the early eighteenth century: Kelly's in 1721 and Ramsay's in 1737. The former was printed in London and its title is significant: *A Complete Collection of Scotish Proverbs Explained and made Intelligible to the English Reader*. The latter, instead, was published in Edinburgh and is titled *A Collection of Scots Proverbs, more complete and correct than any heretofore published*. The volume is dedicated 'To the Tenantry of Scotland, Farmers of the Dales, and Storemasters of the Hills' and the title page bears the Latin and Scots renderings of the same proverb: 'Vox populi vox dei / That maun be true that a' Men say': a rhyming dictum which implicitly attests the truthfulness of the book's contents. Finally, five pages are devoted to the 'Explanation of the Words less frequent amongst our Gentry than the Commons', thus also making a sociolinguistic observation.

Kelly had also paid special attention to his reading public and made this explicit both on the title page and in the Introduction. The title page bears an epigraph by Lord Bacon which says: 'The Genius, Wit, and Spirit of a Nation, are discovered by their Proverbs'; not an authentic proverb, then, but an Englishman's opinion of the value of proverbs, as if to justify the collection as such. Subsequently the author often emphasised his role as editor in a detailed description of what he selected and what he omitted. He stated that at first he had wanted to collect 'none but those which I knew to be Native, Genuine, *Scotish* Proverbs', but, having found that many also belong elsewhere, he 'set down all those for *Scotish* Proverbs, that are used in *Scotland*, and by *Scotish* Men, though many are common to the *English*, and not a few, perhaps, originally of that Nation'. Kelly wishes to focus on authentic Scottish usage, and emphasises that he 'resolved to collect none but those which had been the

---

52 Biographical notes on David Fergusson are also provided by Motherwell (in Henderson 1832: xiv-xvii). From these we gather that he was born in Dundee and died on 23 August 1598. It is Motherwell's notes again that set the first printed edition of Fergusson's collection in 1642 and that outline its bibliographical history (pp. xxi–xxii).

result of prudent Observation, or carried in them some moral Instruction, or, at least, were odd and comical in the Expression'.[53]

Kelly's collection is not in alphabetical order, but an index is provided. His editorial work is also explained where spelling conventions are described; his choices are justified in terms of intelligibility to his English readers and Kelly also tries to fend off objections from Scots:

> I have written the English Words in the Margin that correspond to the Scotish in the Proverb. And I have spelled the Scotish Words that differ from the English only in Accent and Pronunciation as the English do: except where the Rhyme and Decorum of the Proverb necessarily require it to be otherways. ... I know my Countrymen will quarrel with me for this, as spoiling a great deal of the Briskness and Vigour of the Phrase; but I am not without Apprehensions that if I had spelled them as they pronounce them, they themselves would have found some difficulty in reading of them, whereas here they will find none.

Kelly also included English and Latin dicta, and finished his Introduction with another note that is interesting from the psycholinguistic and sociolinguistic point of view:

> If what I have done, be any way grateful, either to the English, whom I honour and esteem; or to the Scots, whom I love and affect, I shall be well pleased.

The verbs that Kelly associates with Scottish and English readers respectively reflect the different kind of prestige that was becoming increasingly perceptible in Scotland: overt prestige for English and covert prestige for Scots.

While Fergusson's collection had stopped at 940 entries, Kelly's reaches almost 3,000 (Hislop 1868: i), but his attempt to domesticate Scots forms was criticised both by his contemporaries and by later commentators: Hislop quotes Motherwell's remark, according to which Kelly's rendering of the Scottish dialect was 'most barbarous' (Hislop 1868: viii). Ramsay particularly was to resent so much interference with language: in the preface to his collection he alluded to Kelly's collection as 'a large book ... fou of errors, in a style neither Scots nor English'. His collection of about 2,200 items, instead, claimed authenticity in the highest degree, and he strongly recommended it to his readers:

---

53 Discussing his sources, Motherwell (in Henderson 1832: xxvi – xxvii) underlines Kelly's indebtedness to Alexander Montgomerie's poem *The Cherrie and the Slae*, which Kelly himself describes as 'a book so commonly known to *Scottish* men, that a great share of it passes for proverbs'. A further sociolinguistic reference is in Kelly's statement that 'It is written in native genuine Scotch, and, to them who understand it, very fine and taking'; this implies that, no matter how good the text may be, the language in which it is written inevitably restricts the number of its potential readers.

I desire you, for the thriving and pleasure of you and yours, to use your een and lend your lugs to these *guid auld says*, that shine with wail'd sense, and will as lang as the world wags. Gar your bairns get them by heart; ... How usefou it will prove to you ... when you forgather with your friends at kirk or market, banquet or bridal! By your proficiency, you'll be able, in a proverbial way, to keep up the soul of a conversation, that is baith blythe and usefou.

As a matter of fact, his collection does include phrases that were omitted by other collectors on account of their offensiveness: for instance, Mackay (1888) excluded not only proverbs deemed to be rude, but also the proverbs *Freedom's a fair Flower* and *A' Stuarts are no sib to the King*, possibly to avoid any reference to the Jacobite uprisings and to political issues.

In the nineteenth century one of the most important collections was edited by Andrew Henderson and was published in Glasgow in 1832. It is arranged in thematic order and the introduction by Motherwell is an extensive study, which provides very interesting insights into this subject (Dossena 1999/2000). Subsequent collections were published by Alexander Hislop (1862) and by Andrew Cheviot (1896) – in both cases the title pages underline the presence of 'notes and parallel phrases' (Cheviot) and 'explanatory and illustrative notes and a glossary' (Hislop), again implicitly emphasising a supposed unintelligibility of original forms. Hislop's collection is more interesting because it allegedly collates the works of Fergusson, Kelly and Ramsay and, in addition to this, the compiler points to literary texts and to items he collected personally, thus joining two very different sources of information:

Large additions have been made from various sources, such as the works of Sir Walter Scott, Galt, Hogg, and other national writers, while not a few have been picked up and registered as they fell from the lips of friends and strangers with whom the compiler came in contact (1862: x).

On the other hand, Hislop did not only include Scots proverbs, but also proverbs of English, Classical, Eastern and Continental origin. As regards his notes, the compiler devoted a few paragraphs in the introduction to the doubts he had had about inserting them ('also in deference to opinions which have been expressed as to the propriety of adding notes to a collection of proverbs at all'), but he claimed that they would, 'at least, tend to relieve the monotonous or catalogue effect, ... which is apt to be felt by many readers when perusing works arranged in alphabetical order'. Instead, what was taken for granted was the presence of 'a simple but comprehensive Glossary ... containing and explaining the meaning of the Scottish words to be found in the book' (1868: xi).

Collections continued to be published in the latter part of the century. In one of these, published anonymously around 1880, we find that the overall content appears to be sufficiently close to original forms, with few traces of anglicisation in spelling, grammar or vocabulary:

- A wee moose will creep aneath a muckle corn stack
- Better a wee ingle to warm ye than a big fire to burn ye
- Gin ye hadna been amang the craws ye wadna hae been shot
- Gin ye hae pain tae yer pech ye're sair made
- He caresna wha's bairns greet gin his laugh
- Ilka blade o'grass keps its ain drap o' dew
- Ilka craw thinks its ain bird whitest
- Ilka man buckles his belt his ain gait

Even what appear to be patriotic sayings are included in the collection: *Let them that scorn the tartan fear dark* and *Oppression will make a wise man mad*.

In the same decade Charles Mackay published *A Dictionary of Lowland Scotch with an introductory chapter on the poetry, humour, and literary history of the Scottish language and an appendix of Scottish Proverbs* (1888). Again, the association of Scots is with poetry, antiquity and humour. Mackay openly stated this when he said that 'The design of this Dictionary was not to include all Scotticisms, but only those venerable by their antiquity, quaint in their humour, touching in their simplicity, or admirable in their poetic meaning' (1888: xxvi). The lexical choices of the author signal the important changes that had been taking place in the attitude towards Scots – from strict prescriptivism to the acceptance of Scots in literary forms of expression: the use of 'Scotticism', the dreaded proscribing label, seemed to lose its negative connotation when it was linked to such positive adjectives as 'venerable', 'touching' and 'admirable', and to ideas of humour, antiquity and poetry, the three areas of usage to which Scots had been restricted by then.

Mackay emphasised the closer connection of Scots with the older 'Anglo-Teutonic' vocabulary which is described as obsolete in English, but still fully comprehensible in Scotland (1888: xii), thus assigning it an aura of respectability that had also been stressed by those English scholars who wished to emphasise the Anglo-Saxon lineage of English (Dury 1992; Milroy 1996).[54] Another positive feature of 'Scoto-Teutonic' was, in Mackay's view, its deletion of 'all harsh or unnecessary consonants. Thus it has *loe*, for love; *fa'*, for fall; *wa'* for wall; ... and many hundreds of similar abbreviations which ... soften the roughness of the expression' (1888: xiii). Mackay ascribed these features to the influence of Low Dutch on the Scottish tongue, and he claimed this ascendancy is also recognisable in the Scots use of diminutive suffixes:

Another source of the superior euphony of the Scoto-Teutonic is the single diminutive in *ie*, and the double diminutive in *kie*, formed from *och*

---

54 It is possibly in this cultural framework that Motherwell (in Henderson 1832: lxiv–lxv) associates some phonological features of proverbs with Scandinavian influences upon language, since many of them are just 'rymes running in a rattling row'; he then quotes the saying *To rime a rat to death* to claim that it may be 'a vestige of Scandic superstition, referring to the magical powers ascribed to the Gothic runes'.

or *ock*, or possibly from the Teutonic *chen* ... as *wife, wifie, wifoch, wifikie* ...; *bairn, bairnie, bairnikie* ... &c.[55]

The attempt to provide Scots with historical dignity was pursued then through an attempt to locate the origin of Scottish vocabulary in various European languages. In his treatment of Scots proverbs, however, Mackay owed much to the standardising trend that had been dominant for many decades. First of all, his collection allegedly reflects Allan Ramsay's, since the title is 'Allan Ramsay's Collection of Scottish Proverbs', but in fact it turns out to be only a selection from it. Already on the first page, nine of Ramsay's proverbs are omitted from Mackay's collection:

- A bawdy Dad makes a begging Bairn-time
- A Bit But and a Bit Benn, makes a mim Maiden at the Board End
- Abundance of Law breaks nae Law
- A braw Whore is like a dirty house with a clean Door
- A cumbersome Cur is hated by his Neighbours
- A dear ship lies lang in the Harbour
- A drink is shorter than a tale
- Ae foot in a Bawdy house and anither in a hospital
- Ae Fool makes mony

Further on we find that acceptability was also improved through linguistic devices that limited the use of apostrophes signalling those deletions that had been praised in the introduction. Local forms were also used very sparingly: the Scots adjectival numeral *ae* is used 11 times at the beginning of proverbs, and this where other Scots features also appear quite prominently, as, for instance, in:

- Ae bird in hand is worth ten fleeand
- Ae half of the warld kenna how the ither half live
- Ae man may lead a horse to the water, but four and twenty winna gar him drink
- Ae scabbed sheep will smit the hale hirdsel

In *fleeand* we recognise one of the few occurrences of the Scots participial suffix *-and*, standardised elsewhere, as in *A gawn foot's aye getting*; the suffix *-it* instead of *-ed* was also avoided, as in *A bonny bride is soon busked, and a short horse is soon whisked*.

Vocabulary was possibly modified in order to enhance phonological effects of internal rhyme, alliteration and assonance, as in *A toom purse makes a*

---

55 At this point Mackay inserted a footnote in which he identified similar suffixes in Dutch and Flemish, extracting them 'from the *Grammaire Flamande* of Philippe La Grue (Amsterdam 1745): -*Manneken*, little man; *wyfken*, little wife; *vrouwtje*, little woman; *Mejsgie*, little girl (Scottice, *Missie*); ... *scheepje*, little boat (Scottice, *boatie*); *vogeltje*, little bird, or *birdie*' (1888: xiii).

tartling merchant; or in order to avoid its cultural specificity, as in *A twapenny cat may look at a king*, in which *twapenny* substitutes *bawbee* (Hislop). In other cases 'improvement' reversed the meaning of the proverb itself – see, for instance, *Bairns are certain care, but nae sure joy*, in which the substitution of one adjective is crucial – Henderson had, in fact, reported this as *Bairns are certain care, but nae sma' joy* (1832: 2), though in other cases he was not to prove so sensitive towards childhood, as when he included *The death o' ae bairn winna skail a house* (p. 11) or *The best that can happen to a poor man, is that ae bairn die and the rest follow* (p. 48).

Among Scots items that seldom appear in the collection are the distributive pronoun *ilka* (*He's silly that spares for ilka speech*), generally rendered with 'every' (*Every man wears his belt his ain gate*) and the intensifier *unco* (*He's unko fu' in his ain house that canna pike a bane in his neighbour's*). In general, Mackay's use of Scots plural forms (*You shape shoon by your ain shachled feet*) and of a singular verb with a plural subject (*Your een's no marrows*) point to linguistic reliability. Besides, Fergusson's version in Ruddiman's edition of the proverb *He that will not when he may, shall not when he wald* is made to sound more authentic through the agglutination of the verbs and the negative forms: *He that winna when he may, shanna when he wad*.

On the other hand, the Scots conjunctions *gin* and *an* were typically substituted with 'if': *If marriages be made in heaven, ye have had few friends there*. Almost complete rephrasing occurred when an item was perceived to be difficult to understand:

- They that see you a' day winna break the house for you at night (Henderson's version was a less than flattering *They that see you in daylight winna rin awa wi' you in the dark*)
- Wishers and waddlers were never good house hauders[56]

As late as the beginning of the twentieth century collections were published in which 'the homely pithy speech of the village folk' (Wilson 1915: 4) was presented together with vocabulary lists, notes on the grammar and phonology of the dialect, riddles, rhymes and songs. In *Lowland Scotch as Spoken in the Lower Strathearn District of Perthshire* (1915), *The Dialect of Robert Burns as Spoken in Central Ayrshire* (1923) and *The Dialects of Central Scotland* (1926), all edited by James Wilson, the title clearly shows that these works are explicitly linguistic descriptions of dialects,[57] in which the proverbs, like the rhymes, riddles and songs previously mentioned, are illustrative of their geographical

---

56 This had appeared in John Davies' collection (1612?) as *Wishers and Woulders are no good Housholders* (Motherwell, in Henderson 1832: l) and it is actually rephrased as *Wishers and woulders are poor house holders* by Henderson (p. 97).

57 In each of these Wilson actually adopts a phonetic spelling, in order to represent the phonological realisation of different items: cf. 'Dhe neerur dhe kirk, dhe fawrur fay grais. The nearer the church, the farther from grace' (1923: 92).

specificity. In previous collections, instead, geographical distribution of proverbs was never mentioned, and indeed Motherwell (in Henderson 1832: lxxxv) had identified the correction of this defect as a possible way of improving the collection in the event of a new edition.

Though Ramsay had complained of Kelly's style, describing it as 'neither Scots nor English', it is also true that it has always been notoriously difficult to draw a line between the two varieties and that the best depiction is that of a continuum ranging from broad Scots to English via Anglicised Scots. This appears to be most prominent in collections of proverbs, which should be set in the wider cultural context of the late eighteenth and nineteenth centuries – a time when increasing attention was given to national antiquity and to popular culture, though in a rather 'domesticated' form.

An age of transition

The above analysis has attempted to identify connections between different trends. A complex picture emerges, in which apparent contradictions are reconciled in an extremely fluid linguistic situation. At the turn of the century a number of factors, ranging from literary taste to fashion to historical and political circumstances, made it possible for Scots to acquire a new status – not in a strictly defensive sense, because English maintained, and even increased, its overt prestige – but in a way that made Scottish speakers recover a deep awareness of the value of their own variety as a means for the expression of feeling, sentimentality and authenticity. In some cases this was actually interpreted in an openly patriotic and nationalistic sense. For instance, the failure of the Jacobite movement marked Scottish cultural life through a wave of sentimental song that conveyed the idealised perception of a lost cause. Thus antiquarianism came to be associated with patriotism. This phenomenon is clearly visible in the establishment of the Society of Antiquaries of Scotland in 1780, allegedly due to the 'truly patriotic spirit' of the 11th Earl of Buchan (Jones 1997a: 272–273).

In a more general sense, the shift from strict prescriptivism to a 'vernacular revival' – or better, a reassessment of original linguistic features – was related to a kind of tradition which 'soon dwindled down into facile sentimentality to join the other streams which flowed into the torrent of tartanry which increased steadily throughout the nineteenth century' (Daiches 1964: 35), and the outcome somehow 'forged' Scotland's image of itself, its history, its tradition and its language.[58] The dualism which opposed politeness and spontaneity, correctness and 'vulgar speech', was to continue and to be reinforced by extraordinarily popular literary models until it was perceived to be so real that it found its way into didactic manuals.

58 An often quoted, though controversial, presentation of the history of 'tartanry' is included in the study by Trevor-Roper (1983); cf. also McCrone (1989: 174–195). On the association between tartan and Jacobitism, cf. Nicholson (1998).

CHAPTER SIX

The Nineteenth Century:
Antiquity, Propriety and Bad Language

Travelogues, literature and linguistic concerns

The sociolinguistic trends begun in the late eighteenth century developed into the nineteenth century, when greater emphasis was placed on 'pure Saxon' forms and on picturesque elements of Scottish culture. At the same time, this attitude caused Scots to be perceived as even more 'exotic' than before: typically, commentators stressed the specificity and difficulty of Burns' language, a difficulty that was often related to the poet's social background.[1] Yet it was owing to this very specificity that his writing was considered to be so genuine, as may be gathered from 'a poet of Nature's own making'. Indeed, the merit of that 'homely rustic jingle' was ascribed to its authenticity and its sharpness: 'In that rough dialect, in that rude, often awkward metre, so clear and definite a likeness!' (Carlyle 1828/1897: 485).

Linguistic preoccupation apparently went hand-in-hand with the fashionable search for the picturesque and the sublime, which persisted through the period of the Napoleonic wars – when the Continent was virtually off-limits – and reached a turning point during the Victorian age. For the Romantics the chief attraction in Scotland was possibly the isle of Staffa, first discovered a few decades before and inevitably associated with the Ossianic cult through 'Fingal's Cave',[2] an impressive grotto that was to inspire painters like Turner and musicians like Felix Mendelssohn-Bartholdy, in addition to a series of more or less literary imitators (cf. Mitchell 1999: 160). Mendelssohn visited Scotland in the summer of 1829 and provided many poetic accounts in his evocative

---

1 If Mackenzie had called Burns 'our rustic bard', in the nineteenth century Thomas Carlyle labelled him 'the Peasant Poet' in his article 'Burns' that appeared in the *Edinburgh Review*, no. 96, in 1828 (in Cochrane 1897: 482). According to Carlyle, Burns was 'Without help, without instruction, without model; or with models only of the meanest sort. ... with no furtherance but such knowledge as dwells in a poor man's hut, and the rhymes of a Ferguson or Ramsay for his standard of beauty' (1828/1897: 481).

2 Joseph Banks announced his discovery in 1772 and immediately linked the island to the Ossianic fashion, stating that 'There is a cave ... which the natives call the Cave of Fingal'. This was probably a misunderstanding, but it corresponded so well to what the public expected that even today it is one of the most fascinating tourist attractions in the British Isles. Bray (1986/1996: 97) even suggests that Banks' discovery may have played a part in Johnson's decision to visit Scotland the following year.

letters. At Abbotsford he met Sir Walter Scott and the literary, pictorial, and musical elements of Mendelssohn's imagination often merged in his compositions. Describing, in a letter written from the Hebrides, the manner in which the waves break on the Scottish coast, he noted down the opening bars of the Hebrides Overture (also known as *Fingal's Cave*, first performed in London in 1832). He then dedicated his Symphony No. 3 in A Minor-Major, or Scottish Symphony, as it is called, to Queen Victoria, who also visited Staffa in 1847.

Victoria was possibly the figure who did most to promote a certain popular image of Scotland that is still with us today, but it was George IV who re-opened the royal road to Scotland in 1822. As a matter of fact, no royal visits had taken place since James VII and II's stay in 1681/82, and Walter Scott's own popularity and commitment[3] played a considerable part in persuading the King to cross the Border. Twenty years later Queen Victoria also 'discovered' the Highlands and she commented on the language of the Gaelic boat songs sung at one entertainment, describing it as 'so guttural and yet so soft' (quoted by Cadell 1977: 25). In fact, this comment seems to suggest that she transposed a certain view of landscape – quite rugged and wild, yet so alluring for many visitors – to language; it may have set the most significant and permanent seal on an idea of Highland life that was untrue, but which appealed to the wide southern public, since it conferred an aura of authenticity on popular novels, brought wildernesses closer to a domestic setting, those who had been identified as rebels, dangerous Jacobites, becoming romantic heroes instead.

In addition to the accounts related to royal visits, numerous travelogues were published throughout the nineteenth century. As we saw, the interest in Scotland's antiquities had begun in the late seventeenth-early eighteenth century: already Martin Martin's works *A Late Voyage to St. Kilda* (1698) and *A Description of the Western Islands of Scotland* (1703) made reference to this, and indeed his journeys appear to have been made mainly at the request of Sir Robert Sibbald, the antiquary. Although earlier journeys had been made into the Highlands, it was only in the eighteenth century that their accounts became popular, as is the case with Sir Donald Monro's *Description of the Western Isles of Scotland* (1549), a few copies of which were only printed in 1774. While Thomas Pennant's accounts had a more naturalistic focus (Youngson 1973 and 1974), an antiquarian focus was a common denominator in Bishop Pococke's letters of 1760 (Youngson 1973: 2).

The raging fashion for antiquity also gave rise to satire (Brown 1980: 10);[4]

---

3 Apart from his literary fame, Scott was also very popular because of his role in the rediscovery of the Scottish regalia in 1818.

4 Remarkable were, for instance, Burns' lines 'On the Late Captain Grose's Peregrinations through Scotland, Collecting the Antiquities of that Kingdom', in which he appealed to the 'Land o'Cakes, and brither Scots' to treasure whatever trifling object they might be tempted to throw away, because 'A chield's amang you, taking notes, /And, faith, he'll prent it'. Then in 1821 William Coombe published in London *The Tour of Dr Prosody in search of the Antique and the Picturesque, through Scotland*, which is often reminiscent of Johnson's jaunt.

nonetheless, this interest was made explicit in the 1829 reprint of Petruccio Ubaldini's *Descrittione del Regno di Scotia*, originally published in 1588, as the editor stated:

> It is obvious [Ubaldini] has borrowed so largely from Hector Boece, that his book is little more than an enlarged paraphrase of that historian's *Scotorum Regni Descriptio*[5] .... Although this certainly detracts greatly from the value and originality of the *Descrittione*, it is still one of those *curious trifles* which Walpole describes as at all times acceptable to the antiquary, and as such alone it is presented to the Bannatyne Club (1588/ 1829: vii).

In the nineteenth century Scottish literature achieved what is arguably its zenith, with authors like Scott, Hogg and Stevenson (to name only those who achieved worldwide reputation) producing masterpieces in English, in Scots, and in both languages at once.[6] Indeed, together with antiquities and Ossian, the success of Scott's novels was an incredible boost to the recognition of Scotland as a tourist destination. This is shown in Theodor Fontane's accounts (1860/1989: 129 and 159), in which explicit reference is made to Rob Roy and to the 'Fair Maid of Perth'. However, Fontane, who visited Scotland in 1858, was also a keen observer of how Highland culture had been changing in the light of Lowland expectation. He remarked on the widespread presence of tartan items in an Inverness shop (1860/1989: 183), and even Culloden Moor is first presented through a quotation from Burns' 'Drumossie Moor' (1860/ 1989: 187). As regards the metropolitan face of Scotland, his notes on the Old Town of Edinburgh and on its *Spukhäuser* (1860/1989: 22, 83) seem to anticipate Robert Louis Stevenson's *Edinburgh: Picturesque Notes* (1879).

Foreign observers also linked Scottish culture to other European realities; for instance, the Genevan Louis-Albert Necker de Saussure, whose *Voyage en Ecosse et aux Iles Hébrides* (1821) outlined both geological similarities and religious affinity between Scotland and Calvinist Switzerland (Utz 1992 and 1995).[7] Of course the Ossianic quest had been one of the main interests during

---

5 Indeed, Hume Brown openly defines it as 'a barefaced appropriation of Hector Boece, with scarcely an independent statement which we may regard as the result of his own observation' (1891: xiii).

6 The various ways in which one language or the other was used for stylistic purposes has been analysed in a thorough survey by Emma Letley (1988). As regards the present study, this theme is deliberately left aside, as my main purpose is to investigate language use and linguistic attitudes in non-literary contexts. On the other hand, it is acknowledged that the role of literature was obviously crucial in influencing speakers' perceptions of 'pure forms' and of dialect: for instance, another important consequence of Scott's success was that language became crystallised in a stereotypical view of quaintness, since his Scots-speaking characters were generally old, or uneducated, or their stories were set in the past.

7 Necker also established a political connection, calling Wallace 'le Guillaume Tell d'Ecosse' (Utz 1995: 35).

Necker's tour, which took place in 1807, so in his work we find a chapter on Gaelic, but Lowland Scots also drew his attention. Necker highlighted its phonological, lexical and morphological specificity (guttural consonants, Norse and French borrowings, diminutives) and concluded that it was not 'a bastard jargon, but an English dialect' (Utz 1992: 63; 1995: 52–53).

As a matter of fact, travelogues did occasionally include remarks on linguistic differences between English and Scots, but these were typically seen as a source of puzzlement for English visitors. The image that was provided generally fitted the stereotype of the shrewd mountaineer whose sense of humour strikes the townspeople as a curiosity even when the anecdotes refer to gentry or indeed noblemen. In this sense the accounts published by Catherine Sinclair (1859) appear to be emblematic:[8] the kind of Scots that is represented in her accounts is promptly recognisable as the kind of dialect made popular by Scott's novels, but no attempt appears to have been made to achieve accuracy, so that the language of both Highlanders and Lowlanders is reported in the same way, with the exception of Doric, as shown in the following paragraphs:

> Two country folk in Bamff-shire working together while a grand equipage passed by, one said, 'Fa's tat, Janet?' 'Och, do ye no' ken him? Tat's Lord Fife!' 'Lord Fife!' she exclaimed, 'fa's he?' 'Do ye no mind him? Braco tat was!' 'Braco!' she cried, 'tat's him tat has his cellars fu' o' goud, and pits it by in spade fu's.'

> When Foote first travelled in Scotland, he asked a Highland theatrical prompter about the habits of his country, and at last said, 'I conclude, then, that with about £300 a-year, one may live here like a gentleman?' His informant thoughtfully replied, 'I canna tell ye, for I never ken'd a man here wha spent the half o' that sum, an' I dinna ken what may come into ony body's head wha wad attempt to squander the hale o't.' (Sinclair 1859: 338)

On the other hand, these accounts also stressed the romantic aspect of the scenery, and though they often recurred to stereotypes such as the fact that 'Some of the poor in Skye have scarcely a notion of any food but oatmeal' (Sinclair 1859: 181), they contributed to the creation of an idealised picture of Scotland which persists to this day: rough landscape with ruins, intriguing ghost stories, excellent whisky, deer-stalking and 'idle tourists'.[9]

---

8 For instance, on one occasion the author says: 'I was recently amused to hear that the late Lord Dalhousie, not being able at once to understand the difference between St. Peter's and the Vatican, a friend made it plain by saying, "Why, my lord, only recollect that St. Peter's is the kirk, and the Vatican the manse"' (1859: 307).

9 We owe this label to Sinclair (1859: 305). The extent to which this view clashed with reality is possibly shown by the fact that the overwhelming success of Scott's Waverley novels coincided with the time of the Highland Clearances (Ward 1998: 193-194; Dossena 2000/2001).

Still on the linguistic level, Catherine Sinclair mentioned the following peculiarities of what she called 'our dialect':

> An English clergyman, anxious to make himself acquainted with our customs ... but not knowing enough of our dialect, to be aware that in many parts of the north, the letter 'i' is pronounced like an 'e', stopped one day where some women were collected round a pond of muddy water, preparing it, in fact, for steeping lint, and inquired anxiously what they were doing. The reply led him to suppose that some unheard-of penance was inflicted in the Highlands at particular seasons, as the women replied ..., 'We are preparing for Lent, Sir!' ... On another occasion, a stranger was amazed to hear a strict divine, when intending to inculcate on his congregation the propriety of receiving a hint properly, deliver his advice in these words, 'My friends! Be ready at all times to take a hunt;' and I remember seeing an Englishman quite perplexed, when told at a party in Scotland, that all the guests were 'kent people,' not meaning to imply that they came from the county of Kent, but merely that they were well-known personages. (1859: 97–98)

In addition to phonology and morphology, vocabulary differences were frequently presented as a source of misunderstanding between English and Scots:

> In Scotland a sore is called an 'income;' and an English tourist would be rather perplexed if a beggar came up to him ... asking charity ... 'because she had a great *income* on her hand'. A legacy to any charitable fund is called a 'mortification;' and you might hear a truly benevolent person say ... 'he is happy to hear the blind have got a great mortification in Mr. Smith's will.' If a Scotch person says, 'will you speak a word to me,' he means, will you listen; but if he says to a servant, 'I am about to give you a good *hearing*,' that means a severe scold. The Highland expression for two gentlemen bowing to each other, amused us extremely on a late occasion, when a Scotchman said to his friend, 'I saw your brother last week exchange hats with Lord Melbourne in Bond Street!' (Sinclair 1859: 98–99)

Similarly, some nineteenth-century travelogues humorously introduced the topic of midges: according to Roberts (1991: 102): 'It could be argued that Scotland became a target of humour at about the same time as shooting became fashionable through Victoria and Albert taking up summer residence at Balmoral'.

Humorous travelogues also appeared at the beginning of the twentieth century: an example is Sir Archibald Geikie's *Scottish Reminiscences*, published in 1904, in which various episodes are reported and dialogues including dialect sentences are quoted in order to enhance the comic effect. A similar technique was also adopted by Ratcliffe Barnett in his *Reminiscences of Old Scots Folk* (1913). From the sociolinguistic point of view, in Geikie's text we find one comment which describes a speaker's Doric as 'pure and racy' (1904: 295) and a rather perfunctory observation on the decline of Gaelic in the Highlands (1904: 268), although the author does point out that it is unfortunate that 'the Sassenach hardly ever takes the trouble to learn even a smattering of Gaelic' (1904: 269).

Echoing eighteenth-century prescriptivists, Scottish observers often stressed the necessity to overcome the provincial accent. Hugh Miller, referring to the turn of the century in his article 'Edinburgh an Age Ago', of 1856, pointed out that

> The intellect of the country ... required only a fitting vehicle in which to address that extended public to which the Union had taught our country-men to look; ... Scotsmen bred in Scotland had great difficulty in mastering that essentially foreign language the English. (Miller 1856/1897: 377)[10]

Previously, Elisabeth Isabella Spence had expressed the following remark:

> I cannot help thinking that the grace of oratory is restrained by the Scotch accent. It is true, in polished circles, all vulgar and broad idiom is banished, yet a certain high tone accompanies the articulation, which from the mouth of females, in the estimation of the English, who are never capable of feeling the force and *naiveté* of their language, seem to divest them of that softness of address which ought to characterise them. (1811: 156–157)

The sociolinguistic value of an 'appropriate' accent appeared to be specially prominent for lady-speakers, whose 'softness of address' was blurred by provincial intonation, though this might actually be seen as a sign of linguistic 'force and naiveté', but for the reaction of English listeners. Consequently, it was highly recommended that the local accent should be discarded, and the author provided her readers with two success stories: one is her own uncle's, 'a native of Aberdeen, a country said to have the worst accent in Scotland',[11] whose elocution as a preacher had been praised by Garrick himself (1811: 159), while the other refers to 'a lady not far removed from Glasgow, who, without being educated, or passing any time in England, had overcome all provincial accent and high tone; ... her fine sense taught her, that elegance of speech and softness of manners, are amongst the most winning qualifications of a woman' (1811: 159–160).

Elisabeth Spence thus identifies linguistic propriety with the kind of accomplishment that can turn a woman into a lady, but at this point she reveals her

---

10 Hugh Miller (1802–1856) is described by Cochrane (1897: 529) as 'one of the most remark-able of our self-taught writers'; in 1834 he published *Scenes and Legends in the North of Scotland* and in 1840 he was called to Edinburgh as editor of the *Witness* newspaper.

11 However, Spence then hastens to add that she does not agree with this opinion (1811: 159).

debt to eighteenth-century views,[12] since she inserts a note in which she explains that 'Dr Beattie, with great liberality, dwells in several of his letters on the disadvantages, not merely in speaking, but particularly in writing, under which a Scotsman labours from his provincial idiom' (1811: 160). We recognise the same kind of approach – indeed, the same words – that had appeared in the Regulations of the Select Society:[13] the presentation of linguistic 'improvement' as a source of social benefits and success.

By mid-century the decline of the vernacular appeared to be impossible to stop, and Henry Cockburn even observed:

> Every year makes me the more afraid that henceforth Burns' glory must contract, not extend; and this solely because the sphere of the Scotch language, and the course of Scotch feelings and ideas, is speedily and rapidly abridging, even in Scotland. The lower orders still speak Scotch, but even among them its flavour is not so fresh and natural as it was fifty years ago, particularly in towns (also quoted by Fyfe 1942: 402).

Cockburn's view was deeply pessimistic, and indeed he found that the vernacular ought to be treated 'as a dead language', teaching it 'as a regular branch of education', lest readers and speakers should lose an opportunity to understand 'the habits and characters of one of the most picturesque of European nations' and lest Scotland should lose itself: 'Instead of being what we are, we become a poor part of England' (also quoted by Fyfe 1942: 403).[14]

As we see, there are two key themes represented here: on the one hand, we have an appreciation of Scottish culture as an element of national(istic) identity, while on the other Scotland's picturesque nature is portrayed according to canons that had become increasingly popular and that encompassed language. Further on, Cockburn described Scots as a 'picturesque and delightful language', the loss of which is regarded as 'a national calamity' (quoted by Fyfe 1942: 423). This observation was actually taken up by Sir Archibald Geikie (1904: 368–369), who expressed his regret at the 'decay of the old national language – the Doric of Burns and Scott'. The reference to literary models is significant, as is the remark that even in the country the younger generations cannot read Burns' poems without referring to a glossary. Although local accents persist, Geikie finds that the loss of old words and phrases is specially deplorable[15] and the 'affectation of what is supposed to be English

12 On the issue of the relationship between grammar and politeness, see also Fitzmaurice (1998).
13 Cf. Chapter 4.
14 A similar fear had been expressed by Sir John Sinclair, but rather than advocate the preservation of Lowland Scots features he had stressed the importance of asserting identity through those that were in fact Highland symbols, such as tartan (cf. Devine 1994: 98).
15 Another account published in 1909, Holmes' *Literary Tours in the Highlands and Islands of Scotland*, also took comprehension of Burns' poetry as a measurement of linguistic diffusion. He found that 'Very fine Scotch is still spoken in the rural districts of Ayrshire', where 'Burns's dialect words are in daily use, at least by the older generation' (1909: 103). However, this

pronunciation ... is sometimes irresistibly ludicrous'. In Geikie's remarks we also note that he appears to refer to the use of 'overt Scotticisms' in upper-class speech:

> I can remember men and women in good society, who if they did not ordinarily speak pure Scots, at least habitually introduced Scots words and phrases, laying emphasis on them as telling expressions, for which they knew no English equivalents (Geikie 1904: 369).

The number of these, however, had been decreasing considerably, and since the time of Lord Cockburn linguistic decay is said to have made 'huge strides'. Cockburn's anecdotes of elderly ladies using Scots expressively (1856/1971: 58–67) were then resumed in an undated anonymous text (Anon. n.d.: 2; 29-31). The linguistic focus is provided in comments relating to change in dialect 'and, in consequence, ... change in regard to Scottish humour or wit' (Anon. n.d.: 4), and both changes are described with regret:

> I cherish a great love of the old Scottish language. How expressive, how beautiful are many of its turns! You can't translate them. ... I cannot help thinking that a change of national language involves also a change of national character. ... There was a dry Scottish humour which we fear [Scots speakers'] successors do not inherit. (Anon. n.d.: 25–26; 33)

In the description of language change, the author inevitably mentioned Beattie's and Sinclair's collections of Scotticisms, pointing out the extent to which the decrease in their number is related to their occurrence in the usage of 'less refined' speakers:

> We mark in the course of fifty years how some disappear altogether; others become more and more rare, and of all of them we may say, I think that the specimens of them are to be looked for every year more in the descending classes of society. (Anon. n.d.: 36)

Possibly in order to 'entertain' his audience, the author then went on to present a letter in which a number of Scotticisms were included, so that readers might see 'the sort of puzzle it would be to a young person of the present day – one of what we may call the new school' (Anon. n.d.: 37). A letter was then presented which might be the reply to the former; however, this was also written in a style claimed to be just as incomprehensible, due to its recurrent 'fast' – i.e., fashionable – phraseology.

---

remark shows that the situation is changing, and Holmes is indeed in agreement with Geikie when he foresees that 'Book-English will soon push out the relics of the old Scotch tongue. Burns will soon be read by lexicon, even in the shire of Ayr' (1909: 104). Holmes further defended the educated variety of Scottish speech, stating that 'intelligible differences of vocalisation, pitch, and even of vocabulary, are allowable, and at times positively charming' (1909: 105).

Concerning the connection between humour and Scots language, the author also presented a series of stories relating to ministers, beadles, lairds and English travellers in the Highlands. An instance of these is the following, in which the Highlander is made to speak broad Scots:

> An English traveller had gone on a fine Highland road so long, without having seen an indication of fellow travellers, that he became astonished at the solitary character of his journey. ... Our traveller at last coming up to an old man breaking stones, he asked him if there was any traffic in this road – was it at *all* frequented; 'aye', he said, 'it's no ill at that, there was a cadger body yestreen, and there's yoursel to-day.' (Anon. n.d.: 46)

Prescriptivism and 'improvement'

As regards non-literary prose, Donaldson (1986 and 1989) has shown how vital the use of Scots was in the local press.[16] It is therefore possible that, as Williamson (1983: 59) suggests, in many contexts both learners and teachers could 'dialect-switch', although inspectors constantly stressed the fact that the focus was to be on teaching 'English' – cf. also Bailey (1987b). Paterson (1855: 145) claimed that Scots was taught in Ayrshire schools until the Union; however, the terminological confusion that is so obvious even in official records prevents us from accepting this statement at face value. The issue of education and literacy is also taken up by Houston (1989), but the role of English in relation to Scots is not discussed in his paper. Similarly, Anderson (1995: 212–220) describes the teaching of Scottish history in post-Union schools, but only mentions the linguistic problems that concerned the Gaelic-speaking communities.

In fact, in the nineteenth century the role of English as a social dialect became increasingly pervasive. McKnight (1968: 406) attributes the first definition of propriety to George Campbell's *Philosophy of Rhetoric* (1776), in which it was claimed that 'Good usage must be *national* and *reputable* and *present*'. At the same time, the idealisation of rural dialects as 'pure' and therefore 'agreeable' continued in opposition to an increasing stigmatisation of the 'coarseness' of urban working-class accents,[17] although at the turn of the century the use of Scots on the part of judges was still regarded as a sign of authority and, as Kay puts it, 'a reaction against the fashion for precious gentility' (1986: 108).[18]

16 In these texts the characters who are made to speak Broad Scots are often set in humorous contexts, as may be seen from the pseudonyms with which they are presented (cf. Tammy Trampalot, 'just come hame frae a grand pedestrian toor i' the Hielands' – Donaldson 1989: 38) or through the predicaments in which they find themselves (cf. the Jeems Kaye episodes from the Glasgow 'comic' paper *The Bailie* – Donaldson 1989:157–177). A similar trend in contemporary local newspapers is discussed by McClure (1993: 2) and Smith (1995/96: 153).

17 As a matter of fact, Aitken (1982: 41) points out that 'Bad Scots [= urban working-class dialect] comes to notice after the Industrial Revolution'.

18 Kay is here referring to Lord Braxfield and Lord Kames, expressive utterances of both of whom he quotes; the former allegedly was a model for Archie's father in Robert Louis Stevenson's

Prescriptive works continued to be published with significant titles that stressed their sociolinguistic approach; among these, we may cite *The Vulgarities of Speech Corrected: with Elegant Expressions for Provincial and Vulgar English, Scots and Irish; for the use of those who are unacquainted with grammar* (London, 1829); *Scotticisms Corrected* (London, 1855); Alexander Mackie's *Scotticisms Arranged and Corrected* (Aberdeen, 1881); and David Masson's *Use and Abuse of English: a Handbook of Composition* (Edinburgh, 1896; revised by Rosaline Masson in 1924). The popularity of these booklets is shown by the number and frequency of their editions and revisions (cf. Bailey 1996 and Görlach 1999). Their format and low cost also contributed to their diffusion; the structure of their contents clearly emphasised their function as 'usage guides', rather than attempts to describe linguistic varieties, and in some cases the authors actually referred to other 'Dictionaries and works on Grammar' (Anon. 1855: 64).

As Klein (1993) points out, the search for 'politeness' evokes a social context in which a theory of 'conversational manners' has been established. Consequently, the idea of 'politeness' does not only apply to lexical and grammatical correctness, but also to a concept of 'pragmatic correctness' that is typically metropolitan in its outlook. Along similar lines, the development of eighteenth-century prescriptivism in a more and more socially evaluative sense has been outlined by Fitzmaurice (1998). This type of sociolinguistic focus is actually quite obvious in many nineteenth-century grammars. In a booklet published in 1829 in London, *The Vulgarities of Speech Corrected*, we find 'Tell the servant *to speak to me*' classified as 'vulgar Scotch': the 'correct English' form being given as 'Tell the servant I want to speak to him' (p. 240). The first sentence is not ungrammatical in itself, but in the second sentence the introduction of a clause with a verb expressing volition provides a completely different sociological perspective on the pragmatic expression of authority. In fact, McKnight, who dates the publication of this book in 1826, defines it as 'a book of speech etiquette' (1968: 502) and associates the attitude of its anonymous author with those of the scholars who promoted the Society for Pure English in the twentieth century (1968: 505).

The most striking feature of the earliest booklets is their lack of systematic organisation of content, since nouns, verbs, prepositions, adjectives, idioms and syntactic features all appear in random order, as in Hume's list. Indeed, many of Hume's examples are taken almost verbatim. For instance, in *The Vulgarities of Speech Corrected* (1829) there are more than 200 entries arranged in two columns, 'Vulgar Scotch' and 'Correct English', in which a number[19] of

---

Weir of Hermiston, a novel in which the contrast between the father, a very strict judge, and his sensitive son is also mirrored in the latter's use of English as opposed to the former's use of Scots. Anecdotes of Braxfield's forceful use of Scots were also reported by Cockburn (1856/ 1971: 113–117).

19 I have identified 25 items, i.e. 12.5% of the total number, included with no or minimal variations in the new list.

Hume's Scotticisms are included, among them the following:

- p. 234 – *Annual rent* of money   Interest of money.
- p. 235 – *He craved* him *for debt*   He dunned him.
- p. 236 – *Dubiety*   Doubt.
- p. 236 – *Fresh* weather   Open weather.
- p. 238 – *Butter and bread*   Bread and butter.
- p. 239 – *Proven – Improven*   Proved – Improved.
- p. 240 – *Paper, pen, and ink*   Pens, ink, and paper.

In *Scotticisms Corrected* (1855), which contains 565 entries, occur the following items, together with many others that had also been included in Hume's list:[20]

- 3.   Has the tailor brought my *big* coat? say, *great* coat.
- 18.   He has handed him over the *superplus*: say, the *surplus*, or *overplus*.
- 22.   He showed me great *discretion*: say, *civility*.
- 44.   He was very angry *at* me: say, *with* me.
- 66.   Come and sit *into* the fire: say, *near* the fire.
- 92.   The story may be read in *Herodote*: say, in *Herodotus*.
- 230.   I *think much shame at him*: say, I *am much*, or, *greatly ashamed of him*.

Unlike Hume's list, these works present entries that are often expanded into sample sentences, or even into anecdotes, since they have an explicitly didactic aim and therefore need to be made as memorable as possible. For example, Mackie's text claims: 'This little volume is intended as a school book, and, … as a book of reference in the home' (Mackie 1881: vii). The author then acknowledges his sources (Beattie, first of all, but also Mitchell, Angus, Bain and Sprague) and arranges his contents according to the type of errors: incorrect grammar (as in: W*ere you ringing?* instead of 'Did you ring?'); pleonasm (as in: *No passage down this way*); impropriety in the use of single words (as in: *I do not mind that I ever saw you before*); 'violation of idiom, where words individually correct are given in un-English combinations' (1881: 3).

What is specially interesting in this text is the adamantly prescriptive attitude of the author, who admits that Scots 'may be pithy, … but the usage of polite society in England holds supreme sway in Literature, and we must follow the fashion of the time' (1881: 3). Even though the choice between Scots *butter and bread* and English 'bread and butter' is 'a matter of convention … [,] still the Scotch must yield to English usage. … So, "who *do you sit under?*" might easily be justified as figurative language, but being without the stamp of English authority, it must give way to "whose church do you attend?"' (1881: 3–4).

20 Although in this case the percentage of entries taken from Hume's list is lower (7.4%, i.e. 42 items out of 565), it is still interesting to see that they are reported in a very similar way.

In Masson's book Scotticisms only form a part of the third chapter (1896/ 1929: 41-52), together with 'English colloquialisms, slang, vulgarisms' and 'advertisement English', whereas the other chapters focus on more general rules of usage (punctuation, common errors, figures of speech, English verse and rules of composition). However, their independent status as stigmatised elements puts them in the tradition of the previous prescriptive lists. Also in this case the 103 marked items are placed in a sample letter with annotations; as in the case of the instances quoted by Anon. (n.d.), both sender and addressee are women, as if it were implied that it is particularly women who should (and actually do) aim at prestige forms. This time, however, there does not appear to be any age difference between the two correspondents, since the aim is not to present different varieties (one geographically marked, the other socially marked) in the same framework, but simply to provide a context for 'errors' to be singled out.

As regards the relationship of this list with Hume's, this is made explicit in the Preface to the first edition, where the author also outlines the changes that have taken place:

> It is a century and a half since David Hume compiled a list of the Scot-ticisms ... then most common; and later lists are to be found in various places. In looking at the older lists, one is struck by the fact that many of the Scotticisms reported to have been once in use have either totally disappeared or ceased to be thought of as Scotticisms. Not a few real Scotticisms, however, some of them not mentioned at all in the older lists, do survive (1896/1929: vi-vii).

It is beyond the scope of the present study to provide an exact list of what 'new' Scotticisms appear in Masson's list that had not occurred in any of the previous sources. However, it is interesting to observe that the author also mentions the fact that some items have 'ceased to be thought of as Scotticisms', thus signalling that they had become geographically (if not socially) unmarked. The use of overt Scotticisms is also described, though the prescriptive attitude remains prominent:

> Even if a Scotticism or a provincialism be grammatically defensible, – even if it be a better and more expressive phrase than its national equivalent, as it often is, – it must be avoided.
>
> A Scotticism is a word or expression which is used only by Scottish persons, and which, being regarded as peculiar and provincial, is there-fore inadmissible, unless used consciously and with a purpose. (1896/ 1929: 40)

Lexicography

The persistence of the antiquarian fashion into the nineteenth century was also reflected in the continuing search for 'pure Saxon' in linguistic matters. Thomas Guthrie praised the way in which children had once been taught in Scotland by means of the Shorter Catechism and the Book of Proverbs, because especially the latter contains 'quite a repertory of monosyllables and pure Saxon — 'English undefiled' ' (quoted by Fyfe 1942: 517).

A similar line was followed by James Paterson, whose *Origin of the Scots and the Scottish Language* (1855) argued in favour of Pictish as the original 'Scottish dialect' (1855: 109) and linked 'Dano-Saxon', i.e. 'the northern Saxon of England', to Icelandic, 'which is the elder branch of the Teutonic, and, of course, the senior of the Anglo-Saxon' (1855: 119). Paterson thus acknowledged Scandinavian influence on Scots, especially on poetic language, but he also claimed that Scots was not 'wholly indebted to the Gothic ... the great body of the people, ancient Picts and Britons, being Celtic' (1855: 135), 'hence the blending of both characteristics in the poetry, music, and language, of the Scots' (1855: 137). At the same time, Paterson emphasised the number of Gaelic words borrowed into Scots; as regards morphology, instead, he referred to Alexander Geddes' 'Dissertation on the Scoto-Saxon Dialect' which had appeared in the first volume of the *Transactions of the Society of Antiquaries of Scotland* (1855: 150). This dissertation stressed the role of diminutives and augmentatives in Scots, categories which brought the language close to classical models, but lamented the lack of inflexion and attributed this defect to the influence of Chaucer, 'for in Wiclef, who preceded him but a few years, we find many traces of pure Saxonism' (1855: 153). In general, Geddes found the 'Scoto-Saxon' more harmonious than the Anglo-Saxon[21] and indeed Paterson himself pointed out that 'We have often listened with delight to the Scottish language, when spoken by some octogenarian of the higher and better educated classes' (1855: 165).[22]

Paterson's theory challenged a previous one, according to which the Scandinavian influence had been paramount in the development of Scots;[23] this

---

21 In this respect the only drawback that is acknowledged is the persistence of the 'guttral ch'; even this, however, may 'become a beauty in the hand of a skilful orator' (1855: 155). Paterson followed Geddes' text very closely (cf. Geddes 1792), though he did not take up Geddes' view according to which 'The neglect of cultivating the Scoto-Saxon tongue has been attended with some detriment to the English language; that many words and phrases of great energy and beauty are still preserved in the former which the latter wants, and which all its borrowed treasure but imperfectly supplies' (1792: 404). Finally Geddes included a passionate appeal to collect 'The old terms as soon as possible, and from the mouths of the oldest inhabitants' (1792: 439).

22 The identification of the speaker appears to be highly significant: first of all, he or she is an elderly person, which evokes a time when language was 'less corrupt', and, secondly, their usage expresses prestige in relation to their social status and their level of education.

23 On this controversy cf. also Collin (1862).

theory had been based on Bede's account of early settlements in Britain and had been put forward by John Pinkerton and James Sibbald, the eighteenth-century antiquaries. It was then taken up by one of the leading figures in Scottish lexicography, John Jamieson, who claimed that the Picts had Scandinavian origins and presented his views on the origin of Scots in a very lengthy study of etymologies of names and place-names in the 'Introduction' to his *Etymological Dictionary of the Scottish Language*, which appeared in two volumes in 1808[24] (1808/1840: xii–xiii; cf. also Kidd 1993: 251).

This early instance of modern Scottish lexicography on historical principles was seen as a laudable attempt to preserve old forms.[25] Indeed, Walter Scott praised Jamieson as an antiquary, but he also described him as a man 'full of auld Scottish cracks' (Brown 1980: 38). This also allows us to observe the connection between antiquarianism and nationalism: the search for antiquity implicitly meant a search for authenticity, originality, and consequently higher status, almost to compensate for the disappointment that the Union had engendered.

The biographical note at the beginning of the 1840 edition emphasises the fact that Jamieson had at first held the widespread view that Scots was just a corrupt dialect of English; however, an exchange with the Danish professor Grim Thorkelin had led him to investigate the matter in considerable depth. Thorkelin claimed that during his stay in Angus and Sutherland he had come across 'between three and four hundred words purely Gothic' (1808/1840: 8).[26] Jamieson thus began to collect 'all the remarkable or uncouth words of the district'. When he learned that the Vicar of Epsom, the Rev. Mr Boucher, was pursuing the same activity, he considered selling his materials to him, but then he realised that his competitor's view of Scots would 'degrade it to the level of the English provincial dialects', so the transaction did not go ahead and the competition was finally ended by Boucher's death.[27]

At the outset, Jamieson identified the specificity of Scottish vocabulary in the legal register, but then he also stated that his work would 'serve to mark the difference between words which may be called classical, and others merely colloquial; and between both of these, as far as they are proper, and such as

---

24 A *Supplement* of two further volumes was published in 1825, then an edition in two volumes appeared in 1840; a four-volume edition was issued with additions in 1879-1882 and another *Supplement* was released in 1887.

25 However, Skeat (1912/1968: 43-44) criticised the introductory 'Dissertation on the Origin of the Scottish Language' as a piece of writing 'in which wholly mistaken and wrongheaded views are supported with great ingenuity ... a notable feat of card-building'. The latter comment is taken from the introduction to the 1879 edition.

26 Thorkelin's words are quoted explicitly, so that the emphasis laid on the link between Scots and Gothic, and the consequent antiquity of the former, is highlighted. Inevitably, there is also the typical disparaging reference to Johnson's supposed contempt for the Scottish language, which is ascribed to 'ignorance or prejudice'.

27 The whole text of the biographical note is, in fact, a patriotic celebration of Jamieson's achievement as Scotland's 'National Lexicographer' (1808/1840: 9).

belong to a still lower class, being mere corruptions, cant terms, or puerilities' (1808/1840: ii). Jamieson purports to identify social varieties in Scots, thus highlighting the existence of a 'proper' standard and of vulgar speech.

Consequently, for the 'colloquial' items he included quotations of humble origin, and his use of 'mean' sources marked a turning point in the history of lexicography.[28] Towards the end of the century, though, criticism was also directed at Jamieson's apparent lack of system. For instance, in 1898 J. B. Montgomerie-Fleming wrote a letter to the editor of the *Glasgow Herald* in which he summarised the problem as follows:

> We all know the story of the decent old Scotchman who, having unexpec-
> tedly succeeded to a considerable fortune, thought it the correct thing to go
> in for a library, and, being found one day deep in a dictionary, declared it
> to be 'a rale interestin' wark, if it just had an index tae it'. Well, Jamieson
> really almost requires an index. (Montgomerie-Fleming 1899: vii)

Montgomerie-Fleming's criticism is introduced with a jocular anecdote complete with humorous 'verbatim' quotation of the protagonist's words, but what is specially interesting is that Montgomerie-Fleming compares Jamieson's dictionary with a newer one, which was to leave a very deep mark in the history of lexicography: Murray and Bradley's *New English Dictionary on Historical Principles* (which had reached letter 'H'), about which Montgomerie-Fleming states that he has found it 'a remarkably good *Scotch* dictionary' (1899: iv).[29]

The *New English Dictionary* would subsequently become world famous as the *Oxford English Dictionary* (OED), and it is intriguing to follow Murray's career both as a lexicographer and as 'the founder of the modern study of Scots, both historical and descriptive' (Aitken 1995/96: 14).[30] As a matter of fact, Murray had also been praised by D. T. Holmes (1909: 104) as the author of 'an illuminating grammar of the language, indicating the various dialects of the Lowlands and their geographical areas'. Holmes was referring to Murray's seminal work *The Dialect of the Southern Counties of Scotland* (1873), a text that was to influence all subsequent studies of the history and the description of Scots.

Aitken (1995/96: 29) points out that Murray was not a linguistic nationalist and actually identified Scots with the northern part of the northern English

---

28 In this sense Jamieson's Dictionary also has an important encyclopaedic value, since many entries provide ethnological information that might otherwise have been lost. This was also to play a significant role in the shaping of McDiarmid's poetry, as is pointed out by Milton (1995/ 96).

29 Aitken (1995/96: 34) ascribes the prominence of the Scots element in the *OED* to the longer tradition of recording Scots rather than other non-standard varieties, opposing this theory to the supposition that this may be due to the provenance of two of the four editors, namely Murray and Craigie.

30 A very compact bio-bibliographical account is provided by Aitken (1995/96), but cf. also Murray (1977).

dialect – thus challenging Jamieson's (and many others') view of Scots as a language – but was against literary corruption of dialect.[31] His new approach to the historical perspective went beyond the previous debates on the Pictish or Saxon origin of Scots and directed its research to the mutual roots of Scots and Northern English; it provided valuable insights into Scots phonology, morphology and syntax. In addition to this, Murray was the first to outline a dialect map that was adopted and adapted by later commentators, including the editors of the *Scottish National Dictionary* and the *Concise Scots Dictionary*, in which the so-called 'Highland Line' marked the geographical distribution of Scots dialects and Highland English.

Into the new century

In spite of literary appreciation and increasing scholarly attention, towards the turn of the century the undesirability of Scots features in speech and prose writing had become so steadfast an idea that the actual survival of Scots was doubted: Robert Louis Stevenson was to describe Scots as a dying language more than a century after the *literati*'s quest for linguistic purity, and even today academic estimates of the actual knowledge and use of the language are often controversial.

When Stevenson introduced the Scots poems in *Underwoods* (1887), he acknowledged both the new dialectological trends that had been establishing themselves and his freedom to use whatever variety of Scots would suit his literary purpose. The exactness of the one and the anarchy of the other – apparently irreconcilable – were reunited in a text the linguistic purity of which was professedly dubious, but which would provide a contemporary instance of an 'illustrious and malleable tongue', by then – apparently – inexorably waning:

> Among our new dialecticians, the local habitat of every dialect is given to the square mile. I could not emulate this nicety if I desired; for I simply wrote my Scots as well as I was able, not caring if it hailed from Lauderdale or Angus, from the Mearns or Galloway; if I had ever heard a good word, I used it without shame; and when Scots was lacking, or the rhyme jibbed, I was glad (like my betters) to fall back on English. ... Let the precisians call my speech that of the Lothians. And if it be not pure, alas! what matters it? The day draws near when this illustrious and malleable tongue shall be quite forgotten; and Burns's Ayrshire, and Dr. Macdonald's Aberdeen-awa', and Scott's brave, metropolitan utterance will be all

31 Aitken (1995/96: 30) mentions that Murray's favourite example of this was Burns' celebrated 'Scots wha hae', which he called 'fancy Scotch', i.e. 'the English 'Scots who have' spelled as Scotch ... The vernacular is ... 'Scots at hes', which Burns evidently considered ungrammatical'. On Burns' linguistic attitude, see Chapter 5.

equally the ghosts of speech. Till then I would love to have my hour as a native Maker, and be read by my own countryfolk in our own dying language: an ambition surely rather of the heart than of the head, so restricted as it is in prospect of endurance, so parochial in bounds of space.

The modernity of these comments is also reflected in Stevenson's discussion of orthographic conventions in his Scots poems:

The Scots tongue has an orthography of its own, lacking neither 'authority nor author.' Yet the temptation is great to lend a little guidance to the bewildered Englishman. Some simple phonetic artifice might defend your verses from barbarous mishandling, and yet not injure any vested interest. So it seems at first; but there are rocks ahead. Thus, if I wish the diphthong OU to have its proper value, I may write OOR instead of OUR; many have done so and lived, and the pillars of the universe remained unshaken. But if I did so, and came presently to DOUN, which is the classical Scots spelling of the English DOWN, I should begin to feel uneasy; and if I went on a little farther, and came to a classical Scots word, like STOUR or DOUR or CLOUR, I should know precisely where I was – that is to say, that I was out of sight of land on those high seas of spelling reform in which so many strong swimmers have toiled vainly. To some the situation is exhilarating; as for me, I give one bubbling cry and sink. The compromise at which I have arrived is indefensible, and I have no thought of trying to defend it. As I have stuck for the most part to the proper spelling, I append a table of some common vowel sounds which no one need consult; and just to prove that I belong to my age and have in me the stuff of a reformer, I have used modification marks throughout. Thus I can tell myself, not without pride, that I have added a fresh stumbling-block for English readers, and to a page of print in my native tongue, have lent a new uncouthness. SED NON NOBIS.

To describe phonological remarks as summarised in a table 'which no one need consult', but which lends 'a new uncouthness' to the Scots language, is a superbly ironic way of signalling a feature which had by then become recurrent in anthologies of Scots poems and in Scots books. The exotic character of Scots as a literary language was stressed through ubiquitous glossaries, and spelling and pronunciation guides. It appeared that Pinkerton's aim to destroy Scots as a language with everyday currency, while preserving it as a literary medium, had been virtually achieved; in Stevenson's view, one day posterity would find Scots words as incomprehensible as runes:

> ...
> Their sense, that aince was braw an' plain,
> Tint a'thegether,

> Like runes upon a standin' stane
> Amang the heather.
>> ('The Maker to Posterity', *Underwoods*, 1887)

And yet, his skilful use of Scots in his fiction and even in his private correspondence[32] proved that Scots was still a powerful medium (cf. McClure 2000: 33–37). In fact, literary Scots had actually been praised in the essay on Robert Burns that appeared in the *Cornhill Magazine* in 1879 and was then included in *Familiar Studies of Men and Books*, of 1882:

> Burns, like most great artists, proceeded from a school and continued a tradition; only the school and tradition were Scotch, and not English. While the English language was becoming daily more pedantic and inflexible, and English letters more colourless and slack, there was another dialect in the sister country, and a different school of poetry tracing its descent, through King James I., from Chaucer. The dialect alone accounts for much; for it was then written colloquially, which kept it fresh and supple; and, although not shaped for heroic flights, it was a direct and vivid medium for all that had to do with social life.

As a matter of fact, this perception of Scots as a 'direct and vivid medium for all that had to do with social life' was to prove very relevant also in the following century.

---

32 This is particularly significant in the letters addressed to Charles Baxter in the Thomson/Johnson saga – cf. Booth/Mehew (1994) and Dossena (2002).

CHAPTER SEVEN

Vernacular Items and Contemporary Usage

Descriptions of Scots in the early twentieth century

The value of Scots as a poetic medium, especially in the days of Dunbar, was emphasised in many studies,[1] so this provided further opportunities for a philological approach to the language. One of the earliest in the twentieth century was George Gregory Smith's *Specimens of Middle Scots* (1902), in whose Introduction we find a 75-page description of Middle Scots phonology, vocabulary and syntax and of its relationship with Celtic, Scandinavian, French and Latin.

While the Scandinavian influence on Scots had also been outlined by Flom (1900), the Gothic background was stressed by Colville (1909: vi), who claimed that 'The speech of Bishop Wulfila's flock is as intelligible to the Scot now as, say, that of the Cumberland dalesman'. Colville described his task as 'scholarly and patriotic' (1909: v) and, after tracing an outline of the convergence between Scots and English, deplored the loss of vernacular forms with instances of expressive usage in different circumstances and complemented his exemplification as follows(1909: 86–87):

This comparative list shows how difficult it is to do justice in English to a group of graphic descriptive epithets:

Scots.		English.
blate,	feebly rendered as	coy, shy
gleg,	'	'cute
dweeble,	'	pliable, lithe
dowie,	'	sad, in Elizabethan and Miltonic sense
fikie,	'	fastidious
furthie,	'	abundantly hospitable
couthie,	'	kindly
fashiss,	'	ill to please
wersh,	'	insipid
bauch,	'	dull (in surface)
croose,	'	cocky.

1 A notable exception is perhaps Chiari, who stated: 'The greatest works of Scottish literature, with the exception of those of Dunbar and Burns, have been written in the English language' (n.d.: 84).

The English presentation of negative qualities wants the vigour of these:-

Scots.	*English.*
feckless	feeble
fushonless	without virtue or grit
menshless	immoderate, insatiable
thowless	handless
wairdless	thriftless
taebetless	benumbed

As far as phonology is concerned, in 1912 William Grant published a text which, in spite of an apparently descriptive title, *The Pronunciation of English in Scotland*, was certainly prescriptive in its aim to be 'a Phonetic Manual for the use of students in Scottish Training Colleges and Junior Student Centres, ... teachers of English of all grades in ... Scottish schools, to lawyers and ministers and all those who, in the course of their calling, have to engage in public speaking' (1912/1970: v). The didactic aim was also extended to learners of English as a foreign language:

> Foreigners, too, may find that the more conservative pronunciation of educated Scotland as depicted in this volume, is easier to acquire than the Southern type of English, and all students of language should be interested in the study of the Scottish variety of Standard English. (Grant 1912/1970: v)

Grant's model was 'the speech of the educated middle classes of Scotland' (1912/1970: vi), and although the sociolinguistic attitude is reminiscent of older views, this acknowledgement of the existence of a Scottish variety of Standard English and a scientific approach to its description are remarkably modern.

As we saw in the case of Wilson (1915, 1923 and 1926), the scholars' focus was mainly on the peculiarities of specific dialects. This, for instance, was also the case with Watson's study (1923), the subtitle of which clearly stated the limits of the investigation, both in terms of geographical distribution and in terms of methodological selectivity: *The Roxburghshire Word-Book, Being a Record of the Special Vernacular Vocabulary of the County of Roxburgh, with an Appendix of Specimens*. On the other hand, the linguistic competence in the vernacular of Aberdeenshire schoolchildren was taken to be the expression of the liveliness of Scots vocabulary in 1930, when William Will published a paper read at a meeting of the Vernacular Circle of the Burns Club of London, in which he presented an account of how lexical loss and lexical change had been taking place in North-East Scotland. Some Scots forms appear in the very first part of his paper:

The family lum hats, raikit oot only for marriages and funerals, may be left to accumulate a little more Scottish dust. ... although a number of expressive words are dwinin, Scots is far from being kistit. If, as some language undertakers say, the doric is dead, we meet in the presence of a very lively corp. (Will 1930: 1)

This opening, laced with Scots forms to signal the vitality of the language under discussion, is possibly a way to capture the attention of the audience. However, Will does consider both words that seem to have fallen out of use (e.g., *bauckie*, bat) and reasons why they may have been lost. For instance, the fact that children learn the English names of plants and animals from books at school (Will 1930: 24) is singled out as something that will cause old local forms to be forgotten. The survey is thus intended to outline ways in which certain items of vocabulary disappear and to launch an appeal for their retention, lest 'our people in the not distant future [should be] unable to read the literature of their own land, without a glossary' (Will 1930: 33).

Once more, the link between language and literature was perceived to be specially valuable, hence the Scottish Education Department was called upon to promote the study of modern Scots literature in schools (1930: 34). This, however, did not necessarily imply a reassessment of Scots as an everyday spoken language. In 1909 Holmes commented on the book, *Wee Macgregor*, 'a brave and amusing attempt to phonograph the talk of a Glasgow boy of the lower middle class', saying that 'the unlovely speech employed by the author is, happily, quite unlike the careful and deliberate speech of the educated citizen of Glasgow or Paisley' (1909: 104–105).

At the same time, anthologies of vernacular verse are good instances of the patriotic attitude that characterised the 'Vernacular Revival' in the first half of the twentieth century. Among these, Henderson explicitly referred to Hugh MacDiarmid's belief that 'old words and idioms [could] be used in modern verse' and attacked the habit of complacent enjoyment of pastoral lyrics associated with Burns Suppers, stating that 'Burns's success chained Scots to the parish pump' (1931: 4–5). In order to overcome this type of parochialism, it was important that the vitality of Scots as a speech-medium should be acknowledged and that schools should 'make a far more liberal use of Scottish Literature' (1931: 4, 10). An appeal to schoolteachers was also included in the Introduction to a later anthology (Macwhannell 1937: 16), but with a totally different starting point: schools were seen as places where Scots literature should be preserved because 'the Vernacular, ... though not now a spoken language, is still a language of literature – brimful of couthy and sappy words and pithy phrases' (1937: 15).[2]

The lexicographic enterprises of the nineteenth century were providing a fruitful background for a series of other collections aimed at the preservation

2 Cf. also Williamson (1983: 76).

of vernacular forms. One of the earliest was the *Scots Dialect Dictionary*, compiled by Alexander Warrack in 1911, with an introductory chapter by William Grant. Both authors acknowledged the relevance that Jamieson's, Murray's and Craigie's studies had had in the preparation of this work, which – although allegedly 'a popular Dictionary' (1911: vi) – comprised an interesting awareness of variation across space within the same area, hence the Introduction focused on the morpho-syntactic and phonological features of Scots dialects and referred to the Dialect Committee, whose collections of lexical items and their usage would contribute forming the basis of the *Scottish National Dictionary*.

Robson (1937) began an analysis of the story of 'Mansie Wauch, Tailor in Dalkeith', which had appeared in Blackwood's *Edinburgh Magazine* in October 1824, in order to collate the MS, the printer's proof, and the book-form, so that the phonology of early nineteenth-century Scots could then be studied. However, it appears that the project never went beyond its preparatory stage.

After Warrack's *Dictionary*, Grant and Dixon published a very systematic and thorough study of Scots grammar and syntax: their *Manual of Modern Scots* (1921) has proved of considerable interest to the present day. Lexicography was dramatically enhanced by the work of W. A. Craigie, the third editor of the *Oxford English Dictionary* (*OED*) who would subsequently become one of the main editors of *Dictionary of the Older Scottish Tongue* (*DOST*) and *Scottish National Dictionary* (*SND*).[3] His investigation certainly benefited from the co-operation with Murray, and this also ensured that the standards of the *OED* and of the Scots dictionaries would be comparable. The contribution of Scots to English (especially owing to the success of Burns' poetry and Scott's novels) was also acknowledged: Craigie (1937) listed 108 items and discussed their introduction into southern texts. As in the case of Johnson's Dictionary, it was vocabulary generally pertaining to Highland life and culture (e.g., *clan, slogan*), natural scenery (e.g., *fell*) or the supernatural (e.g., *bogle, wraith, eerie*). Murison (1964: 47) similarly stressed the ethnological value of preserving Scots words through works like the *SND* on the grounds that 'whatever the speech of this country at the beginning of the next century, it is very doubtful whether it will be anything that is recognisably Scottish, at least in the ordinary historical meaning of that term'.[4] Valuable material was also acquired through the work that produced the 'Survey of Scottish Dialects' (McIntosh 1952).

---

3 The challenge and enthusiasm of the pioneering days of these major achievements may be seen in papers like Craigie's (1925), but cf. also Aitken (1964). The highly significant connection between the *OED* and the *DOST* and *SND* (and the ways in which the two Scottish dictionaries supplement the English one) has been outlined by Aitken (1987b). Cf. also Murison (1987) for a brief historical overview of Scottish lexicography.

4 The variety and expressive forcefulness of Scots vocabulary are also key points in McClure's passionate defence of the language (1988: 50–51; 53–59).

Subsequently, booklets which were possibly less scholarly, but which witnessed a continuing and unrelenting interest in vernacular forms, continued to appear. Among these we may refer to Mackinnon (1966), whose *Lowland Scots Glossary* is organised thematically, includes a few idioms and proverbs, and even presents a short table of irregular verbs, 'some adjectives ..., a few adverbs ... [and] a few regular verbs'. Although spelling and pronunciation are also discussed very briefly in the Preface, the overall impression is of a rather haphazard collection of relatively familiar items, in which vocabulary is displayed as a curio. A similar attitude emerges from the Introduction to a modern reprint of the 1858 *Handbook of the Scottish Language* by Cleishbotham the Younger, which addresses the reader with the following question:

> Supposing someone offered you a large *usqueba* and a *broun*. Called you a *clump* or a *taupie*. Or threatened to give you a *nyte* with *nivvil*. Well, would you have a clue what he was talking about? (1858/1975: i)

Another 'Selection of Scots Words arranged as an English-Scots Dictionary' published in 1947 actually stated that the author wished 'more to entertain than to educate' (Jarvie 1947: 5), while a 'handy guide to Scots' of 1968 listed vocabulary, place-names, 'strange matters' and even included a 'mixtie-maxtie quiz' on the booklet's contents (Graham 1968).

Contemporary descriptions of Scots in relation to SSE (Scottish Standard English)

The grammar and vocabulary of Scots have also been described by Murison (1977): his view of the future of Scots was rather pessimistic and, as a matter of fact, he even pointed out that 'To write a full grammar of a language now sorely in decay and so confused with standard English' (1977: 38) was beyond the scope of the specific chapter in his book; however, his notes on usage and pragmatic meaning are certainly very valuable. In addition to this, the *Edinburgh History of the Scots Language* (Jones 1997) has provided a dramatic improvement in the scholarly approach to Scots, and Smith (1999: xii) announces two books which should also prove of considerable interest: *A Book of Older Scots* by Graham Caie and Jeremy J. Smith, and *An Introduction to Older Scots and Scottish English* by Anne King.

In recent times, Purves also provided a very short study, but 'offered on the grounds that "*bannocks is better nor nae breid*"' (1997: 5). In particular, this booklet is to be a valuable starting point for the study of the debate on Scots orthography, as it includes a chapter on 'The Spelling of Scots' (1997: 57–61), an Appendix with 'The Scots Style Sheet', 'As proposed at the Makkars' Club meeting on April 11, 1947, in a hostelry in Edinburgh' (1997: 63) and another Appendix with 'Recommendations for Writers in Scots' endorsed by the Scots Language Society and 'agreed at a meeting of Scots *makkars* in the School of Scottish Studies in Edinburgh in 1985' (Purves 1997: 65).

Within this framework, the lively debate on spelling that has been going on in *English World Wide, Scottish Language* and other journals (cf. McClure 1985b; McClure *et al.* 1985; Macaulay 1991b; Stirling 1994; McClure 1997)[5] and the latest developments in Scottish lexicography – discussed by Robinson (1987), Macleod (1992/93, 1993 and 1998) and Dareau (1998) – bear witness to the vitality of Scots as a medium of communication in a wide range of contexts. However, Romaine (1994: 118–119) has underlined to what extent even today schoolchildren's forms of speech may be 'corrected' more or less forcefully, and indeed the issue of 'dialect erosion', especially in urban areas, has been investigated by Macafee (1987, 1994a and 1994b).[6] As the author correctly points out, in the case of vocabulary, 'the crucial problem is sampling, ... Depending on the words selected, very different results can be obtained' (Macafee 1994b: 69). As a matter of fact, in the last twenty years several investigations have been carried out, in order to assess the extent to which passive knowledge and active use of Scots vocabulary are still widespread in different social strata; however, they all start from a list of items which are assumed to be (or perhaps <u>not</u> to be) known to the informants, so that the researcher may then see whether the starting presupposition is correct and whether any traits are receding.

One of the earliest studies based on this methodological approach is described by Sandred (1983 and 1985); his analysis of 27 'Scotticisms' includes both lexical items and grammatical features, so we find *dreich, dour* and *kenspeckle* discussed together with *dinna, gaed,* and *That's me having to do the whole thing over again*; as regards the last item, the author claims that 'This is the first item where we have an example of idiomatic Scottish use of general English words' (1983: 68) and describes it as 'unknown [as a Scotticism] to no less than fourteen informants'. According to Sandred's investigation, 'the special Scottish character was covert to everyone in the LWC group' and 'to a few informants in the other social-class groups (UWC=3, LMC=2, UMC=4),[7] who classified it as "good English"' (1983: 68–69).

---

5 In this context, it is perhaps ironic to observe that strict adherence to original orthography had been suggested by Pinkerton as a means of forcing people to read English versions of Scottish poems and, as a result, unlearn Scots: 'Nothing can take [Scots] so much out of the hands of the vulgar as a rigid preservation of the old spelling. Were there no Scotish books that the common people in Scotland could read, their knowledge of the English would increase very rapidly. But while they are enraptured with Barbour's History of Bruce, Blind Hary's Life of Wallace, and the works of Sir David Lindsay, books to be found in modern spelling at this day in almost every cottage of Scotland, their old dialect will maintain it's ground. ... The old Scotish poets ought to be regarded in the same light as Chaucer and the old English ones; and who suspects that the perusal of the latter can injure the purity of English conversation or writing?' (1786: 1/ xvii-xviii).

6 Attitudes to Glaswegian have also been investigated by Ruf (1996), though this study focuses on radio broadcasts and the perception of a local accent.

7 LWC = Lower Working Class, UWC = Upper Working Class, LMC = Lower Middle Class, UMC = Upper Middle Class.

Other recent investigations of linguistic awareness, attitude and pressure towards anglicisation on the part of families and teachers, lexical survival and phonological specificity have been carried out by Macaulay (1978), Reid (1978), Romaine (1975 and 1978), Abercrombie (1979), Aitken and McArthur (1979), McClure (1980), Aitken (1984a), Riach (1984), Johnston (1983, 1984 and 1985), Pollner (1985a, 1985b and 1985c), Melchers (1985 and 1999), Lawrie (1991), Menzies (1991), Iacuaniello (1992/93) and Macafee / McGarrity (1999).

Not all of these studies are equally exhaustive – for instance, in several cases interviews were carried out with or questionnaires were returned by a relatively small number of informants. However, the main point that appears to emerge most frequently is possibly the issue of covert prestige of local forms. This is shown quite clearly when it is reported that 'classmates were sometimes critical because [the informant] spoke properly' (Iacuaniello 1992/93: 64). At the same time, the association of rural varieties with 'Good Scots' and a common misunderstanding of Scots as Gaelic[8] (Iacuaniello 1992/93: 66) show how little awareness there is even at university level of the specific linguistic situation of Scotland. A similarly worrying lack of clarity concerning the distinction between Scots and SSE does not appear to be uncommon among teachers and inspectors (cf. Steele 1998). One then inevitably agrees with Kirk (1992/93) on the urgent need to acquire tools on the basis of which scholars may describe contemporary Scots in the same scientific way as the Helsinki Corpus of Older Scots has allowed.

An attempt to describe the contemporary range of Scots usage by providing informants with lists of lexical items and asking them to classify them consciously does not appear to be based on a very appropriate methodological approach, as it does not imply observation of the informants' actual usage, but their response in terms of some given categories which may reflect whatever sociolinguistic perceptions have become associated with certain features. Instead, it is certainly more fruitful to collect a corpus of 'natural' language, either formal or informal, but as spontaneous as possible, and then identify the features that appear to be most frequent and productive. To this end a crucial step has been taken with the Miller-Brown Corpus of Scottish English.

The Miller-Brown Corpus of Scottish English: experimental findings

The Miller-Brown Corpus of Scottish English (henceforth MBC) is a corpus of over 250,000 words collected in the late 1970s at the University of Edinburgh, Department of Linguistics – cf. Brown and Miller (1980). It is made up of

---

8 I experienced a similar misunderstanding on my first visit to the new Scottish Parliament in summer 1999: I mentioned to one of the wardens in the Visitors' Centre that there were no signs or documents available in Scots and my attention was drawn politely to all the signs in Gaelic.

dialogues (conversation, short narratives and jokes) from male and female informants. These were secondary school pupils from state schools in Edinburgh and a small town in East Lothian, and from a private school in Edinburgh; another group of informants included first-year undergraduates and a university porter. Two interviewers took part in the project; it is important to notice that both of them are Scottish, of Scottish parents, as this was considered essential to elicit spontaneous conversation.

It is also quite relevant to remark that most informants were about 18 years old, though there were long contributions from three older informants as well. This is quite interesting, because it may show that supposedly traditional elements of language may acquire such relevance, or maybe they are so ingrained in everyday speech that even younger people use them, though they might be expected to use more standard language. The transcripts of the dialogues are stored on computer, and they are unpunctuated; only pauses are represented by obliques; to facilitate the analysis of the corpus, they were subdivided into ten parts, or files.[9]

The importance of the MBC should also be emphasised because it seems to be the first corpus of spoken SSE based on natural conversation.[10] Another corpus of SSE, the so-called Map-Task corpus, collected at the Human Communication Research Centre of Edinburgh University in the late 1980s, consists of 128 unscripted dialogues, but they are all based on a task in which two people are given maps with different details, and one gives enough information to the other to complete his/her map. This is obviously quite unlike natural conversation: in fact, the language that is used in these exchanges appears to be very selective, with attention given to details, checking of information and constant communication maintenance. Consequently, the pragmatic functions that are most prominent in this corpus are specific, and lexical choices are also careful; this may prove very interesting in certain respects, but it hardly provides a snapshot of everyday spoken language.

The conversations in the MBC, instead, clearly exemplify the phenomena of code-switching and code-mixing observed in the speech of Scottish speakers that were mentioned in Chapters 1 and 2, hence Dossena (1996, 1998a and 1998b) investigated the extent to which Scots features occur within English utterances with a specific communicative aim. This may depend on the Scots item having a slightly different meaning from the English one, or it may be dictated by homogeneity with the interlocutor's own style.

9 These are labelled as follows: MBC1to10, MBC11to2, MBC21to3, MBC31to4, MBC41to5, MBC51to6, MBC61to7, MBC71to8, MBC81to9 and MBC91to9. In this analysis the line number of the occurrence, together with the indication of the file in which it was recorded, is provided at the end of each quotation.

10 As we saw, previous research on SSE was based on special field studies, with interviews and recordings collected specifically for the kind of research that was being carried out; however, none of these recordings seems to have been published *per se*.

The former case is exemplified by *kirk*, which occurs only seven times in the MBC, while its English equivalent *church* appears 67 times: almost ten times as frequently. The two words may appear in the same exchange, indeed in the same sentence, but with a different meaning, which shows that they are not always exactly interchangeable:

(1) I'm a member of the kirk just locally here the kirk o'field church which is the parish of Dumbiedykes area (MBC1to10, line 96)

In this case *kirk o'field* appears to be the name of the church being discussed, as *kirk* is often associated with a name: in Edinburgh, for instance, we have the Tron Kirk, the High Kirk of St. Giles and the Greyfriars Kirk.

However, as we said, the corpus also exemplifies a case of wavering from one item of vocabulary to the other not because a different meaning is attributed to either, or because a special stylistic connotation is needed, but as a way to adapt one's speech to the interlocutor's own lexical choices:

(2) <X A34> ... our own church session decided that they would give him a present ...
<X J35> ... do the the kirk session[11] feel that they are expected ...
<X A35> I don't know not being on the kirk session but ...
(MBC51to6, line 1256)

This form of adjustment to the interlocutor's speech may of course be seen as a stylistic choice, and indeed one informant's comment is very interesting in this respect:

(3) There's an example of me shifting the now I would very rarely say yeah ye ken but speakin to you I use it in normal eh I wouldnae say yeah I would always say aye if you see what I mean (R59, MBC31to4)

In addition, phonological adjustments may occur; again, it may be revealing to focus on the words of a speaker:

(4) I tell you talking aboot Scots I find a difference between Edinburgh and say here ken in the dialect in the especially in certain words that you that are quite common things like the use of the velar fricative for instance it's still used here quite I mean I dinnae say nicht bricht but when I worked in the mill I used to say straicht and waicht and things like that (yeah) oh aye because I used to say what's the waicht o that reel keep that straicht and things like that but it's I would say that before I went to work in the mill I didnae I didnae use these terms but I fell into I got into the habit o daein it ... but then after I left I got oot the habit again (R45-R46, MBC31to4)

---

11 In this case it should be pointed out that 'kirk session' is the correct term and could therefore be classed as a cultural Scotticism.

Other overt Scotticisms, instead, appear quite often in the MBC as the normal choice and unaffected by waverings and adjustments to the interlocutor. The use of *wee*, for instance, is much more widespread than the use of *small, little,* and *tiny*, and it may collocate with one of these other adjectives or even with a diminutive:

(5) I shot this tiny wee rabbit (MBC1to10, line 2758)

(6) there's a wee kiddies' pool (MBC1to10, line 2712)

In the MBC *wee* has a total of 234 occurrences, whereas *small* has 67, *little* 104 and *tiny* 6: it is as if the choice of a more familiar item of vocabulary emphasised the small size of the child, animal, or object being discussed.

Also the use of the suffix *-ie* to produce diminutives proves very interesting; as in the case of *wee*, the effect is to reduce the distance, either social or psychological, from the noun involved (cf. Dossena 1998b). It is often found in proper names (*Lizzie, Jamie, Dougie, Davie, Robbie,* etc.) and in nouns like *laddie, lassie* and *kiddie,* to which we may add various others: for instance: *wifie* (= woman), *mannie, thingie* and *placie*.

An analysis of the frequency of these nouns is revealing, and we may summarise their occurrences as follows:

Lexeme	occurrences		
	singular	plural	total
Lassie	15	6	21
Wifie	14	1	15
Mannie	12	0	12
Laddie	7	5	12
Kiddie	6	4	10

An interesting case is provided by an analysis of the occurrences of *wifie* (= *woman*);[12] in the corpus this item generally occurs in narratives of amusing episodes,

(7) it hit the this wifie who was putting her coins in the wee thing that you get the ticket out of (MBC61to7, line 1714)

in ironic questions,

(8) why is she an old wifie that hangs out the window with her hair in curlers (MBC41to5, line 91)

or in negative remarks, indeed, insults:

(9) that wifie is a bitch (MBC91to9, line 1382).

---

12 Although this form also exists in southern English, in that variety it only applies as the diminutive form of *wife*.

In all three cases the diminutive appears to downgrade the theme of the utterance, with the result that the idea of the joke is strengthened in the first case,
while the irony and the insult in the other two instances are emphasised by the
obviously familiar/contemptuous form.[13]

Mannie, which might be expected to be the counterpart of *wifie*, does not, in
fact, appear to have exactly the same pragmatic value. Though it does occur
together with *wifie* in the same narrative in MBC61to7,[14] we also find an
instance in which it is used in direct speech, which shows the virtual lack of
intrinsic negative connotations of this item:

>   (10) I thought you were a mannie that works in Edinburgh University
>   (MBC61to7, line 1682)

Differently from *wifie*, *mannie* is also found to collocate with *wee* in contexts
in which there is no clearly negative connotation:

>   (11) ... we had to go up to the wee mannie at the door standing in this
>   great big fancy you know uniform (MBC81to9, line 6178)

Ambivalence is also lacking in the contexts in which *lassie, lassies, laddie* and
laddies occur, since these are generally used in a positive or neutral way:

>   (12) when the lassie that's on the till when she gauns up for her dinner
>   then somebody else takes over (MBC21to3, line 658)

>   (13) the laddie that I muck about wi (MBC21to3, line 1176)

In the case of *kiddie/kiddies*, instead, ambivalence reappears; in the following
example, this item co-occurs with *wee*, which emphasises the young age of the
users of the pool:

>   (14) there's a wee kiddies' pool (MBC1to10, line 2712).

However, *kiddie*, like *wifie*, is also used in a disparaging sense in the
following turns of the same speaker. The negative value of *kiddie* is stressed by
the adjective that is used in the second turn, *kideous*, a piece of linguistic
invention that apparently joins *kid* and *hideous*.

>   (15) <S80> Euan's a kiddie ...
>   <S81> ... he's absolutely kideous ... (MBC71to8, lines 981–984)

As far as full affirmatives are concerned, *aye* (or *ay*) is generally placed in the
category of overt Scotticisms, so this should have a special stylistic effect, but

---

13 Milton (1992: 225) discusses a poem by J.C.Milne, 'Dominie', in which he identifies 'the use of
   the (characteristically North-East Scots) double diminutive [in *mannikies*] to describe the
   Inspectors as they go about their self-important work'. This kind of humorous/contemptuous
   diminutive is also found in Jacobite songs and ballads: most famously, the diminutive *Johnnie*
   in the well-known text of *Hey, Johnnie Cope* is an instance of this.
14 Cf. 'one bus stopped you see and the mannie got out' (MBC61to7, line 1704).

the analysis of the MBC shows that its distribution is much higher than we might expect from an overt Scotticism. As a matter of fact, *yes* occurs 777 times, whereas *ay(e)* occurs 529 times: this means that *yes* shares 59.5% of all occurrences, whereas *ay(e)* shares 40.5% .

Of course the implication may be that *yes* is slightly more formal, whereas *ay(e)* creates a stronger bond between the listener and the speaker by stressing the common cultural background. However, the use of both forms within the same exchange (with the same interlocutors, on the same topic, in the same situation, etc.) seems to refute this:

(16) Aye yes I had to write it out all again (MBC9 1to9, line 1069)

(17) <X A4> Oh yes yes
     <X K5> Actually ...
     <X A5> Aye I know ... (MBC1to10, line 672)

This mixture, alternation or free variation seems to apply to negative adverbs as well. According to Miller (1993:114), 'in Scots, the verb in a sentence is negated by the independent words *no* and *not* ... or by the dependent forms *nae* and *n't*, which are always attached to other words .... In the conversations corpus *no* is most frequent with BE, and next most frequent with *'ll*, the reduced form of *will* ..., and *'ve* and *'s*, the reduced forms of *have* and *has* .... *Nae* is added to all the modal verbs and to DO .... Educated speakers prefer *n't* to *nae*, certainly in formal contexts, but forms like *isnae* can be heard in informal circumstances from educated speakers'.

Again, we find that choices are made not only on a lexical level, but this time on a grammatical level, too, according to stylistic purposes that may not always be conscious, with instances of the different forms occurring in the same context:

(18) I don't know I dinnae really ken what it'll be this summer (MBC3 1to4, line 141)

(19) I don't know where she went to school ... I dinnae think she could produce a sortae polite form ... she just doesnae know any other form (MBC8 1to9, line 3114)

Compounds may also be affected: *naebody* occurs seven times, whereas *nobody* occurs 26 times, yet the two forms seem to be interchangeable in the same conversation:

(20) <X MS22> ... there's nobody has a good word to say about him
     <X A11> he's ignorant ...
     <X MS23> and naebody liked him (MBC1 1to2, line 530)

It might be argued that in this example the third sentence, being a repetition, inserts a Scots word to emphasise the meaning; however, already in the first sentence the syntactic structure followed the Scots pattern. Moreover, (18) does not only show what might look like a free variation of negative forms, but also two alternative verbs, *know* and *ken*, the latter being the traditional Scots form.

According to the data provided in the corpus, *ken* seems more widespread in its negative form: *ah/I dinnae/dinnay ken* has 33 occurrences against the 16 occurrences of *ah/I ken*; however, both are greatly outnumbered by the English forms *I know* (223 occurrences) and *I don't know* (286 occurrences). Besides, *dinnae* never collocates with *know*, nor does *don't* collocate with *ken*: this may be for euphonic reasons, but it also shows cohesion within the speakers' integrating language systems. Nonetheless, the two forms may be found in the same context, without any clear reason why the speaker should use first one and then the other, self-correction being excluded by the order in (18) and by the exchange in (24), where the second speaker's use of the Scots form seems to confirm the first speaker's statement while avoiding repetition and certainly not correcting it:

(21) <X K20> Ah ken
     <X M45> How's that
     <X K21> Ah don't know (MBC1to10, line 1215)

(22) I ken I know and most of us (MBC61to7, line 554)

(23) <X S74> I ken he is ...
     <X K80> I mean ...
     <X S75> I know you are ... (MBC81to9, line 387)

(24) <X M52> So you know everybody there
     <X ML25> Aye I ken them aw now (MBC21to3, line 678)

A similar case of interchangeability seems to apply to *hame* and *home*, the former also appearing in compound forms:

(25) I hardly get any hamework for physics (MBC1to10, line 1880)

(26) <LM59> oh ah've moved home now ...
     <PS43> really ...
     <LM60> ... ah just moved hame ... ah'm livin on a livin awae fae home grant an ah'm livin at hame ...
     <LM65> ... ah did write an tell them ah had moved back home ...
     (MBC41to5, lines 1902ff.)

To this we may add that an overall view of the MBC allows us to note that this wavering between two alternative forms does not only concern content words, but also grammar words, which are normally unstressed and therefore less likely to be given a special stylistic connotation, and even interjections, although these are not really part of the sentence structure. In fact, the use of these Scots forms can be seen more in terms of interference:

(27) <X K82> Och yes naturally
<X S88> Well we knew that already
<X K83> Oh but we're not ... (MBC71to8, line 492)

(28) <X K85> Och they're both the same
<X S106> I'd probably use both yes
<X W52> ...
<X K86> Oh just miss out the rest (MBC71to8, line 5659)

(29) <X J121> Och I don't know

...

<X J123> Oh no (MBC21to3, line 2622)

(30) the boy down the road fae me (MBC21to3, line 1172)

(31) <X A209> Aye apart frae a few o them
<X M177> Do any of them wear jeans
<X A210> Lindsay used to last year he's been smarter this year apart
from when he's on outdoor education ... (MBC11to2, line 2752)

(32) Everybody was petrified frae him (MBC11to2, line 2821)

As we saw in (20), also in the case of (32) we observe a Scots grammatical form, in which *frae* substitutes *by*.[15]

This kind of corpus-based study allows us to see that speakers seem to go beyond code-switching and code-mixing: in fact, we might even call this 'code-blending', since it is virtually impossible to decide which factors determine the change. In Smith's view, 'choosing Scots or English is ... in one sense a statement of social solidarity' (Smith 1996: 167–168), and indeed this relates to Milroy's description of language change as being socially originated (1992 and 1993), an issue briefly discussed also by Paterson (1992). It is true that very often the speakers' perception of the topic, of the interlocutors, of the situation, and of their own role in that situation, influences their linguistic behaviour in ways that are seldom acknowledged consciously if they are not elicited clearly. However, the systematicity of this phenomenon allows further interpretations. Perhaps the use of Scots features as a stylistic choice should be interpreted in a much broader sense: not only linked to cultural connotations or as a special communication device, but also as a tool for variety on the speaker's own part, as a characteristic that allows for richer expression and enhanced vividness of discourse.

15 As shown in the first part of this study, Miller (1993: 131) discusses these cases of exchanged prepositions together with other instances of morpho-syntactic variation connected with lexical variation (for example, the use of *how* instead of *why*).

Concluding remarks

What has been outlined in this study is certainly not a brief history of the complex relationship between English and Scots, but an overview of some aspects of this relationship, especially those concerning prescriptive lexical usage and the way in which users' perceptions of Scots forms attributed prestige to English or acknowledged the value of Scots as an expressive literary medium.

The vast complexity of the situation has only allowed us to consider the phenomena that have had the greatest impact. The process of language change that continuously affects and is determined by the speakers' and writers' selections of certain items, their adaptation of existing ones, or indeed their creation of new possibilities will certainly provide new opportunities for future investigation. Scots does not seem to be disappearing, as the belief was in the nineteenth century and at some stages in our own times, though much may still be done to overcome a proscribing attitude. As in the past, the debate on linguistic issues has taken on distinctly socio-political overtones; for instance, Douglas (1995: 2–3) observes:

> Those who claim Scots is just a form of English are often the same people who say they cannot understand anyone who speaks Scots, even if it is only Scots-accented English. ... I want to denounce the poisonous racism inherent in the system by which generations of Scots have been taught to reject their own language. 'Speak properly' has long meant for Scottish school-children 'Speak English'. This is a monstrous piece of cultural oppression.

Along similar lines, though more moderately, Watson (1998) has discussed the role of Scottish culture in post-colonial Britain, while Finlay (1998b) has focused on the relationship between devolution and cultural themes that may go beyond stereotypes. This sets itself in the context of a wider ongoing debate about the concept itself of a standard language,[16] and strategies have also been suggested to advance the status of Scots at various levels. On the other hand, Aitken (1980) has warned against the dangers of language planning that, no matter how well meant, is still in the hands of a minority of speakers. This in itself may be unacceptable even for speakers of the variety being promoted, a view that is also shared by Miller (1998: 56).

The publication of the New Testament in Lorimer's translation (1983) has provided an opportunity to rediscover the linguistic flexibility of Scots, but – as Gibson (1988: 211) reminds us – 'It is too literary a production, and it has come too late to be a genuinely religious or even a popular event'. The 1987 reprint of Waddell's translation of the Psalms, which dates back to 1871, also

16 Cf., among others, Trudgill (1998), McArthur (1998) and Davies (1999).

appears to be a scholarly achievement, rather than an effective means to restore Scots as a religious language.[17]

A certain degree of institutional support has already been granted both to Scots and to Gaelic,[18] though the latter can certainly count on greater attention. In education, it would appear that much progress has been made since Withrington *et al.* (1974) discussed the situation. Nowadays Scots is actively encouraged in schools by the 5–14 Curriculum Guidelines.[19] The oldest Scottish universities – Aberdeen, Edinburgh, Glasgow and St. Andrews – all now teach Scots, and the Scots literary heritage is increasingly prominent within the curriculum; in addition to this, the language is widely represented by the Scots Language Resource Centre in Perth and by several associations such as the Scottish Text Society, the Saltire Society, and the Association for Scottish Literary Studies.

According to a report published by the General Register Office (Scotland),[20] in 1996 the number of Scots speakers was estimated at 1.5 million; however, the official census has never included a question on Scots. Although in recent years there has been increasing pressure (especially on the part of the Scots Leid Quorum at the University of Aberdeen) to include one in the 2001 census (Macafee 1997b: 515), the issue has not been taken up institutionally, allegedly due to the difficulty of collecting reliable data when users are expected to report on their own proficiency in a certain language.

In fact, official data collected through the census would prove very valuable to measure and monitor the health of the language. As far as positive nurturing is concerned, some new developments give cause for cautious optimism. The new political situation and Scotland's own parliament[21] should increase popular awareness of the language's history and potentiality for renewed uses, not only in literature, but also within the framework of today's rich plurality of registers, accents and varieties.

---

17 Corbett (1999: 124), however, stresses the innovative aspects of Waddell's translation in relation to earlier Victorian versions of biblical texts and to twentieth-century Lallans writers.

18 Cf. Fenton and MacDonald (1994: 175-180); as far as Gaelic is concerned, updated information is also available in the website of the Scottish Executive: <http://www.scotland.gov.uk >.

19 This has been received very favourably, as acknowledged by the Scottish Consultative Council on the Curriculum (1999). The extent to which the curriculum nowadays gives greater attention to Scots is discussed by Niven and Jackson (1998) and new materials are being published to this end (cf. MacGillivray 1997).

20 The report is available from Ian Máté, GRO (Scotland), Ladywell House, Ladywell Road, Edinburgh EH12 7TF.

21 The creation, within the Scottish Parliament, of a Cross-Party Group on Scots and current language policy is discussed by McClure and Dossena (forthcoming).

Conclusion

When I began to investigate how the concept of 'Scotticism' had developed, the first elements that soon became evident were the clearly connotative value that this term might have and, at the same time, its high degree of subjectivity. What was an overt Scotticism for one speaker could be covert for another; one might use it in an appreciative sense, another might avoid its usage altogether. A preliminary survey of studies carried out by means of questionnaires such as were discussed in Chapter 7 showed that, in approaching this subject, I would need to deal with phenomena which were clear indexes of sociolinguistic attitudes and that the labels used to describe their occurrence could be controversial in themselves. This resulted in a decision to investigate 'Scotticisms' by means of the methodological tools made available by corpus linguistics – that is, to focus on a computerised collection of dialogues, in order to assess the extent to which certain items did occur in everyday speech and, if so, in what contexts. To this end, the Miller-Brown Corpus of Scottish English proved an invaluable source of data. The social context within which the corpus had been collected ensured that both explicit linguistic comments and spontaneous conversation could occur in the same exchange, allowing me to identify patterns of usage relating to individual items and, at the same time, what kind of attitudes could be expressed by the speakers themselves.

In order to assess the connection between attitudes and usage, however, the first step would be to investigate the ways in which the linguistic situation of present-day Scotland has been discussed. The very fact that scholars have felt the need to define Scottish English (while in no other cases do we find similar worries about possible definitions of Canadian, Australian or New Zealand English), whether in relation to English or to Scots (with which it can even be confused), also hints at the sociological complexity of several issues. It could actually be argued that 'the Scottish language means different things to different people':[1] this might have a metaphorical meaning (speakers attach different values to different varieties) or indeed a literal one (the label 'Scottish language' could be interpreted as Scots by some speakers and as Scottish English by others). These views on language in contemporary Scotland would

---

1 This comment was actually made in the Scottish Parliament during the debate on whether there should be a question on Scots in the 2001 Census (January 2000).

then have to be discussed in the light of their historical development, as language ideology (and the linguistic labels that it forges) is closely connected to socio-political factors that transcend immediate linguistic phenomena.[2] In particular, the role of Scots in the history of Scottish English would be a crucial theme.

It would be incorrect to assume that the history of Scots has always followed a smooth and constant path of increasing anglicisation. For instance, commentators have often stressed that throughout the sixteenth century Central Scots was perceived to be the national norm; in fact, recent studies (Meurman-Solin 2000a) have shown that other competing norms were also available in different geographical areas. In general, though, it was mainly due to historical 'accidence' at around the times of the Union of the Crowns and of Parliaments that Scots appeared to lose its status as a 'standard' at which educated speakers should aim. This concerned phonology and, possibly to a greater extent, grammar and vocabulary, which were typically singled out as the areas in which 'provincialisms' were most likely to appear. The recurring label for this type of 'error' was 'Scotticism'. To this end, my study began with an overview of this concept as defined by contemporary scholars, so that this could then be related to its historical background.

Concerning present-day Scottish English, Aitken's distinction between overt and covert Scotticisms was to prove specially fruitful. Although other scholars compiled different lists of what lexical items and features belonged to either category (indeed, each individual speaker might draw up slightly different lists), this gave me an opportunity to assess the actual occurrence of these items in a corpus of spontaneous conversation and to relate these (purely descriptive) lists to the lists of 'Scotticisms to avoid' compiled in previous centuries.

As a matter of fact, grammarians and commentators of the past had generally focused on specific features in order to stigmatise them or (on a different, contrasting plan) to recommend their usage in literary texts, according to the more general trends in the cultural framework of their epochs. From the sociolinguistic point of view, it was the concept of 'linguistic propriety' that had the greatest impact on eighteenth- and nineteenth-century grammars, dictionaries and educational approaches to the 'vernacular'. Although the success of poets like Ramsay, Fergusson and Burns, and of novelists like Scott and Stevenson, allowed Scots to regain ground as a literary language, the view that English was the language needed 'to get on in the world' had become so steadfast in the minds of Scottish speakers that the decline of Scots as an everyday medium could only be regretted in terms of loss of a quaint, peculiar relic of a past that had been increasingly sentimentalised. The 'vernacular

---

2 On this point, cf. Watts (2000: 31): 'One of the most fruitful ways to carry out historical linguistic research is ... to view the process of standardisation as an object of inter-disciplinary research'.

revivals' of the twentieth century were equally restricted to the circle of literary composition – simultaneously, the richness and variety of Scots lexis was perceived to be constantly declining. The most frequent complaint was that very soon hardly anyone would be able to read Burns' poems without a glossary. In fact, glossaries had also been appended to collections of Scots poems in previous centuries; the sense of progressive lexical loss thus largely depended on a perception of Scots as an outlandish dialect, possibly acceptable in literature (a linguistic world apart by definition), but quite unsuitable for 'polite' expression. This kind of dualistic attitude seems to characterise the comments that were to prove most influential even to this day. At about the same time, however, Scots also earned a certain degree of scholarly attention. The possibility that it might be shown to be closer to Anglo-Saxon than English, the latter irretrievably 'frenchified' after the Norman Conquest, gave Scots an aura of respectability associated with greater antiquity. On this basis the first investigations of Scots vocabulary were started, which would then result in the publication of Jamieson's *Dictionary* of 1808.

Nowadays Scots is still used throughout the country with varying degrees of distinctiveness; however, the two trends observed in the past still appear to influence speakers' attitudes. On the one hand, there is distinct awareness of the ancient historical roots of this language, which was at one point the language of the court, of the law and of poetry; on the other, the pervasiveness of English prevents many speakers from realising that Scots is not just a dialect used in informal contexts, but a variety, the expressive potentiality of which might indeed become more apparent in a wider range of uses.

In this study I have attempted to outline the complex historical development of language ideology in Scotland in relation to linguistic sources, such as grammars and dictionaries, but also to documents like travelogues and collections of proverbs, in which individual lexical items could be singled out in order to give authenticity to the narration or to make the proverb more memorable. All of these have been discussed in the framework of their more general socio-political context, as it is undeniable that such milestones in Scottish history as the Unions of the Crowns and of Parliaments, the Reformation and the Jacobite defeat contributed enormously to changes in linguistic attitudes on the part of Scottish speakers. The eighteenth century was indeed a crucial point in this respect. While prescriptivists like Sheridan encouraged the process of anglicisation, some commentators like Adams saw that the complete disappearance of Scots would be an immense cultural loss. Both attitudes were then maintained throughout the nineteenth and the twentieth centuries and, as a result of this, the situation today appears to be even more complex. On the one hand, the risk of increasing anglicisation (and consequent loss of specifically Scottish vocabulary) is somehow limited by various cultural projects and initiatives aimed at favouring the use of Scots; these, however, might protect a crystallised kind of literary Scots which does not necessarily coincide with ordinary usage.

Throughout the centuries, the relationship with Gaelic on the one hand and with English on the other has placed Scots in a unique position in terms of the range within which speakers could adopt expressive modalities of each individual language, inscribing features of one in the context of the others in relation to different situational and pragmatic constraints. Consequently, the connection between Scots and Scottish English still appears to be as fruitful as ever. Speakers do not just seem to code-switch between one and the other; their stylistic adjustments to context, topic and interlocutor encompass different aspects of both codes at the same time. In this sense, then, the linguistic situation of present-day Scotland has proved to be a fascinating field of research, in which the interaction of different varieties can be studied in terms of their mutual influence – the way in which features of lexis, syntax and phonology have been adopted from one into the other and, perhaps even more interestingly, the way in which speakers and writers convey meaning by means of a careful, though spontaneous, selection of individual traits. The result is an intriguingly opalescent code, in which even elements that do not appear to be particularly prominent convey different shades of meaning and varying degrees of speaker-listener involvement.

References

Abercrombie, D. (1979), 'The Accents of Standard English in Scotland', in Aitken / McArthur, eds., pp. 68–84.

Adam Smith J. (1970), 'Some Eighteenth-Century Ideas of Scotland', in Phillipson / Mitchison, eds., pp.107–124.

Adams, J. (1799), *The Pronunciation of the English Language*, repr. in *English Linguistics 1500–1800*, Alston, R.C. (ed.), London, The Scolar Press, 1974.

Agutter, A. (1988a), 'The Dangers of Dialect Parochialism: The Scottish Vowel Length Rule', in Fisiak, ed., pp. 1–21.

— (1988b), 'Standardisation in Middle Scots', *Scottish Language*, 7, pp. 1–8.

Aird, T. (1845/1897), 'Lyric Poetry – Scottish Poetry', in Cochrane, ed., pp. 500–501.

Aitken, A. J. (1964), 'Completing the Record of Scots', *Folklore*, 75, pp. 34–36.

— ed. (1973), *Lowland Scots*, Edinburgh, Association for Scottish Literary Studies.

— (1979), 'Scottish Speech: a Historical View with Special Reference to the Standard English of Scotland', in Aitken / McArthur, eds., pp. 85–118.

— (1980), 'New Scots: The Problems', in McClure *et al.*, pp. 45–63.

— (1981), 'The Scottish Vowel-Length Rule', in Benskin / Samuels, eds., pp. 131–157.

— (1982), 'Bad Scots: Some Superstitions about Scots Speech', *Scottish Language*, 2, pp. 30–44.

— (1984a), 'Scottish Accents and Dialects', in Trudgill, ed., pp. 94–114.

— (1984b), 'Scots and English in Scotland', in Trudgill, ed., pp. 517–532.

— (1985/1996), 'Introduction', in Robinson, ed., pp. ix – xli.

— (1987a), 'The Extinction of Scotland in Popular Dictionaries of English', in Bailey, ed., pp. 99–135.

— (1987b), 'The Lexicography of Scots: The Current Position', *Review of Scottish Culture*, 3, pp. 91–96.

— (1991), 'Progress in Older Scots Philology', *Studies in Scottish Literature*, XXVI, pp. 19–37.

— (1992a), 'Scots', in McArthur, ed., pp. 893–898.

— (1992b), 'Scotticism', in McArthur, ed., pp. 900–901.

— (1992c), 'Scottish English', in McArthur, ed., pp. 903–905.

— (1994), 'Progress in the Study of Modern Scots since 1948', in Fenton / MacDonald, eds., pp. 1–40.

— (1995/96), 'James Murray, Master of Scots', *Review of Scottish Culture*, 9, pp. 14–34.

— (1997), 'The Pioneers of Anglicised Speech in Scotland: A Second Look', *Scottish Language*, 16, pp. 1–36.

Aitken, A.J., A. McIntosh and H. Pálsson, eds. (1971), *Edinburgh Studies in English and Scots*, London, Longman.

Aitken, A. J. and T. McArthur, eds. (1979), *Languages of Scotland*, Edinburgh, W.and R. Chambers.

Algeo, J. (1989), 'Americanisms, Briticisms, and the Standard: An Essay at Definition', in Trahern, ed., pp. 139–157.

Anderson, J. (1993), 'Morphology, Phonology and the Scottish Vowel-Length Rule', *Journal of Linguistics*, 29, pp. 419–430.

Anderson, J.H. (1996), *Words That Matter: Linguistic Perception in Renaissance English*, Stanford, Ca., Stanford University Press.

Anderson, M. L., ed. (1957), *The James Carmichael Collection of Proverbs in Scots – From the Original Manuscript in the Edinburgh University Library*, Edinburgh, Edinburgh University Press.

Anderson, R. D. (1995), *Education and the Scottish People, 1750–1918*, Oxford, Clarendon Press.

Andrews, M. (1989), *The Search for the Picturesque – Landscape Aesthetics and Tourism in Britain, 1760–1800*, Aldershot, Scolar Press.

Angus, W. (1800), *A Pronouncing Vocabulary of the English Language*, Glasgow, D. Niven, repr. in *English Linguistics, 1500–1800*, Alston, R.C. (ed.), London, The Scolar Press, 1974.

Anon. (1829), *The Vulgarities of Speech Corrected: with Elegant Expressions for Provincial and Vulgar English, Scots and Irish; for the use of those who are unacquainted with grammar*, London, F.C. Westley.

— (1855) *Scotticisms Corrected*, London, John Farquhar Shaw.

— (1880?), *Scotch Proverbs and Sayings. Alphabetically Arranged. Collected from the Best Sources*, Edinburgh, Hugh Jamieson.

— (n.d.), *Scottish Manners: Lecture on Some of the Changes which have taken place in the Manners and Habits of Scotland during the Last Fifty Years*, n. p.

Arnovick, L. K. (1997), 'Proscribed Collocations with *Shall* and *Will*: the Eighteenth-Century (Non)Standard Reassessed', in Cheshire / Stein, eds., pp. 135–151.

Bailey, R.W. and M. Görlach, eds. (1982), *English as a World Language*, Cambridge, Cambridge University Press.

Bailey, R.W., ed. (1987a), *Dictionaries of English: Prospects for the Record of Our Language*, Cambridge, Cambridge University Press.

— (1987b), 'Teaching in the Vernacular: Scotland, Schools, and Linguistic Diversity', in Macafee / Macleod, eds., pp. 131–142.

— (1991), 'Scots and Scotticisms: Language and Ideology', *Studies in Scottish Literature*, XXVI, pp. 65–77.

— (1992), *Images of English: A Cultural History of the Language*, Cambridge, Cambridge University Press.

— (1996), *Nineteenth-Century English*, Ann Arbor, The University of Michigan Press.

Bald, M.A. (1926a), 'The Anglicisation of Scottish Printing', *Scottish Historical Review*, 23, pp. 107–115.

— (1926b), 'Vernacular Books Imported into Scotland', *Scottish Historical Review*, 23, pp.254–267.

— (1927), 'The Pioneers of Anglicised Speech in Scotland', *Scottish Historical Review*, 24, pp. 179–193.

— (1928), 'Contemporary References to the Scottish Speech of the Sixteenth Century', *Scottish Historical Review*, 25, pp. 163–179.

Ball, M.J. and J. Fife, eds. (1993), *The Celtic Languages*, London / New York, Routledge.

Barber, C. (1993), *The English Language: A Historical Introduction*, Cambridge, Cambridge University Press.

Barisone, E., ed. (1989), *Il trattato delle due donne maritate e della vedova*, Genova, Il melangolo.

Basker, J.G. (1993), 'Scotticisms and the Problem of Cultural Identity in Eighteenth-Century Britain', in Dwyer / Sher, eds., pp. 81–95.

Bauer, L. (1997), 'Attempting to Trace Scottish Influence on New Zealand English', in Schneider, ed., vol. 2, pp. 257–272.

Beal, J. (1996), 'The Jocks and the Geordies: Modified Standards in Eighteenth-Century Pronouncing Dictionaries', in Britton, ed., pp. 363–382.

— (1997), 'Syntax and Morphology', in Jones, ed., pp. 335–377.

Beattie, J. (1779/1787), *Scoticisms, Arranged in Alphabetical Order, Designed to Correct Improprieties of Speech and Writing*, Printed for W. Creech, Edinburgh, and T. Cadell, London.

— (1788), *The Theory of Language*, repr. in *English Linguistics, 1500–1800*, Alston, R.C. (ed.), London, The Scolar Press, 1974.

Benskin M. and M. L. Samuels, eds. (1981), *So Meny People Longages and Tonges: Philological Essays in Scots and Medieval English presented to Angus McIntosh*, Edinburgh, the Editors.

Bermúdez-Otero, R., D. Denison, R. Hogg and C.B. McCully, eds. (2000), *Generative Theory and Corpus Studies: A Dialogue from 10th ICEHL*, Berlin, Mouton de Gruyter.

Biber, D. (1995), *Dimensions of Register Variation – A Cross-Linguistic Comparison*, Cambridge, Cambridge University Press.

Blake, N. F. and C. Jones, eds. (1984), *English Historical Linguistics: Studies in Development*, Sheffield, Centre for English Cultural Tradition and Language, University of Sheffield.

Blank, P. (1996), *Broken English: Dialects and the Politics of Language in Renaissance Writings*, London, Routledge.

Bohn, H.G. (1855), *A Hand-Book of Proverbs comprising an entire republication of Ray's Collection of English Proverbs, with his addtions from foreign languages and a complete alphabetical index ...*, London, H.G. Bohn.

Booth B. A. and E. Mehew, eds. (1994/1995), *The Letters of Robert Louis Stevenson*, New Haven and London, Yale University Press.

Boswell, J. (1786), *The Journal of a Tour to the Hebrides*, in MacGowan, ed., pp. 147–486.

Boulton, J.T. ed. (1971/1995), *Samuel Johnson: The Critical Heritage*, London / New York, Routledge.

Bradley, H. and R. Bridges (1927), *S.P.E. Tract No. XIV on the Terms Briton, British, Britisher*, Oxford, Clarendon Press.

Bray, E. (1986/1996), *The Discovery of the Hebrides: Voyages to the Western Isles, 1745–1883*, Glasgow, Collins; Edinburgh, Birlinn.

Britton, D., ed. (1996), *English Historical Linguistics 1994*, Amsterdam / Philadelphia, John Benjamins.

Broadie, A. (1997), *The Scottish Enlightenment: An Anthology*, Edinburgh, Canongate.

Broun, D., R. J. Finlay and M. Lynch, eds. (1998), *Image and Identity: The Making and Re-Making of Scotland Through the Ages*, Edinburgh, John Donald.

Brown, E. K. and J. E. Miller (1980), *Scottish English*, End of Grant Report to the Social Science Research Council.

Brown, I.G. (1980), *The Hobby-Horsical Antiquary. A Scottish Character, 1640–1830*, Edinburgh, National Library of Scotland.

Brown, K. (1991), 'Double Modals in Hawick Scots', in Trudgill / Chambers, eds., pp. 74–103.

Brunner, K. (1949), 'Did Dr Johnson Hate Scotland and the Scottish?', *English Studies*, 30, pp. 184–190.

Buchanan, J. (1757), *Linguae Britannicae Vera Pronuntiatio*, repr. in *English Linguistics, 1500–1800*, Alston, R.C. (ed.), London, The Scolar Press, 1968.

Buffoni, F. (1992), *Ramsay e Fergusson precursori di Burns: poesia pastorale e poesia vernacolare nel Settecento scozzese*, Milano, Guerini.

Bulloch, J.M. (1921/1970), 'The Delight of the Doric in the Diminutive'; reprinted in Craigie, ed., pp. 125–151.

Burchfield, R., ed. (1994), *The Cambridge History of the English Language*, vol. 5, Cambridge, Cambridge University Press.

Burn, J. (1777/1786), *A Pronouncing Dictionary of the English Language*, repr. in *English Linguistics, 1500–1800*, Alston, R.C. (ed.), London, The Scolar Press, 1974.

Cadell, P. (1977), *Royal Visits to Scotland*, Edinburgh, National Library of Scotland.

Cameron, E.A. (1998), 'Embracing the Past: The Highlands in Nineteenth-Century Scotland', in Broun / Finlay / Lynch, eds., pp.195–219.

Carlyle, T. (1828/1897), 'Burns', in Cochrane, ed., pp. 480–493.

Carter J.J. and J.H. Pittock, eds. (1987), *Aberdeen and the Enlightenment*, Aberdeen, Aberdeen University Press.

Cheshire, J., ed. (1991), *English Around the World – Sociolinguistic Perspectives*, Cambridge, Cambridge University Press.

Cheshire, J. and D. Stein, eds. (1997), *Taming the Vernacular: From Dialect to Written Standard Language*, London / New York, Longman.

Cheviot, A. (1896), *Proverbs, Proverbial Expressions, and Popular Rhymes of Scotland Collected and Arranged with Introduction, Notes and Parallel Phrases*, Paisley, Alexander Gardner.

Chiari, J. (n.d.), *Impressions of People and Literature*, Edinburgh / London, The Moray Press.

Chitnis, A.C. (1976), *The Scottish Enlightenment: A Social History*, London, Croom Helm.

Cleishbotham the Younger (1858/1975), *The Old Scots Tongue*, Kirkintilloch, Lang Syne Publishers.

Cleland, John (1766), *The Way to Things by Words, and to Words by Things; being a sketch of an attempt at the retrieval of the Antient Celtic, or, primitive language of Europe*, London, repr. in *English Linguistics 1500–1800*, Alston, R.C. (ed.), London, The Scolar Press, 1968.

Clement, R. D. (1984), 'Gaelic', in Trudgill, ed., pp. 318–342.

Clingham, G., ed., (1991), *New Light on Boswell*, Cambridge, Cambridge University Press.

Clyde, R. (1995), *From Rebel to Hero: The Image of the Highlander, 1745–1830*, East Linton, Tuckwell Press.

Cochrane, R., ed. (1897), *The English Essayists*, Edinburgh, W. P. Nimmo, Hay and Mitchell.

Cockburn, H. (1856/1971), *Memorials of His Time*, Edinburgh, Adam and Charles Black / James Thin.

Coles, E. (1676), *An English Dictionary*, repr. in *English Linguistics, 1500–1800*, Alston, R.C. (ed.), London, The Scolar Press, 1971.

Colgan, M. (1987), 'Ossian: Success or Failure for the Scottish Enlightenment?', in Carter / Pittock, eds., pp.344–349.

Collin, Z. (1862), *An Essay on the Scoto-English Dialect*, Lund, Berlings Printing Office.

Colville, J. (1909), *Studies in Lowland Scots*, Edinburgh / London, W. Green and Sons.

Connor, J. (1998), 'Elder Brother in the Muse', *Studies in Scottish Literature*, 30, pp. 59–66.

Cooper, L. (1936), 'Johnson on Oats', *Publications of the Modern Language Association*, 52, pp. 785–802.

Corbett, J. (1997), *Language and Scottish Literature*, Edinburgh, Edinburgh University Press.

— (1999), *Written in the Language of the Scottish Nation: A History of Literary Translation into Scots*, Clevedon, Multilingual Matters.

Craig, D. (1961), *Scottish Literature and the Scottish People, 1680–1830*, London, Chatto and Windus.

Craigie, W.A., ed. (1919), *The Maitland Folio Manuscript*, vol. I, pp. 159–161, Edinburgh, Scottish Text Society N.S. 7.

— ed. (1921/1970), *The Scottish Tongue*, College Park, Maryland, McGrath.

— (1925), 'The Earliest Records of the Scottish Tongue', *Scottish Historical Review*, 22, pp. 61–67.

— (1937), 'Northern Words in Modern English', *Society for Pure English Tract no. L*, Oxford, Clarendon Press.

Craigie, W.A., A.J. Aitken *et al.* (1931–2002), *Dictionary of the Older Scottish Tongue*, Oxford, Oxford University Press.

Crawford, R. (1992), *Devolving English Literature*, Oxford, Clarendon Press.

— ed. (1998), *The Scottish Invention of English Literature*, Cambridge, Cambridge University Press.

Crowley, T., ed. (1991), *Proper English?*, London / New York, Routledge.

Crozier, A. (1984), 'The Scotch-Irish Influence on American English', *American Speech*, 59:4, pp. 310–331.

Culpeper, J. (1997), *History of English*, London / New York, Routledge.

Curley, T.M. (1987), 'Johnson's Last Word on Ossian: Ghostwriting for William Shaw', in Carter / Pittock, eds., pp. 375–431.

Currie, J., ed. (1846), *The Complete Works of Robert Burns, with an Account of his Life and a Criticism on his Writings, to which are prefixed some observations on the character and condition of the Scottish peasantry*, Halifax, William Milner.

Daiches, D. (1964), *The Paradox of Scottish Culture: the Eighteenth Century Experience*, Oxford, Oxford University Press.

— (1986/1996), 'The Scottish Enlightenment', in Daiches / Jones / Jones, eds., pp. 1–42.

— (1996), 'Robert Burns', *ScotLit*, 14, Spring, pp.1–2.

Daiches, D., P. Jones and J. Jones, eds. (1986/1996), *The Scottish Enlightenment, 1730–1790. A Hotbed of Genius*, Edinburgh, The Saltire Society.

Dareau, M. (1998), 'DOST towards the Millennium', *Scottish Language*, 17, pp. 1–9.

Davies, A. (1999), 'Standard English: Discordant Voices', *World Englishes*, 18:2, pp. 171–186.

Deanina, C. (1763), *Extract form an Essay on the Progress of Learning among the Scots ..., Published Lately in the Italian Language, by Carlo Deanina, a Piedmontese. Transmitted in a Letter from Rome, dated February 5th*, n.p.

Deumert, A. and W. Vandenbussche, eds. (2003), *Germanic Standardizations – Past to Present*, Amsterdam, Benjamins.

Devine, T.M., ed. (1989), *Improvement and Enlightenment*, Edinburgh, John Donald.

— (1994), *Clanship to Crofters' War: The Social Transformation of the Scottish Highlands*, Manchester, Manchester University Press.

Devitt, A. J. (1989), *Standardizing Written English: Diffusion in the Case of Scotland, 1520–1659*, Cambridge, Cambridge University Press.

Donaldson, W. (1986), *Popular Literature in Victorian Scotland: Language, Fiction and the Press*, Aberdeen, Aberdeen University Press.

— (1989), *The Language of the People: Scots Prose from the Victorian Revival*, Aberdeen, Aberdeen University Press.

Dorian, N. (1981), *Language Death: the Life Cycle of a Scottish Gaelic Dialect*, Philadelphia, University of Pennsylvania Press.

— (1993), 'Internally and Externally Motivated Change in Language Contact Settings: Doubts about Dichotomy', in Jones, ed., pp. 131–155.

Dossena M., (1996), 'Overt Scotticisms in the Vocabulary of Scottish Standard English: a Matter of Style?', *Linguistica e Filologia*, 2, pp. 5–21.

— (1997a), 'The Search for Linguistic Excellence in Eighteenth-Century Scotland', *Textus*, X, 2, pp. 355–376.

— (1997b), 'Attitudes to Scots in Burns' Correspondence', *Linguistica e Filologia*, 4, pp.91–103.

— (1998a), 'Portraiture and Self-Portraiture in Scottish Standard English', *Linguistica e Filologia*, 6, pp. 27–42.

— (1998b), 'Diminutives in Scottish Standard English: A Case for Comparative Linguistics?', *Scottish Language*, 17, pp. 22–39.

— (1999/2000), 'Sense, Shortness and Salt: Ideas of Improvement in Eighteenth- and Nineteenth-Century Collections of Scottish Proverbs', *Review of Scottish Culture*, 12, pp. 93–106.

— (2000/2001), 'The Voice of Witnesses in Nineteenth-Century Accounts of the Highland Clearances', *Review of Scottish Culture*, 13, pp. 40–50.

— (2001a), '*For the aduancement of the commoun weilth*: Hypotheses in Scots Scientific Discourse of the 16th – 17th Centuries. A Preliminary Investigation', *Scottish Language*, 20, pp. 47–65.

— (2001b), '*The cruel slauchtyr that vas cruelly exsecutit*: Intensification and Adverbial Modality in the Helsinki Corpus of Older Scots – A Preliminary Overview. *Neuphilologische Mitteilungen*, 102, 3, pp. 287–302.

— (2002), "A strong Scots accent of the mind': The Pragmatic Value of Code-Switching between English and Scots in Private Correspondence – A Historical Overview', *Linguistica e Filologia* 14, pp. 103–127.

— (2003), 'Scots', in Deumert and Vandenbussche, eds, pp. 383–404.

— (forthcoming), 'Scotticisms in Johnson's Dictionary: A Lexicographer's Perceptions of a Sociolinguistic Change in Progress', *Atti del Convegno Nazionale di Storia della Lingua Inglese*, Genova 1997.

Dossena, M. and C. Jones, eds. (2003), *Insights into Late Modern English*, Bern, Peter Lang.

Douglas, S. (1995), *The Scots Language and Its European Roots*, Perth, The Scots Language Resource Centre.

Drescher, H.W. (1968), 'Johnson in Scotland', *Anglia*, 86:1/2, pp. 113–123.

Dressler, W. U. and L. Merlini Barbaresi (1994), *Morphopragmatics: Diminutives and Intensifiers in Italian, German, and Other Languages*, Berlin / New York, Mouton de Gruyter.

Dunbar, W. (1508), *The Tretis of the Tua Mariit Wemen and the Wedo*, in Barisone, ed., 1989.

Durkacz, V. E. (1983), *The Decline of the Celtic Languages*, Edinburgh, John Donald.

Dury, R. (1992), 'Saxonism and the Preference for 'Native' Vocabulary', in Pantaleo, ed., pp. 133–146.

Dwyer J. and R. B. Sher, eds. (1993), *Sociability and Society in Eighteenth-Century Scotland*, Edinburgh, The Mercat Press.

Dwyer, J. (1998), *The Age of the Passions*, East Linton, Tuckwell Press.

Elphinston, J. (1771), *Animadversions upon Elements of criticism: calculated equally for the benefit of that celebrated work, and the improvement of English stile: with an appendix on Scoticism*, London: Sold by W. Owen.

Fenton, A. (1995), *Craiters... Or Twenty Buchan Tales*, East Linton, Tuckwell Press.

Fenton A. and D. A. MacDonald, eds. (1994), *Studies in Scots and Gaelic*, Edinburgh, Canongate Academic.

Fenyö, K. (2000), *Contempt, Sympathy and Romance: Lowland Perceptions of the Highlands and the Clearances during the Famine Years, 1845–1855*, East Linton, Tuckwell Press.

Fergusson, D. (1785), '*A Collection of Scottish Proverbs*, The greatest part of which were at first gathered together by Mr David Fergusson, some time Minister at Dunfermline: And put into an Alphabetical Order after he departed this life, anno 1598', in Ruddiman, ed., unnumbered pages.

Filppula, M. (1991), 'Subordinating *And* in Hiberno-English Syntax: Irish or English Origin?', in Ureland / Broderick, eds., pp. 617–631.

— (1997), 'Cross-Dialectal Parallels and Language Contacts: Evidence from Celtic Englishes', in Hickey / Puppel, eds., pp. 943–957.

— (1999), *The Grammar of Irish English: Language in Hibernian Style*, London / New York, Routledge.

Finlay, R. J. (1998a), 'Caledonia or North Britain? Scottish Identity in the Eighteenth Century', in Broun / Finlay / Lynch, eds., pp.143–156.

— (1998b), 'Devolution and Scottish Culture: Setting a New Agenda', *The European English Messenger*, VII, 2, pp. 18–20.

Fisiak, J., ed. (1988), *Historical Dialectology – Regional and Social*, Berlin / New York, Mouton de Gruyter.

Fissore, V., ed. (1993), *In Transit Between Two Words* [sic], Torino, Tirrenia.

Fitzmaurice, S. M. (1998), 'The Commerce of Language in the Pursuit of Politeness in Eighteenth-Century England', *English Studies*, 79:4, pp. 309–328.

Flom, G.T. (1900), *Scandinavian Influence on Southern Lowland Scotch*, New York, Columbia University.

Fontane, T. (1860/1989), *Jenseit des Tweed. Bilder und Briefe aus Schottland*, Frankfurt a. M., Insel.

Frank, T. (1994), 'Language Standardization in Eighteenth-Century Scotland', in Stein / Tieken-Boon van Ostade, eds., pp. 51–62.

Fyfe, J.G. (1942), *Scottish Diaries and Memoirs, 1746–1843*, Stirling, Eneas Mackay.

Gachelin, J.M. (1995), 'From the Permanence of Scots to the Revival of Diachrony', *English Today*, 44:11/4 (October 1995), pp. 51–54.

Garioch, R. (1983), *Complete Poetical Works*, ed. by R. Fulton, Edinburgh, Macdonald.

Geddes, A. (1792), 'Three Scottish Poems, with a previous Dissertation on the Scoto-Saxon Dialect', *Archaeologia Scotica: or Transactions of the Society of Antiquaries of Scotland*, vol. 1, pp. 402–468.

Geikie, A. (1904), *Scottish Reminiscences*, Glasgow, James Maclehose and Sons.

Gibson J. (1988), 'The Bible in Scotland Today: Retrospect and Prospect', in Wright, ed., pp. 208–220.

Gillies, W., ed. (1989), *Gaelic and Scotland – Alba agus A'Ghàidhlig*, Edinburgh, Edinburgh University Press.

Glauser, B. (1974), *The Scottish-English Linguistic Border: Lexical Aspects*, Bern, Francke.

Glendening, J. (1997), *The High Road: Romantic Tourism, Scotland, and Literature, 1720–1820*, London, Macmillan.

Görlach, M. ed. (1985a), *Focus on Scotland*, Amsterdam / Philadelphia, John Benjamins.

— (1985b), 'Scots and Low German: The Social History of Two Minority Languages', in Görlach, ed., pp. 19–36.

— (1987), 'Lexical Loss and Lexical Survival: The Case of Scots and English', *Scottish Language*, 6, pp. 1–20, reprinted in Görlach (1990), pp.123–143.

— (1988a), 'The Study of Early Modern English Variation – the Cinderella of English Historical Linguistics?', in Fisiak, ed., pp. 211–228.

— (1988b/1990), 'The Development of Standard Englishes', in Görlach (1990), pp. 9–64.

— (1990), *Studies in the History of the English Language*, Heidelberg, Carl Winter Universitätsverlag.

— (1991a), *Englishes: Studies in the Varieties of English, 1984–1988*, Amsterdam / Philadelphia, John Benjamins.

— (1991b), 'Scotland and Jamaica – Bidialectal or Bilingual?', in Görlach, 1991a, pp. 69–89.

— (1991c), *Introduction to Early Modern English*, Cambridge, Cambridge University Press.

— (1995a), *New Studies in the History of English*, Heidelberg, Carl Winter Universitätsverlag.

— (1995b), 'Dialect Lexis in Early Modern English Dictionaries', in Görlach 1995a, pp. 82–127.

— (1996a), 'And Is It English?', *English World-Wide*, 17:2, pp. 1–22.

— (1996b), 'Morphological Standardization: The Strong Verbs in Scots', in Britton, ed., pp. 161–181.

— (1997a), 'Language and Nation: The Concept of Linguistic Identity in the History of English', *English World-Wide*, 18:1, pp. 1–34.

— (1997b), *The Linguistic History of English*, London, Macmillan.

— (1998a), *Even More Englishes: Studies 1996–1997*, Amsterdam / Philadelphia, John Benjamins.

— (1998b), 'Text-types and the History of Scots', in Görlach (1998a), pp. 55–77.

— (1998c), 'Celtic Englishes?', in Görlach (1998a), pp. 78–100.

— (1999), *An Annotated Bibliography of 19th-century Grammars of English*, Amsterdam / Philadelphia, John Benjamins.

Gotti, M. (1996), 'The Canting Terms of Coles' Dictionary', *Linguistica e Filologia*, 3, pp. 231–252.

— (1997), 'The 'Hard Words' of Levins' Dictionary', in Hickey / Puppel, eds., pp. 483–501.

Graham, W. (1968), *The Handy Guide to Scots*, Edinburgh, The Ramsay Head Press.

Grant, W. (1912/1970), *The Pronunciation of English in Scotland*, College Park, Maryland, McGrath.

Grant, W. and J.M. Dixon (1921), *A Manual of Modern Scots*, Cambridge, Cambridge University Press.

Grant, W. and D.D. Murison, eds (1931–76), *The Scottish National Dictionary*, Edinburgh, Scottish National Dictionary Association.

Green, D. ed. (1984), *Cobbett's Tour in Scotland*, Aberdeen, Aberdeen University Press.

Green, T.H. and T.H. Grose, eds. (1964), *Essays Moral, Political, and Literary by David Hume*, Aalen, Scientia.

Greig, J.Y.T., ed. (1932), *The Letters of David Hume*, Oxford, Clarendon Press.

Grillo, R.D. (1989), *Dominant Languages – Language and Hierarchy in Britain and France*, Cambridge, Cambridge University Press.

Gunn, J.S. (1970), 'Twentieth-Century Australian Idiom', in Ramson, ed., pp. 49–68.

Häcker, M. (1998), *Adverbial Clauses in Scots: A Semantic-Syntactic Study*, Berlin / New York, Mouton de Gruyter.

Hanway, M.A. (1776/1974), *A Journey to the Highlands of Scotland*, New York / London, Garland.

Harvie Wood, H. (1977/1991), Introduction to James Watson's *Choice Collection of Comic and Serious Scottish Poems*, Edinburgh, Scottish Text Society.

Haugen, E.R, J.D. McClure and D. S. Thomson, eds. (1981), *Minority Languages Today*, Edinburgh, Edinburgh University Press.

Hayashi, T. (1978), *The Theory of English Lexicography, 1530–1791*, Amsterdam / Philadelphia, John Benjamins.

Henderson, A. (1832), *Scottish Proverbs, with an Introductory Essay by W. Motherwell*, Edinburgh, Oliver and Boyd.

Henderson, R.A. (1993), 'Scottish Identity and the Languages of Scotland', in Fissore, ed., pp. 53–84.

Henderson, T. (1931), *A Scots Garland: An Anthology of Scottish Vernacular Verse*, Edinburgh, Grant and Murray.

Hewitt, D. (1987), 'James Beattie and the Languages of Scotland', in Carter / Pittock, eds., pp. 251–260.

Hickey, R. and S. Puppel, eds. (1997), *Language History and Linguistic Modelling*, Berlin / New York, Mouton de Gruyter.

Hickey, R., M. Kytö, I. Lancashire and M. Rissanen, eds. (1997), *Tracing the Trail of Time*, Amsterdam / Atlanta, GA, Rodopi.

Hill Burton, J. (1846), *Life and Correspondence of David Hume*, Edinburgh, William Tait.

Hislop, A. (1862/1868), *The Proverbs of Scotland with Explanatory and Illustrative Notes and a Glossary, New Edition, Entirely Revised and Supplemented*, Edinburgh, Alexander Hislop and Co.

Hobsbawm, E.J. and T. Ranger, eds. (1983), *The Invention of Tradition*, Cambridge, Cambridge University Press (trad. it.: *L'invenzione della tradizione*, Torino, Einaudi, 1987).

Holmes, D. T. (1909), *Literary Tours in the Highlands and Islands of Scotland*, Paisley, Alexander Gardner.

Houston, R. A. (1989), 'Scottish Education and Literacy, 1600–1800: An International Perspective', in Devine, ed., pp. 43–61.

Hudson, V. B. (1946), 'Johnson and the Scots', in *The Times Literary Supplement*, 13th April 1946.

Hughes, A. and P. Trudgill (1996), *English Accents and Dialects: An Introduction to Social and Regional Varieties of English in the British Isles*, 3rd edition, London, Arnold.

Hume, D. (1752), 'Scotticisms', in *Political Discourses*, Edinburgh, unnumbered pages, and in Green / Grose, eds., 1964.

Hume Brown, P. (1891), *Early Travellers in Scotland*, Edinburgh, David Douglas.

Hunter, G., ed. (1960), 'David Hume: Some Unpublished Letters, 1771–1776', *Studies in Literature and Language*, Houston, University of Texas.

Iacuaniello, F. (1992/93), 'Linguistic Awareness and Attitudes in a Sample of Scottish Speakers', *Scottish Language*, 11/12, pp. 62–71.

Iamartino, G. (1995), 'Dyer's and Burke's Addenda and Corrigenda to Johnson's *Dictionary* as Clues to its Contemporary Reception', *Textus*, VIII, 2, pp. 199–248.

Jack, R.D.S. (1994), 'Burns as Sassenach Poet', in Simpson, ed., pp. 150–166.

— (1997), 'The Language of Literary Materials: Origins to 1700', in Jones, ed., pp. 213–263.

Jackson Young, M. (1997), 'The Penniless Pilgrimage', *The Scots Magazine*, April 1997, electronic edition available at: <http://www.scotsmagazine.com>

Jamieson, J. (1808/1840), *An Etymological Dictionary of the Scottish Language ... to which is prefixed A Dissertation on the Origin of the Scottish Language*, 2nd edition edited by J. Johnstone, Edinburgh, William Tait.

Jarvie, J.N. (1947), *Lallans*, London, Wren Books.

Jeffares, A.N., ed. (1969), *Scott's Mind and Art*, Edinburgh, Oliver and Boyd.

Johnson, S. (1755/1773), *A Dictionary of the English Language*, re-edited by McDermott, A., ed. (1996), *A Dictionary of the English Language on CD-ROM*, Cambridge, Cambridge University Press.

— (1775/1824), *A Dictionary of the English Language*, London, Offor *et al.*

— (1775), *A Journey to the Western Islands of Scotland*, in MacGowan, ed., pp. 3–145.

Johnston, P.A. (1983), 'Irregular Style Variation Patterns in Edinburgh Speech', *Scottish Language*, 2, pp. 1–19.

— (1984), 'Variation in the Standard Scottish English of Morningside', *English World-Wide*, 4:2, pp. 133–185.

— (1985), 'The Rise and Fall of the Morningside / Kelvinside Accent', in Görlach, ed., pp. 37–56.

— (1997a), 'Older Scots Phonology and its Regional Variation', in Jones, ed., pp. 47–111.

— (1997b), 'Regional Variation', in Jones, ed., pp. 433–513.

Jones, C., ed. (1991), *A Treatise on the Provincial Dialect of Scotland, by Sylvester Douglas (Lord Glenbervie)*, Edinburgh, Edinburgh University Press.

— (1993a), 'Scottish Standard English in the Late Eighteenth Century', *Transactions of the Philological Society*, 91:1, pp. 95–131.

— ed. (1993b), *Historical Linguistics: Problems and Perspectives*, London, Longman.

— (1995), *A Language Suppressed: The Pronunciation of the Scots Language in the Eighteenth Century*, Edinburgh, John Donald.

— ed. (1997), *The Edinburgh History of the Scots Language*, Edinburgh, Edinburgh University Press.

— (1997a), 'Phonology', in Jones, ed., pp. 267–334.

— (1997b), 'An Early Eighteenth Century Spelling Book for Ladies', *English Studies*, 78:5, pp. 430–450.

— (2002), *The English Language in Scotland: An Introduction to Scots*, East Linton, Tuckwell Press.

Kastovsky, D., ed. (1994), *Studies in Early Modern English*, Berlin / New York, Mouton de Gruyter.

Kastovsky, D. and A. Mettinger, eds (2000), *The History of English in a Social Context – A Contribution to Historical Sociolinguistics*, Berlin / New York, Mouton de Gruyter.

Kay, B. (1986), *Scots, The Mither Tongue*, London, Grafton Books.

Kelly, J. (1721), *A Complete Collection of Scotish Proverbs Explained and made Intelligible to the English Reader*, London, Printed for William and John Innys at the West End of St Paul's, and John Osborn in Lombard Street.

Kenrick, W. (1784), *A Rhetorical Grammar of the English Language*, repr. in *English Linguistics, 1500–1800*, Alston, R.C. (ed.), London, The Scolar Press, 1974.

Kidd, C. (1993), *Subverting Scotland's Past: Scottish Whig Historians and the Creation of an Anglo-British Identity, 1689–c. 1830*, Cambridge, Cambridge University Press.

King, A. (1997), 'The Inflectional Morphology of Older Scots', in Jones, ed., pp. 156–181.

Kinghorn, A.M. and A. Law, eds (1972), *The Works of Allan Ramsay*, Edinburgh / London, Blackwood.

Kingsmore, R.K. (1995), *Ulster Scots Speech*, Tuscaloosa / London, Univ. of Alabama Press.

Kirk, J.M. (1985), 'Linguistic Atlases and Grammar: The Investigation and Description of Regional Variation in English Syntax', in Kirk / Sanderson / Widdowson, eds., pp. 130–156.

— (1987), 'The Heteronomy of Scots with Standard English', in Macafee / Macleod, eds., pp.166–181.

— (1992/93), 'Computing and Research on Scots', *Scottish Language*, 11/12, pp. 75–131.

Kirk, J.M., S. Sanderson and J.D.A. Widdowson, eds. (1985), *Studies in Linguistic Geography*, London, Croom Helm.

Klein, L. (1993), '*Politeness* as Linguistic Ideology in Late Seventeenth- and Early Eighteenth-Century England', in Stein / Tieken-Boon van Ostade, eds., pp. 31–50.

Klemola, J., M. Kytö and M. Rissanen, eds (1996), *Speech Past and Present – Studies in English Dialectology in Memory of Ossi Ihalainen*, Frankfurt a. M., Peter Lang.

Klemola, J. and M. Filppula (1992), 'Subordinating Uses of *And* in the History of English', in Rissanen / Ihalainen / Nevalainen / Taavitsainen, eds., pp. 310–318.

Klibansky R. and E.C. Mossner, eds. (1954), *New Letters of David Hume*, Oxford, Clarendon Press.

Kniezsa, V. (1997a), 'The Origins of Scots Orthography', in Jones, ed., pp. 24–46.

— (1997b), 'The Influence of English upon Scottish Writing', in Hickey / Puppel, eds., pp. 637–653.

Kremer, D., ed. (1991), *Actes du XVIII Congrès International de la Linguistique et de la Philologie Romanes* (Trier 1986), Tübingen, Niemeyer.

Kytö, M., M. Rissanen and S. Wright, eds. (1994), *Corpora Across the Centuries*, Amsterdam / Atlanta, GA, Rodopi.

Laing, M. (1994), 'The Linguistic Analysis of Medieval Vernacular Texts: Two Projects at Edinburgh', in Kytö / Rissanen / Wright, eds., pp.121–141.

Laing, M. and K. Williamson, eds. (1994), *Speaking in Our Tongues – Proceedings of a Colloquium on Medieval Dialectology and Related Disciplines*, Cambridge, D.S. Brewer.

Lass, R. (1980), *On Explaining Language Change*, Cambridge, Cambridge University Press.

— (1987), *The Shape of English*, London, Dent.

Lawrie, S.M. (1991), 'A Linguistic Survey of the Use and Familiarity of Scottish Dialect Items in NE Fife', *Scottish Language*, 10, pp. 18–29.

Leith, D. (1997), *A Social History of English*, second edn., London, Routledge.

Leneman, L. (1982), 'The SSPCK and the Question of Gaelic in Blair Atholl', *Scottish Studies*, 26, pp. 57–59.

— (1987), 'The Effects of Ossian in Lowland Scotland', in Carter / Pittock, eds., pp. 357–362.

Letley, E. (1988), *From Galt to Douglas Brown: Nineteenth-Century Fiction and Scots Language*, Edinburgh, Scottish Academic Press.

Logan, J. (1831/1843), *The Scotish Gael*, Hartford, S. Andrus and Son.

Lorimer, W. L. (1983/1985), *The New Testament in Scots*, London, Penguin.

Low, D. A., ed. (1974/1995), *Robert Burns: The Critical Heritage*, London / New York, Routledge.

Lowther C. *et al.* (1894), *Our Journall into Scotland, A.D. 1629*, Edinburgh.

Macafee, C. (1985), 'Nationalism and the Scots Renaissance Now', in Görlach, ed., pp. 7–17.

— (1987), 'Language and Modern Life: Notes from Glasgow', in Macafee / Macleod, eds., pp. 182–194.

— (1992/93), 'A Short Grammar of Older Scots', *Scottish Language*, 11/12, pp. 10–36.

— (1994a), *Traditional Dialect in the Modern World: A Glasgow Case Study*, Frankfurt a. M., Peter Lang.

— (1994b), 'Dialect Erosion, with Special Reference to Urban Scots', in Fenton / MacDonald, eds., pp. 69–80.

— (1997a), 'Older Scots Lexis', in Jones, ed., pp. 182–212.

— (1997b), 'Ongoing Change in Modern Scots – The Social Dimension', in Jones, ed., pp. 514–548.

Macafee, C. and I. Macleod, eds. (1987), *The Nuttis Schell: Essays on the Scots Language presented to A. J. Aitken*, Aberdeen, Aberdeen University Press.

Macafee, C. and B. McGarrity (1999), 'Scots Language Attitudes and Language Maintenance', *Leeds Studies in English*, n.s. XXX, pp. 165–179.

Macaulay, D., ed. (1992), *The Celtic Languages*, Cambridge, Cambridge University Press.

Macaulay, R.K.S. (1978), 'Variation and Consistency in Glaswegian English', in Trudgill, ed., pp. 132–143.

— (1985), 'The Narrative Skills of a Scottish Coal Miner', in Görlach, ed., pp. 101–124.

— (1991a), *Locating Dialect in Discourse: The Language of Honest Men and Bonnie Lasses in Ayr*, Oxford, Oxford University Press.

— (1991b), ' 'Coz it izny spelt when they say it': Displaying Dialect in Writing', *American Speech*, 66:3, pp. 280–291.

— (1995/96), 'Remarkably Common Eloquence: The Aesthetics of Urban Dialect', *Scottish Language*, 14/15, pp. 66–80.

— (1997a), 'Ayrshire as a Linguistic Area', in Schneider, ed., vol. I, pp. 159–171.

— (1997b), *Standards and Variation in Urban Speech: Examples from Lowland Scots*, Amsterdam / Philadelphia, John Benjamins.

Macbain, A. (1882), *Grammar and Grammars*, Inverness, W. Mackay.

Macdonald, R. (1994), 'A Dictionary Ramble', *Scottish Language*, 13, pp. 82–87.

MacGillivray, A. (1997), *Teaching Scottish Literature: Curriculum and Classroom Applications*, Edinburgh, Edinburgh University Press.

MacGowan, I., ed. (1996), *Journey to the Hebrides*, Edinburgh, Canongate Books.

MacInnes, J. (1989), 'The Gaelic Perception of the Lowlands', in Gillies, ed., pp. 89–100.

Mackay, C. (1888), *A Dictionary of Lowland Scotch with an introductory chapter on the poetry, humour, and literary history of the Scottish language and an appendix of Scottish Proverbs*, Edinburgh, Ballantyne Press; London, Whittaker and Co.

Mackenzie, H. (1786/1897), 'Extraordinary Account of Robert Burns, The Ayrshire Ploughman', in Cochrane, ed., pp. 278–280.

Mackie, A. (1881), *Scotticisms Arranged and Corrected*, London, Hamilton, Adams and Co; Edinburgh and Glasgow, John Menzies and Co; Aberdeen, A. and R. Milne.

Mackinnon, I. (1966), *Lowland Scots Glossary*, Stirling, A. Learmonth and Son.

MacKinnon, K. (1984), 'Scottish Gaelic and English in the Highlands', in Trudgill, ed., pp. 499–515.

Macleod, I. (1992/93), 'Computers and Scots Lexicography', *Scottish Language*, 11/12, pp. 132–137.

— (1993), 'Research in Progress: Some Problems of Scottish Lexicography', *English World-Wide*, 14:1, pp. 115–125.

— (1998), 'Scots Dictionaries Present and Future', *Scottish Language*, 17, pp. 10–15.

Macleod, I. and A. MacNacail (1995), *Scotland: A Linguistic Double Helix*, European Bureau for Lesser Used Languages.

MacQueen, L.E.C. (1983), 'English Was to Them a Foreign Tongue', *Scottish Language*, 2, pp.49–51.

Macwhannell, N. (1937), *Oor Mither Tongue: An Anthology of Scots Vernacular Verse*, Paisley, A. Gardner Ltd.

Martin, M. (1703/1994), *A Description of the Western Islands of Scotland*, London, Andrew Bell; Edinburgh, Birlinn.

Masson, R. (1896/1929), *Use and Abuse of English: A Handbook of Composition*, Edinburgh, James Thin.

Mather, J.Y. and H.H. Speitel, eds. (1975–86), *The Linguistic Atlas of Scotland*, London, Croom Helm.

McArthur, T. ed. (1992a), *The Oxford Companion to the English Language*, Oxford, Oxford University Press.

— (1992b), 'Celtic Languages', in McArthur, ed. pp. 202–204.

— (1998), *The English Languages*, Cambridge, Cambridge University Press.

McClure, J. D. (1980), 'Western Scottish Intonation: a Preliminary Study', in Waugh / van Schoonefeld, eds., pp. 201–218.

— (1981a), 'Scottis, Inglis, Suddroun: Language Labels and Language Attitudes', *Proceedings of the Third International Conference on Scottish Language and Literature, Mediaeval and Renaissance, Stirling 1981*, Stirling and Glagow, pp. 52–69, reprinted in McClure (1995), pp. 44–56.

— (1981b), 'The Synthesisers of Scots', in Haugen / McClure / Thomson, eds., pp. 91–99, reprinted in McClure (1995), pp.190–199.

— (1983a), *Scotland and the Lowland Tongue*, Aberdeen, Aberdeen University Press.

— (1983b), 'Scots in Dialogue: Some Uses and Implications', in McClure (1983a), pp. 129–148, reprinted in McClure (1995), pp. 86–106.

— (1984), 'Lowland Scots: An Ambivalent National Tongue', *Multilingua*, 3, pp. 143–151, reprinted in McClure (1995), pp. 5–19.

— (1985a), 'The Pinkerton Syndrome', *Chapman*, 41, pp. 2–8, reprinted in McClure (1995), pp. 57–67.

— (1985b), 'The Debate on Scots Orthography', in Görlach, ed., pp. 203–210.

— (1986), 'What Scots Owes to Gaelic', *Scottish Language*, 5, pp. 85–98, reprinted in McClure (1995), pp. 68–85.

— (1987a), "Lallans' and 'Doric' in North-Eastern Scottish Poetry', *English World-Wide*, 8:2, pp.215–234.

— (1987b), 'Language and Genre in Allan Ramsay's 1721 Poems', in Carter / Pittock, eds., pp. 261–269, reprinted in McClure (1995), pp. 161–170.

— (1988), *Why Scots Matters*, Edinburgh, The Saltire Society in association with The Scots Language Society.

— (1993), 'Varieties of Scots in Recent and Contemporary Narrative Prose', *English World-Wide*, 14:1, pp. 1–22.

— (1994), 'English in Scotland', in Burchfield, ed., pp. 23–93.

— (1995), *Scots and its Literature*, Amsterdam / Philadelphia, John Benjamins.

— (1997), 'The Spelling of Scots: A Difficulty', in Schneider, ed., vol. I, pp. 173–184.

— (1998), 'What is the Scots Language?', in Niven / Jackson, eds., pp. 7–18.

— (2000), *Language, Poetry and Nationhood – Scots as a Poetic Language from 1878 to the Present*, East Linton, Tuckwell Press.

McClure, J.D., A.J. Aitken and J.T. Low (1980), *The Scots Language: Planning for Modern Usage*, Edinburgh, The Ramsay Head Press.

McClure, J.D., J.T. Low, J.K. Annand, A.D. Mackie and J.J. Graham (1985), 'Our Ain Leid? The Predicament of a Scots Writer', in Görlach, ed., pp. 181–201.

McClure, J.D. and M.R.G. Spiller, eds (1989), *Bryght Lanternis: Essays on the Language and Literature of Medieval and Renaissance Scotland*, Aberdeen, Aberdeen University Press.

McClure, J.D. and M. Dossena (forthcoming), 'Language policy in Scotland today: the (strange?) case of Scots'. Proceedings of the Conference *Sociolinguistics and Language Planning* (Ortisei, Italy, 12–14 December 2002).

McColl Millar, R. – with the assistance of D. Horsbroch (2000), 'Covert and Overt Language Attitudes to the Scots Tongue Expressed in the Statistical accounts of Scotland', in Kastovsky / Mettinger, eds., pp. 169–198.

— (2003), '"Blind attachment to inveterate customs". Language Use, Language Attitude and the Rhetoric of Improvement in the first *Statistical Account*', in Dossena and Jones, eds., pp. 311–330.

McCrone (1989), *Understanding Scotland: The Sociology of a Stateless Nation*, London / New York, Routledge.

McGuirk, C. (1985/1997), *Robert Burns and the Sentimental Era*, Univ. of Georgia Press / East Linton, Tuckwell Press.

McIntosh, A. (1952), *An Introduction to a Survey of Scottish Dialects*, Edinburgh, T. Nelson and Sons Ltd.

McKnight, G.H. (1968), *The Evolution of the English Language from Chaucer to the Twentieth Century*, New York, Dover Publications; formerly titled *Modern English in the Making* (1928).

McMahon, A.M.S. (1992), 'Lexical Phonology and Diachrony', in Rissanen / Ihalainen / Nevalainen / Taavitsainen, eds., pp. 167–190.

McNicol, D. (1779), *Remarks on Dr Samuel Johnson's Journey to the Hebrides; in which are contained, observations on the antiquities, language, genius, and manners of the Highlanders of Scotland*, London.

Meek, D. (1988), 'The Gaelic Bible', in Wright, ed., pp. 9–23.

Melchers, G. (1985), ' 'Knappin', 'Proper English', 'Modified Scottish': Some Language Attitudes in the Shetland Isles', in Görlach, ed., pp. 87–100.

— (1999), 'Writing in Shetland Dialect', in Taavitsainen / Melchers / Pahta, eds., pp. 331–345.

Melville, A. (1621–1640), *Proverbes*, in Rae Smith, ed., pp. 5–20.

Menzies, J. (1991), 'An Investigation of Attitudes to Scots and Glasgow Dialect among Secondary school Pupils', *Scottish Language*, 10, pp. 30–46.

Meurman-Solin, A. (1989), 'The Helsinki Corpus of Older Scots', in McClure / Spiller, eds., pp. 451–458.

— (1992), 'On the Morphology of Verbs in Middle Scots: Present and Present Perfect Indicative', in Rissanen / Ihalainen / Nevalainen / Taavitsainen, eds., pp. 611–623.

— (1993a), 'Older Scots', in Rissanen / Kytö / Palander-Collin, eds., pp. 75–82.

— (1993b), 'Periphrastic *Do* in Sixteenth- and Seventeenth-century Scots', in Rissanen / Kytö / Palander-Collin, eds., pp. 235–251.

— (1993c), *Variation and Change in Early Scots Prose*, Helsinki, Suomalainen Tiedeakatemia.

— (1994), 'The Helsinki Corpus of Older Scots', in Kytö / Rissanen / Wright, eds., pp. 53–63.

— (1995), A New Tool: The Helsinki Corpus of Older Scots (1450–1700). *ICAME Journal* 19, pp. 49–62.

— (1997a), 'A Corpus-Based Study on *T/D* Deletion and Insertion in Late Medieval and Renaissance Scottish English', in Nevalainen / Kahlas-Tarkka, eds., pp. 111–124.

— (1997b), 'Text Profiles in the Study of Language Variation and Change', in Hickey / Kytö / Lancashire / Rissanen, eds., pp. 199–214.

— (1997c), 'Differentiation and Standardization in Early Scots', in Jones, ed., pp. 3–23.

— (1999), 'Letters as a Source of Data for Reconstructing Early Spoken Scots', in Taavitsainen / Melchers / Pahta, eds., pp. 305–322.

— (2000a), 'Change from Above or Below? Mapping the *Loci* of Linguistic Change in the History of Scottish English', in Wright, L., ed., pp. 155–170.

— (2000b), 'Geographical, socio-spatial and systemic distance in the spread of the relative *who* in Scots', in Bermúdez-Otero / Denison / Hogg / McCully, eds., pp. 417–438.

— (2000c), 'On the Conditioning of Geographical and Social Distance in Language Variation and Change in Renaissance Scots', in Kastovsky / Mettinger, eds., pp. 227–255.

— (2001), 'Women as Informants in the Reconstruction of Geographically and Socioculturally Conditioned Language Variation and Change in 16th and 17th Century Scots', *Scottish Language*, 20, pp. 20–46.

Millar, J. H. (1912), *Scottish Prose of the Seventeenth and Eighteenth Centuries*, Glasgow, James Maclehose and Sons.

Miller, H. (1856/1897), 'Edinburgh an Age ago', in Cochrane, ed., pp. 377–381.

Miller, J. and K. Brown (1982), 'Aspects of Scottish English Syntax', *English World-Wide*, 3:1, pp. 3–17.

Miller, J. (1984), 'Discourse Patterns in Spoken English, *Sheffield Working Papers in Language and Linguistics*, 1, pp. 10–39.

— (1993), 'The Grammar of Scottish English', in Milroy / Milroy, eds., pp. 99–138.

— (1998), 'Scots: A Sociolinguistic Perspective', in Niven / Jackson, eds., pp. 45–56.

Milroy, J. and L. Milroy, eds. (1993), *Real English: The Grammar of English Dialects in the British Isles*, London, Longman.

Milroy, J. (1982), 'Some Connections between Galloway and Ulster Speech', *Scottish Language*, 1, pp. 23–29.

— (1992), 'A Social Model for the Interpretation of Language Change', in Rissanen / Ihalainen / Nevalainen / Taavitsainen, eds., pp. 72–91.

— (1993), 'On the Social Origins of Language Change', in Jones, ed., pp. 215–236.

— (1996), ' Linguistic Ideology and the Anglo-Saxon Lineage of English', in Klemola / Kytö / Rissanen, eds., pp. 169–186.

Milton, C. (1992), 'Language, Class and Education in Twentieth-Century Scottish Writing', *English World-Wide*, 13:2, pp. 219–251.

— (1995/96), 'Shibboleths o the Scots', *Scottish Language*, 14/15, pp. 1–14.

Mitchell, A. (1901), *A List of Travels, Tours, etc., Relating to Scotland*, Edinburgh, From the Proceedings of the Society of Antiquaries of Scotland, vol. XXXV.

Mitchell, S. (1999), 'James Macpherson's *Ossian* and the Empire of Sentiment', *British Journal for Eighteenth-Century Studies*, 22:2, pp. 155–171.

Moessner, L. (1997), 'The Syntax of Older Scots', in Jones, ed., pp. 112–155.

Mohr, V. (unpubl. MS), 'The Lexicographic Archaeology of Scotticisms: Provincialisms and International English', paper presented at the 5th International Conference on Languages of Scotland and Ulster, Aberdeen 1997.

Montgomerie-Fleming, J. B. (1899), *Desultory Notes on Jamieson's Scottish Dictionary*, Glasgow / Edinburgh, William Hodge and Co.

Montgomery, M. (1989), 'Exploring the Roots of Appalachian English', *English World-Wide*, 10:2, pp. 227–278.

— (1997), 'The Rediscovery of the Ulster Scots Language', in Schneider, ed., vol. I, pp.211–226.

Montgomery, M. and R. J. Gregg (1997), 'The Scots Language in Ulster', in Jones, ed., pp. 569–622.

Mugglestone, L. (1995), *'Talking Proper': The Rise of Accent as Social Symbol*, Oxford, Clarendon Press.

Murison, D. (1964), 'The Scots Tongue – The Folk Speech', *Folklore*, 75, pp. 37–47.

— (1969), 'The Two Languages in Scott', in Jeffares, ed., pp. 206–229.

— (1971), 'The Dutch Element in the Vocabulary of Scots', in Aitken / McIntosh / Pálsson, eds., pp. 159–176.

— (1977), *The Guid Scots Tongue*, Edinburgh, William Blackwood.

— (1987), 'Scottish Lexicography', in Macafee / Macleod, eds., pp. 17–24.

Murphy, P.T. (1998), 'Burns, Ossian and Real Scottish Genius', *Studies in Scottish Literature*, 30, pp. 67–75.

Murray, J.A.H. (1873), *The Dialect of the Southern Counties of Scotland*, London, Asher.

Murray, K.M.E. (1977), *Caught in the Web of Words: James Murray and the Oxford English Dictionary*, New Haven / London, Yale University Press.

Nagashima, D. (1988), *Johnson the Philologist*, Osaka, Kansai University of Foreign Studies.

Nevalainen, T and L. Kahlas-Tarkka, eds. (1997), *To Explain the Present*, Helsinki, Société Néophilologique.

Nicholson, R. (1998), 'The Tartan Portraits of Prince Charles Edward Stuart: Identity and Iconography', *British Journal for Eighteenth-Century Studies*, 21:2, pp. 145–160.

Nicolson, A. (1866), *Report on the State of Education in the Hebrides*, Edinburgh, HMSO.

Niven, L. and R. Jackson, eds (1998), *The Scots Language: Its Place in Education*, Dumfries, Watergaw.

Nocera Avila, C., N. Pantaleo and D. Pezzini, eds., (1992), *Early Modern English: Trends, Forms and Texts*, Fasano, Schena.

Ó Baoill, C. (1991), 'Borrowing between Scots and Gaelic', *Scottish Language*, 10, pp. 9–17.

— (1997), 'The Scots-Gaelic Interface', in Jones, ed., pp. 551–568.

Pantaleo, N. (1992a), 'On the Fringes of Early Modern English: Middle Scots Variation in Profane and Religious Writing', in Nocera Avila / Pantaleo / Pezzini, eds., pp. 215–233.

— ed. (1992b), *Aspects of English Diachronic Linguistics*, Fasano (Br), Schena.

— (1997), 'The Polyglot Puzzle: Geographical and Military Lexicon in Barbour's *The Bruce*', *Textus*, X, 2, pp. 287–298.

Parkinson, D. (1995), 'The Entry of Wealth in the Middle Scots *Crying of ane Playe*', *Modern Philology*, 93, 1, pp. 23–36.

Paterson, J. (1855), *Origin of the Scots and the Scottish Language*, Edinburgh, John Menzies; Glasgow, T. Murray and Son; Paisley, R. Stewart.

Paterson, L. (1992), 'Scottish Languages and Scottish Identities', *Scotland's Languages*, 1, pp. 34–36.

Phillipson, N.T. and R. Mitchison, eds. (1970), *Scotland in the Age of Improvement*, Edinburgh, Edinburgh University Press.

Pinkerton, J. (1786), *Ancient Scotish Poems, Never Before in Print ... Prefixed are an Essay on the Origin of Scotish Poetry. A List of All the Scotish Poets with Brief Remarks. And ... an Account of the Contents of the Maitland and Bannatyne MSS.*, London, Printed for Charles Dilly and William Creech at Edinburgh.

Pittock, M.G.H. (1991), *The Invention of Scotland: The Stuart Myth and the Scottish Identity, 1638 to the Present*, London / New York, Routledge.

— (1994), *Poetry and Jacobite Politics in Eighteenth-Century Britain and Ireland*, Cambridge, Cambridge University Press.

Pollner, C. (1985a), *Englisch in Livingston*, Frankfurt a. M., Peter Lang.

— (1985b), 'Old Words in a Young Town', *Scottish Language*, 4, pp.5–15.

— (1985c), 'Linguistic Fieldwork in a Scottish New Town', in Görlach, ed., pp. 57–68.

— (1994), 'The Ugly Sister – Scots Words in Early Modern English Dictionaries', in Kastovsky ed., pp. 289–299.

— (2000), 'Shibboleths Galore: The Treatment of Irish and Scottish English in Histories of the English Language', in Kastovsky / Mettinger, eds., pp. 363–376.

Pollner, C. and H. Rohlfing (1986), 'The Scottish Language from the 16th to the 18th Century: Elphinston's Works as a Mirror of Anglicisation', in Strauss / Drescher, eds., pp. 125–137.

Porter, G. (1999), 'The Ideology of Misrepresentation: Scots in English Broadsides', in Taavitsainen / Melchers / Pahta, eds., pp. 361–374.

Portier, F. (1999), 'Le *Scots Musical Museum* et *A Select Collection of Original Scottish Airs*: Réconstitution ou Falsification?', *Études Anglaises*, 52:1, pp. 53–68.

Pottle, F. A. (1929), *The Literary Career of James Boswell, Esq.*, Oxford, Clarendon Press.

— ed. (1952), *Boswell in Holland, 1763–1764*, London, Heinemann.

— ed. (1966), *James Boswell: The Earlier Years, 1740–1769*, London, Heinemann.

Pottle, M.S., C.C. Abbott and F.A. Pottle, eds. (1993), *Catalogue of the Papers of James Boswell at Yale University*, Edinburgh, Edinburgh University Press, and New Haven, Yale University Press.

Purves, D. (1997), *A Scots Grammar – Scots Grammar and Usage*, Edinburgh, The Saltire Society.

Rae Smith, J., ed. (1899), *Extracts from the Commonplace Book of Andrew Melville*, Aberdeen, John Rae Smith.

Rae, T.I., ed. (1974), *The Union of 1707: Its Impact on Scotland*, Glasgow / London, Blackie and Son Ltd.

Ramsay, A. (1737), *A Collection of Scots Proverbs, more complete and correct than any heretofore published*, Edinburgh; also in Kinghorn / Law, eds., vol. 5, pp. 59–129.

Ramson, W.S., ed. (1970), *English Transported – Essays on Australasian English*, Canberra, Australian National University Press.

Ratcliffe Barnett, T. (1913), *Reminiscences of Old Scots Folk*, London and Edinburgh, T.N. Foulis.

Ray, J. (1674/1768), *A Compleat Collection of English Proverbs*; also in Bohn (1855).

Reddick, A. (1990), *The Making of Johnson's Dictionary, 1746–1773*, Cambridge, Cambridge University Press.

Reed J.W. and F.A. Pottle, eds. (1977), *Boswell: Laird of Auchinleck, 1778–1782*, New York, McGraw-Hill.

Reid, E. (1978), 'Social and Stylistic Variation in the Speech of Children: Some Evidence from Edinburgh', in Trudgill, ed., pp. 158–171.

Rendall, J. (1978), *The Origins of the Scottish Enlightenment*, London, Macmillan.

Riach, W.A.D. (1984), 'Galloway Schools Dialect Survey', *Scottish Language*, 3, pp. 49–59.

Rissanen, M., O. Ihalainen, T. Nevalainen and I. Taavitsainen, eds. (1992), *History of Englishes: New Methods and Interpretations in Historical Linguistics*, Berlin / New York, Mouton de Gruyter.

Rissanen, M., M. Kytö and M. Palander-Collin, eds. (1993), *Early English in the Computer Age: Explorations through the Helsinki Corpus*, Berlin / New York, Mouton de Gruyter.

Roberts, A. (1991), 'Midges a Modern Scourge? The Evidence of Early Accounts', *Review of Scottish Culture*, 7, pp. 95–104.

Robinson, M. (1983), 'Language Choice in the Reformation: The Scots Confession of 1560', in McClure, ed., pp. 59–78.

— ed. (1985/1996), *The Concise Scots Dictionary*, Edinburgh, Chambers.

— (1987), '*The Concise Scots Dictionary* as a Tool for Linguistic Research', in Macafee / Macleod, eds., pp. 59–72.

Robinson, P. (1997), *Ulster Scots: A Grammar of the Traditional Written and Spoken Language*, n.p., The Ullans Press.

Robson, E.H.A. (1937), *Preparations for a Study of Metropolitan Scots of the First Half of the Nineteenth Century, as exemplified in 'Mansie Wauch'* ..., Edinburgh / London, W. Blackwood and Sons Ltd.

Rogers, P. (1991), 'Boswell and the Scotticism', in Clingham, ed., pp.56–71.

— (1995), *Johnson and Boswell, The Transit of Caledonia*, Oxford, Clarendon Press.

Romaine, S. (1975), *Linguistic Variability in the Speech of Some Edinburgh Schoolchildren*, M.Litt. Thesis, University of Edinburgh.

— (1978), 'Post-Vocalic /r/ in Scottish English: Sound Change in Progress?', in Trudgill, ed., pp. 144–157.

— (1982), 'The English Language in Scotland', in Bailey / Görlach, eds., pp. 56–83.

— (1984), 'Some Historical and Social Dimensions of Syntactic Change in Middle Scots Relative Clauses', in Blake / Jones, eds., pp. 101–122.

— (1985), 'The Problem of Short /a/ in Scotland', *English World-Wide*, 6:2, pp. 165–197.

— (1989), *Bilingualism*, Oxford, Basil Blackwell.

— (1994), *Language in Society*, Oxford, Oxford University Press.

Ross, I.S. and S.A.C. Scobie, 'Patriotic Publishing as a Response to the Union', in Rae, ed., pp. 94–119.

Roy, R. (1988), 'The Bible in Burns and Scott', in Wright, ed., pp. 79–93.

Ruddiman, T., ed. (1785) *A Select Collection of Scots Poems chiefly in the broad Buchan dialect to which is added a collection of Scots Proverbs by the Reverend Mr David Fergusson some time minister at Dunfermline*, Edinburgh.

Ruf, A. (1996), *'Yi Canny Talk Right'. Eine soziolinguistische Untersuchung zur Verwendung des Glaswegian am BBC Radio Scotland und Radio Clyde*, Bern, Peter Lang.

Ryskamp, C. and F.A. Pottle, eds. (1963), *Boswell: The Ominous Years, 1774–1776*, London: Heinemann.

Sabban, A. (1982), *Gälisch-Englisch Sprachkontakt*, Heidelberg, Julius Groos.

— (1984), 'Investigations into the Syntax of Hebridean English', *Scottish Language*, 3, pp. 5–32.

— (1985), 'On the Variability of Hebridean English Syntax: The Verbal Group', in Görlach, ed., pp. 125–144.

Sandred, K.I. (1983), *Good or Bad Scots? Attitudes to Optional Lexical and Grammatical Usages in Edinburgh*, Uppsala, Acta Univ. Ups.

— (1985), 'Overt and Covert Prestige: Evaluative Boundaries in the Speech Community', in Görlach, ed., pp. 69–86.

Schneider, E., ed. (1997), *Englishes Around the World: Studies in Honour of Manfred Görlach*, Amsterdam / Philadelphia, John Benjamins.

Scott Douglas, W., ed. (1887), *The Works of Robert Burns*, Edinburgh, James Thin.

Scottish Consultative Council on the Curriculum (1999), *The School Curriculum and the Culture of Scotland: A Paper for Discussion and Consultation* (cf. also the website <http://www.sccc.ac.uk/>

Shaw, W. (1778), *An Analysis of the Galic Language*, repr. in *English Linguistics, 1500–1800*, Alston, R.C. (ed.), London, The Scolar Press, 1974.

Shearer, T. (1995), 'The Nature of Scots', *English Today*, 44:11/4 (October 1995), pp. 18–22.

Shuken, C. (1984), 'Highland and Island English', in Trudgill, ed., pp. 152–166.

— (1985), 'Variation in Hebridean English', in Görlach, ed., pp.145–158.

Simpson, K. (1993), 'Burns and Scottish Society', in Dwyer / Sher, pp. 210–224.

— ed. (1994), *Burns Now*, Edinburgh, Canongate Academic.

— (1998), 'Poetic Genre and National Identity: Ramsay, Fergusson and Burns', *Studies in Scottish Literature*, 30, pp. 31–42.

Sinclair, C. (1859), *Sketches and Stories of Scotland and the Scotch, and Shetland and the Shetlanders*, London, Simpkin, Marshall, and Co.

Skeat, W.W. (1912/1968), *English Dialects from the Eighth Century to the Present Day*, Cambridge, Cambridge University Press / New York, Kraus Reprint Co.

Skene, J. (1597/1681), *De verborum significatione: The Exposition of the Termes and Difficill Wordes conteined in the foure buikes of Regiam Majestatem*, in *The laws and acts of Parliament ... Collected, and extracted, from the publick records of the said kingdom, by Sir Thomas Murray of Glendook ...*, Edinburgh, Printed by David Lindsay.

Skene, W.F., ed. (1867), *Chronicles of the Picts, Chronicles of the Scots, and Other Early Memorials of Scottish History*, Edinburgh, H. M. General Register House.

Smith, A. (1776/1986), *An Inquiry into the Nature and Causes of the Wealth of Nations*, London, Strahan and Cadell; London, Penguin.

Smith, G. G. (1902), *Specimens of Middle Scots with Introduction, Notes and Glossary*, Edinburgh / London, W. Blackwood and Sons.

Smith, J. J. (1994), 'Norse in Scotland', *Scottish Language*, 13, pp. 18–33.

— (1996), *An Historical Study of English – Function, Form and Change*, London / New York, Routledge.

— (1999), *Essentials of Early English*, London / New York, Routledge.

Smith, R. (1995/96), 'The Local Press: What's in it for <u>you</u>?', *Scottish Language*, 14/15, pp.148–157.

Sornicola, R. (1991), 'Origine e diffusione della frase scissa nelle lingue romanze', in Kremer, ed., Band III, pp. 43–54.

Speitel, H.H. (1981), 'The Geographical Position of the Scots Dialect in relation to the Highlands of Scotland', in Benskin / Samuels, eds., pp. 107–129.

Spence, E.I. (1811), *Sketches of the Present Manners, Customs, and Scenery of Scotland, with Incidental Remarks on the Scottish Character*, London, Longman.

Starnes De Witt, T. and G. E. Noyes, (1946), *The English Dictionary from Cawdrey to Johnson, 1604–1755*, The University of North Carolina Press, Chapel Hill. Reprinted (with an introduction by Gabriele Stein) by John Benjamins Publishing Company, Amsterdam / Philadelphia.

Steel, T. (1984), *Scotland's Story*, London, Collins.

Steele, L. J. (1998), *Scots and Scottish English: Sociolinguistics and Education in Glasgow and Edinburgh*, University of Edinburgh, unpubl. Ph.D. thesis.

Stein, D. and I. Tieken-Boon van Ostade, eds. (1994), *Towards a Standard English, 1600–1800*, Berlin / New York, Mouton de Gruyter.

Stevenson, D. (1963/1990), *A Short Scots-Norwegian Wordlist*, unpubl. Ms.

Stevenson, R. L. (1886/1962), *Kidnapped*, ed. by M.R. Ridley, London, Dent.

— (1887), *Underwoods*, London, Chatto and Windus.

— (1889/1984) *The Master of Ballantrae*, ed. by M.R. Ridley, London, Dent.

Stirling, A. (1994), 'On a Standardised Spelling for Scots', *Scottish Language*, 13, pp. 88–93.

Strauss, D. (1998), 'Some Reflections on Burns's Command of English', *Studies in Scottish Literature*, 30, pp. 77–89.

Strauss, D. and H. Drescher, eds. (1986), *Scottish Language and Literature, Medieval and Renaissance*, Frankfurt a. M., Peter Lang.

Sundby, B., A.K. Bjørge and K.A. Haugland (1991), *A Dictionary of English Normative Grammar, 1700–1800*, Amsterdam / Philadelphia, John Benjamins.

Taavitsainen, I., G. Melchers and P. Pahta, eds. (1999), *Writing in Non-Standard English*, Amsterdam / Philadelphia, John Benjamins.

Thomson, R. L. (1984), 'The History of the Celtic Languages in the British Isles', in Trudgill, ed., pp. 241–258.

Tieken-Boon van Ostade, I. (1985), "I will be drowned and no man shall save me': The Conventional Rules for Shall and Will in Eighteenth-Century English Grammars', *English Studies*, 66:2, pp. 123–142.

— (1996), 'Social Network Theory and Eighteenth-Century English: The Case of Boswell', in Britton, ed., pp. 327–337.

Trahern, J. B., Jr., ed. (1989), *Standardizing English: Essays in the History of Language Change*, Knoxville, The University of Tennessee Press.

Trevor-Roper, H. (1983/1987), 'L'invenzione della tradizione: la tradizione delle Highlands in Scozia', in Hobsbawm / Ranger, eds., pp. 19–44.

Trudgill, P. (1974), *The Social Differentiation of English in Norwich*, Cambridge, Cambridge University Press.

— (1974/1995), *Sociolinguistics: An Introduction to Language and Society*, London, Penguin.

— ed. (1978), *Sociolinguistic Patterns in British English*, London, E. Arnold.

— ed. (1984), *Language in the British Isles*, Cambridge, Cambridge University Press.

— (1986), *Dialects in Contact*, Oxford, Basil Blackwell.

— (1998), 'Standard English: What It Isn't', *The European English Messenger*, VII, 2, pp. 35–39.

Trudgill, P. and J. K. Chambers, eds. (1991), *Dialects of English: Studies in Grammatical Variation*, London, Longman.

Trudgill, P. and J. Hannah (1985), *International English: A Guide to Varieties of Standard English*, London, Edward Arnold.

Tulloch, G. (1980), *The Language of Walter Scott: A Study of his Scottish and Period Language*, London, André Deutsch.

— (1989), *A History of the Scots Bible*, Aberdeen, Aberdeen University Press.

— (1997a), 'Scots as a Literary Language in Australia', in Schneider, ed., vol. 2, pp.319–334.

— (1997b), 'Lexis', in Jones, ed., pp. 378–432.

Ubaldini, P. (1588/1829), *Descrittione del Regno di Scotia et delle isole sue adiacenti*, Edinburgh, The Bannatyne Club.

Ureland, S. and G. Broderick, eds. (1991), *Language Contact in the British Isles*, Tübingen, Niemeyer.

Utz, H. (1992), 'A Genevan's Journey to the Hebrides in 1807: An Anti-Johnsonian Venture', *Studies in Scottish Literature*, XXVII, pp. 47–71.

— (1995), *Schotten und Schweizer – Brother Mountaineers: Europa entdeckt die beiden Völker im 18. Jahrhundert*, Bern, Peter Lang.

van Leuvensteijn, J.A. and J.B. Berns, eds. (1991), *Dialect and Standard Language in the English, Dutch, German and Norwegian Language Areas*, Amsterdam, The Netherlands Academy of Arts and Sciences.

Waddell, P. Hately (1871/1987), *The Psalms in Scots* (Introduction and Glossary by G. Tulloch), Aberdeen, Aberdeen University Press.

Ward, I. (1998), 'Scott and the Waverley Constitution: A Study in Literary Constitutionalism', *English Studies*, 79:3, pp. 193–211.

Warrack, A. (1911), *A Scots Dialect Dictionary*, London / Edinburgh, Chambers.

Watson, G. (1923) *The Roxburghshire Word-Book, Being a Record of the Special Vernacular Vocabulary of the County of Roxburgh, with an Appendix of Specimens*, Cambridge, Cambridge University Press.

Watson, R. (1984), *The Literature of Scotland*, London, Macmillan.

— (1998), 'Postcolonial Subjects? Language, Narrative Authority and Class in Contemporary Scottish Culture', *The European English Messenger*, VII, 2, pp. 21–31.

Watts, R. J. (2000), 'Mythical Strands in the Ideology of Prescriptivism', in Wright, L., ed., pp. 29–48.

Waugh, L. R. and C. H. van Schoonefeld, eds. (1980), *The Melody of Language*, Baltimore, University Park Press.

Will, W. (1930), *Our Persistent Speech: An Enquiry into the Life of Certain Aberdeenshire Words*, Aberdeen, William Smith and Sons.

Williamson, K. (1982), 'Lowland Scots in Education: An Historical Survey' – Part I, *Scottish Language*, 1, pp. 54–77.

— (1983), 'Lowland Scots in Education: An Historical Survey' – Part II, *Scottish Language*, 2, pp. 52–87.

— (1992/93), 'A Computer-Aided Method for Making a Linguistic Atlas of Older Scots', *Scottish Language*, 11/12, pp. 138–173.

— (1995/96), 'A Maze of Words. The William Will Fellowship Data-base Project', *Review of Scottish Culture*, 9, pp. 128–138.

— (forthcoming), *ECOS – Edinburgh Corpus of Older Scots*, University of Edinburgh, Institute for Historical Dialectology.

Willis, R.L. (1897), *Journal of a Tour from London to Elgin made about 1790 ... Printed from the Original MS.*, Edinburgh, Thomson Brothers.

Wilson, J. (1915), *Lowland Scotch as Spoken in the Lower Strathearn District of Perthshire*, Oxford, Oxford University Press.

— (1923), *The Dialect of Robert Burns as Spoken in Central Ayrshire*, Oxford, Oxford University Press .

— (1926), *The Dialects of Central Scotland*, Oxford, Oxford University Press.

Wimsatt, W. K. (1946), 'Johnson and Scots', in *The Times Literary Supplement*, 9 March 1946.

Wimsatt, W.K. and F.A. Pottle, eds. (1960), *Boswell for the Defence, 1769–1774*, Melbourne, W. Heinemann.

Withers, C.W.J. (1982), 'Education and Anglicisation: the Policy of the SSPCK toward the Education of the Highlander, 1709–1825', *Scottish Studies*, 26, pp. 37–56.

Withrington, D. J., J. T. Low, P. Trudgill, R. Macaulay, J.Y. Mather and J.D. McClure (1974), *The Scots Language in Education*, Aberdeen, Aberdeen College of Education and Association for Scottish Literary Studies.

Wittig, K. (1958), *The Scottish Tradition in Literature*, Edinburgh, Oliver and Boyd.

Wordsworth, D. (1894/1974), *Recollections of a Tour Made in Scotland A.D. 1803*, Edinburgh, The Mercat Press.

Wright, D. F., ed. (1988a), *The Bible in Scottish Life and Literature*, Edinburgh, The Saint Andrew Press.

— (1988b), "The Commoun Buke of the Kirke': The Bible in the Scottish Reformation', in Wright, ed., pp. 155–178.

Wright, L., ed. (2000), *The Development of Standard English, 1300–1800: Theories, Descriptions, Conflicts*, Cambridge, Cambridge University Press.

Youngson, A. J. (1973), *After the Forty-five: The Economic Impact on the Scottish Highlands*, Edinburgh, Edinburgh University Press.

— (1974), *Beyond the Highland Line – Three Journals of Travel in Eighteenth-Century Scotland: Burt, Pennant, Thornton*, London, Collins.

Index